Offended by Grace

Offended by Grace

Moral Injury and the Disruption of Mercy

G. C. SMITH

RESOURCE *Publications* • Eugene, Oregon

OFFENDED BY GRACE
Moral Injury and the Disruption of Mercy

Resource Publications
An Imprint of Wipf and Stock Publishers
199 W. 8th Ave., Suite 3
Eugene, OR 97401

www.wipfandstock.com

PAPERBACK ISBN: 979-8-3852-8392-7
HARDCOVER ISBN: 979-8-3852-8393-4
EBOOK ISBN: 979-8-3852-8394-1

VERSION NUMBER 07/15/26

For those who have had to live without resolution—

who were given grace that did not feel like grace,
who were asked to move forward when nothing had been repaired,
who continue to carry what remains.

And for those who stayed.

Grace does not resolve the world we understand.
It interrupts it—and asks us to remain.

Contents

PART I

The World We Depend On

(Moral Order, Coherence, and Why We Need It)

Introduction

When Mercy Breaks the World We Understand

We know how to name moral injury when something wrong has been done—when trust is broken, when authority fails, when harm is inflicted and not acknowledged. There is language for that. There are frameworks. There are ways of telling the story that make sense of what has happened and why it matters. Moral injury, as we have come to understand it, is the rupture that occurs when the world violates the moral expectations we depend on to live and act with integrity. It is what remains when something that should not have happened does—and cannot be easily repaired. This book begins there, but it does not stay there, because there is another kind of rupture we rarely name.

It happens when something is given that should not be given—when mercy interrupts consequence, when forgiveness appears before repair, when grace is extended without being earned. These moments are often described as beautiful, redemptive, even holy, and sometimes they are. But before they are received that way, they are often experienced differently. They feel wrong.

There are moments when grace does not land as relief. It lands as disruption. It unsettles the moral structure we rely on to make sense of the world, interrupting the sequence we expect to hold: wrong leads to consequence, harm leads to accountability, guilt leads to cost. Grace breaks that sequence, and when it does, it can feel less like healing and more like a violation.

This is not how we are taught to speak about grace. Grace, in much of our theological language, is described as gift, as freedom, as release—something to be desired, celebrated, proclaimed without hesitation. And yet, when grace arrives in places where we believe it does not belong, the response is rarely simple. People hesitate. People resist. People become angry—not because they do not believe in grace, but because they do, and what they are seeing does not align with how they believe grace should work.

We are more comfortable with injustice than we are with unearned mercy. We know how to protest what is wrong, to name harm, to call for accountability, to demand repair. Even when those demands are not met, they provide a structure within which we can locate ourselves. Grace removes that structure. It refuses to follow the rules we use to survive. It is not proportional, not predictable, not evenly distributed, and because of that, it introduces a different kind of instability.

This book is an attempt to name that instability honestly—not to resolve it, not to defend grace against critique, but to take seriously the fact that grace can be experienced as a form of moral disruption, one that feels, at least initially, like injury.

Consider the moment when someone who has caused harm is forgiven before they have made amends, or when a community is asked to make space for someone they have worked hard to move beyond, or when mercy is extended in a way that seems to bypass the very people who were most affected. These are not abstract scenarios. They are lived realities. And in those moments, the language of grace does not always comfort. Sometimes it wounds.

This is not because grace is wrong. It is because grace does not operate within the moral logic we depend on. It does not preserve balance, ensure fairness, or guarantee that what has been broken will be repaired in ways we can recognize. Instead, it introduces something that cannot be managed, cannot be controlled, cannot be made to fit. And so we resist—not because we are opposed to mercy, but because mercy, when it arrives without explanation or condition, threatens the coherence of the world we have constructed. If grace is real, then the systems we rely on to assign meaning—to determine who deserves what, and when—are not as stable as we thought. That is not a small disruption. It is a profound one.

This is where the connection to moral injury emerges. We often assume that moral injury results from the violation of justice, and it does. But moral injury can also arise when justice is interrupted—when the expected sequence is broken not by harm, but by mercy, when what should follow does not follow and something else appears instead.

In these moments, people experience confusion, anger, and disorientation. They struggle to reconcile what they are seeing with what they believe to be true. They ask questions that do not have easy answers: Why them? Why now? Why like this? And beneath those questions is something deeper: What kind of world is this, if this is how it works?

This book does not attempt to resolve those questions. It does not offer a framework that makes grace easier to accept or a method for integrating mercy into a stable moral system, because grace resists integration. It does not fit.

What this book does instead is create space—space to name the offense of grace without dismissing it, space to recognize that resistance to grace is not necessarily a failure of faith but may be an honest response to disruption, space to explore what it means to live in a world where mercy does not follow the rules we expect it to follow.

We will examine the ways grace unsettles individuals, communities, and institutions. We will consider how it exposes assumptions about fairness, responsibility, and identity. We will look at moments where grace creates more tension than relief, and we will ask what it means to remain present in that tension without rushing toward resolution.

This is not a book about rejecting grace. It is a book about telling the truth about it. Because before grace heals, it destabilizes; before it restores, it disrupts; before it is received as gift, it is often experienced as something else entirely.

If we are willing to begin there—honestly, without defense—then we may discover something important. Not about how to control grace, but about how to live with it, and perhaps, over time, how to receive it.

CHAPTER 1

The Moral Logic of the World

PART 1: THE STRUCTURE WE DEPEND ON

People move through the world with an assumption that events will make sense. This assumption is rarely stated, but it governs how individuals interpret experience. Actions are expected to lead to consequences, harm to accountability, effort to outcome. This sequence is not simply a moral preference; it is a functional necessity. Without it, interpretation becomes unstable.

This structure operates beneath conscious awareness. It is not something most people articulate, but something they rely on continuously. When something happens, they instinctively place it within a pattern. A decision leads to a result. A mistake produces consequence. A wrong action invites response. These connections allow events to be understood not as isolated occurrences, but as part of a coherent system.

Because of this, moral logic becomes a stabilizing force. It does not eliminate difficulty or suffering, but it makes them interpretable. A person can endure disruption if it fits within a sequence that makes sense. The hardship may be painful, but it is not disorienting. It can be located, named, and responded to in ways that restore a sense of order.

This is why the structure is so rarely noticed when it is functioning. Stability tends to disappear from awareness. When things align as expected, there is no need to reflect on the underlying framework that makes that alignment possible. The sequence holds, and so attention moves elsewhere. Life proceeds.

In this way, moral logic functions as a kind of background architecture. It supports experience without drawing attention to itself. It provides the conditions under which meaning can be formed. Without it, events would not only be difficult—they would be unintelligible.

This background nature matters. Because when the structure begins to fracture, the disruption is not immediately recognized as structural. At first, it appears as a problem with a particular event. Something unexpected has occurred. Something does not fit. The person may attempt to interpret the event within the existing framework, assuming that additional information will restore coherence.

This is the first response to disruption: preservation. The person tries to maintain the structure by adjusting their interpretation of the event. They assume misunderstanding, missing context, or temporary exception. This interpretive flexibility allows stability to continue. It prevents the immediate collapse of meaning.

But this flexibility has limits. When disruptions accumulate—when multiple experiences resist integration—the effort required to preserve coherence increases. What once felt natural begins to feel strained. The person must work harder to maintain the sense that events still make sense.

It is at this point that the structure begins to become visible.

The person notices the effort itself. What was once automatic now requires attention. They find themselves thinking through situations that previously would have been understood immediately. They pause longer. They reconsider more often. They begin to recognize that something is not aligning as it should.

This recognition marks a transition. The person is no longer fully inside the structure, but they have not yet stepped outside it. They continue to rely on moral logic, but they are now aware of its instability. This awareness introduces a new layer to their experience. They are no longer simply interpreting events—they are evaluating the framework that allows interpretation.

This evaluation is often subtle. It may appear as hesitation, as a lingering question, as a sense that something has not resolved. It is not always dramatic, but it is significant. Because once the structure is seen, it cannot return to complete invisibility. Even if coherence is restored in later moments, the knowledge remains that it can fail.

There is also a forward dimension to this structure that is often overlooked. Moral logic does not only help people make sense of what has happened; it shapes how they act before anything happens at all. It creates a kind of anticipatory stability. A person does not simply react to the world—they enter it with the expectation that their actions will produce outcomes that make sense.

This expectation allows engagement. It permits risk. It makes trust possible.

When someone acts with integrity, they are not doing so only because it is right in an abstract sense. They are doing so within a framework that suggests integrity will matter—that it will connect to response, that it will be recognized, even if imperfectly. When someone extends trust, they are not acting blindly. They are relying on the expectation that trust will be met in a way that corresponds.

These expectations are rarely stated, but they are deeply embedded. They form the conditions under which participation becomes possible. Without them, action itself would be uncertain. A person would not know how to engage, because they would not know what their engagement would mean.

When these anticipatory conditions hold, the world feels navigable. Not predictable in every detail, but intelligible. A person can move forward with confidence that their actions are connected to outcomes in ways that make sense. Even when those outcomes are difficult, they remain interpretable.

But when these conditions begin to weaken, the disruption extends beyond isolated events. It begins to affect how a person approaches action itself.

They may hesitate. Not because they no longer believe in what is right, but because they are less certain that what is right will connect to what follows. They may still act, but with a diminished expectation that their action will be met in a way that corresponds.

This hesitation is often the first indication that something deeper has shifted. It reflects not a change in belief, but a change in expectation. The person still holds the idea that actions should lead to consequences, but they are no longer confident that this will occur.

Over time, this shift reshapes engagement. The person may continue to participate in the world, but differently. They may become more cautious in their trust, more measured in their investment, more attentive to how events unfold. They are adapting to a world that feels less stable.

This adaptation is not necessarily conscious. It may show up in small ways—a pause before speaking, a reconsideration before acting, a subtle distancing from situations that once felt straightforward. These changes are often gradual, but they accumulate.

And as they accumulate, the person's relationship to moral logic changes.

It is no longer something they simply inhabit.

It becomes something they observe.

Test.

Question.

This shift from inhabiting to observing is critical. It marks the beginning of a different kind of awareness—one in which the structure that once provided stability is no longer taken for granted.

At this point, the person is not yet fully disoriented. They still have access to the framework. They still rely on it. But they are aware that it is not as stable as they once believed.

This awareness introduces a tension that cannot be easily resolved.

The person continues to act as if the structure holds, because they need it to.

But they also recognize that it may not.

This tension—between reliance and uncertainty—is one of the earliest expressions of moral disruption.

It does not yet have a name.

It is not yet fully formed.

But it is present.

And it is here, within this tension, that moral injury begins to take shape.

Not only as something that happens—

but as something that alters how the world is experienced.

PART 2: THE WEIGHT OF EXPECTATION

Expectation shapes how people enter the world before anything has happened. It is not passive but active, structuring engagement in advance. A person does not step into a conversation, a relationship, or a decision as a blank slate. They carry assumptions about how things will unfold—how they will be received, how their actions will be interpreted, and how outcomes will correspond to what they have done.

These assumptions are rarely articulated, but they are deeply embedded. They are formed over time through repeated experiences of alignment. When actions consistently lead to recognizable outcomes, expectation becomes internalized. It no longer requires conscious construction. It operates automatically, guiding perception and behavior without needing to be named.

This is why expectation feels so stable when it holds. It does not demand attention. It simply works. A person acts, and what follows makes sense. There may be difficulty, even conflict, but the sequence remains intelligible. The person can say, “This is hard, but it fits.” And because it fits, it can be endured.

Expectation is not only predictive. It is moral. It reflects not only what will happen, but what should happen. This distinction matters. Prediction can be revised without much disruption. A person can adjust their understanding when new information emerges. But expectation resists revision because it is tied to meaning. It reflects a deeper conviction about how the world is supposed to work.

When expectation holds, it reinforces this conviction. It affirms that actions matter, that responses correspond, that the structure of the world is reliable. But when expectation fails, the disruption is not limited to the event itself. It reaches into the underlying conviction. The person does not simply experience surprise—they experience disturbance.

This disturbance carries a particular quality. It is not only cognitive but emotional. The person does not simply think, “I did not expect that.” They feel that something is wrong. The language that often emerges is not descriptive, but evaluative: “That should not have happened.”

This sense of “should” is central. It reveals that expectation is not neutral. It is anchored in a moral framework. When something violates that framework, the response is not only confusion but resistance. The person pushes back internally against what has occurred, even as they try to make sense of it.

This is why violations of expectation linger. They do not resolve easily. The person returns to the moment, replaying it, reconsidering it, attempting to reconcile it with what should have been. This return is not simply a refusal to move on. It is an effort to restore coherence.

Sometimes, this restoration is possible. Additional context emerges. New information reframes the situation. The person adjusts their understanding, and the sequence can be reestablished. The expectation, though challenged, remains intact.

But when reconciliation does not occur—when the event continues to resist alignment—the expectation itself begins to shift.

This shift is rarely immediate. Expectation is not easily relinquished. It has been built through repeated reinforcement. It is trusted. The person may continue to hold the expectation even in the face of contradiction, attempting again and again to restore alignment.

But over time, this effort becomes more difficult. The person begins to introduce qualifications. What was once assumed becomes conditional. "Usually this is how it works." "Most of the time, this holds." These statements reflect a subtle but significant change. Expectation is no longer absolute.

This change affects how the person engages. They may still act within the expectation, but with less certainty. They continue to hope for alignment, but they prepare for the possibility that it may not occur. This creates a layered orientation. One layer maintains the original expectation; another accounts for its possible failure.

Holding these layers requires effort. The person is no longer moving within a single, stable framework. They are navigating between possibilities. This navigation introduces complexity into what was once straightforward.

Interpretation slows. When something happens, the person does not immediately assign meaning. They evaluate. They consider whether the event aligns with expectation or represents another instance of disruption. This process requires attention. What once felt automatic now becomes deliberate.

This shift from automatic to deliberate interpretation is significant. It reflects a change in how the person experiences the world. They are no longer simply receiving events; they are actively working to make sense of them.

This work is not without cost. It requires cognitive and emotional energy. The person may not always be aware of the effort, but they feel its effects. Engagement becomes more taxing. Participation requires more attention.

Over time, this can lead to a subtle recalibration of investment. The person may begin to limit how much they commit to situations. Not because they no longer care, but because they are adjusting to a world that feels less predictable. They are attempting to remain engaged while managing the uncertainty introduced by disrupted expectation.

This recalibration often appears as caution. The person becomes more attentive to how interactions unfold. They watch for signs of alignment or misalignment. They become more selective in what they trust, more measured in how they respond.

This is not withdrawal. It is adaptation.

The person is finding a way to continue participating in a world where expectation no longer holds consistently. They are adjusting their engagement to account for instability.

But this adaptation has implications. It introduces distance. Not complete disengagement, but a degree of separation. The person is present, but less fully exposed. They are involved, but more guarded.

This guardedness reflects a change in how expectation functions. It is no longer something the person inhabits. It becomes something they monitor.

Monitoring expectation requires constant attention. The person is continually assessing whether the structure is holding. They are tracking alignment, noting discrepancies, adjusting their interpretation accordingly.

This ongoing assessment can become exhausting. It adds a layer of effort to every interaction. What once felt natural now feels managed.

And as this management continues, the person's relationship to expectation shifts further.

They no longer assume that the world will respond in ways that make sense.

They hope it will.

But they are no longer certain.

This difference—between hope and certainty—is subtle but profound.

It marks a transition from stability to contingency.

The person continues to act, but within a framework that is no longer guaranteed.

This is one of the ways moral coherence begins to erode—not through a single rupture, but through the gradual weakening of expectation.

The person still carries the sense of what should be.

But they are increasingly aware that what is may not align.

And this awareness reshapes how they move through the world.

PART 3: WHEN THE SEQUENCE BREAKS

There comes a point when the sequence does not merely strain—it breaks.

This moment is not always dramatic. It is not always marked by a single, catastrophic event. Often, it is recognized not by what happens externally, but by what shifts internally. The person encounters something that cannot be reconciled within the structure they have relied upon, and the usual process of interpretation no longer works.

They attempt to make sense of what has happened. They search for connection, for correspondence, for the link between action and outcome that has guided them in the past. But the link does not appear. The event resists placement. It does not fit within the sequence that has made the world intelligible.

At this point, interpretation begins to fail—not completely, but significantly. The person can still describe what has happened. They can name the event, recount the details, even analyze the circumstances. But they cannot locate it within a framework that gives it meaning. The event remains outside the sequence.

This creates a gap—not only between action and consequence, but between experience and understanding. The person knows what has occurred, but does not know how to hold it. It cannot be integrated into the narrative that has previously allowed events to settle into place.

This inability to place is disorienting. Placement is how meaning stabilizes. When an event can be located within a sequence, it becomes part of a coherent whole. When it cannot, it remains unsettled. It resists closure. It continues to press into awareness.

The person may find themselves returning to the event repeatedly. Not necessarily by choice, but because it has not resolved. It interrupts thought. It reappears in memory. It influences how new situations are perceived. It is no longer simply something that happened; it is something that continues to happen in the absence of resolution.

This persistence changes how the person relates to time. Events are expected to move into the past, to become part of a stable narrative. But when the sequence breaks, the event does not settle. It remains present in a way that disrupts continuity. The past is no longer fully past.

This disruption extends forward as well. If the sequence has broken once, it can break again. This possibility enters awareness. The person begins to approach future situations differently—not necessarily with fear, but with heightened attention. They are aware that coherence is no longer guaranteed.

This awareness reshapes expectation at a fundamental level. The sequence is no longer assumed. It becomes provisional. Something that may hold, but may not. The person continues to hope for alignment, but they no longer rely on it with the same certainty.

This shift affects how they engage with the world. They may become more cautious, more attentive to potential points of disruption. They watch more closely. They evaluate more carefully. They are no longer moving within a structure that holds automatically. They are navigating a structure that may or may not hold.

This navigation requires effort. It introduces a layer of interpretation that was not previously necessary. The person is no longer simply participating; they are managing participation. They are adjusting their engagement in response to the instability they have encountered.

Over time, this can alter their sense of self. Identity is often formed in relation to a coherent moral framework. A person understands themselves as someone who acts, responds, and interprets within a structure that makes sense. When that structure fractures, the sense of self can become less stable.

The person may begin to question not only what has happened, but how they understand what has happened. They may become less certain in their judgments, more tentative in their conclusions. This is not necessarily a loss of moral conviction, but a recognition that the frameworks they have relied upon are not sufficient to account for everything they encounter.

This recognition introduces a new kind of awareness—one that is both unsettling and necessary. The person begins to see the limits of the structure they have depended on. They recognize that it does not hold in every situation. That there are experiences that cannot be fully explained within it.

This is where moral injury begins to take on its full significance.

Moral injury is not only the result of something wrong happening. It is the result of something happening that cannot be accounted for within the structure that gives meaning to what is right and wrong. It is not only a violation of expectation, but a rupture of interpretive capacity.

The person is left holding an experience that does not fit.

They cannot dismiss it.

They cannot fully explain it.

They cannot integrate it.

And so it remains.

This remaining is not passive. It is active. It continues to shape perception, to influence response, to alter how the person engages with the world. It becomes part of how they interpret new situations, even if those situations are unrelated to the original event.

This is why moral injury is not confined to the moment in which it occurs. It extends beyond it. It alters the conditions under which future experience is understood.

The person does not simply move on.

They move forward differently.

They carry with them the knowledge that the sequence can break. That coherence is not guaranteed. That meaning may not always be recoverable in the ways they expect.

This knowledge does not eliminate the need for moral logic. If anything, it intensifies it. The person continues to seek coherence, to look for patterns, to try to reestablish a sense of connection between what happens and what follows.

But the search becomes more effortful.

What was once assumed must now be tested.

What once held automatically must now be evaluated.

This shift from assumption to evaluation marks a profound change in how the person experiences the world.

They are no longer simply living within a moral structure.

They are living in relation to it.

This relational stance is more complex. It requires ongoing attention. It does not allow for the same level of ease or immediacy.

But it is also more honest.

Because it acknowledges that the structure, while necessary, is not complete.

That there are experiences that exceed it.

That there are moments when the sequence breaks, and when it does, something else is required.

The question that emerges at this point is not only how to restore the sequence.

It is how to live when it cannot be restored.

This question does not yet have an answer.

It remains open.

And it is this open question that leads into the next movement of the book.

CHAPTER 2

The Stability of Fairness

PART 1: THE ANCHOR OF PROPORTION

IF MORAL LOGIC PROVIDES the structure through which the world becomes intelligible, fairness is what stabilizes that structure. It is the felt assurance that what happens will correspond, in some meaningful way, to what has occurred. Where moral logic establishes sequence—action leading to consequence, harm to response—fairness gives that sequence emotional and relational credibility. It allows people not only to understand the world, but to trust it.

Fairness is rarely defined explicitly in everyday life. It is assumed, recognized, invoked when violated rather than examined when present. Yet its presence is unmistakable. It is the quiet sense that outcomes are proportionate, that responses reflect events, that what is given or withheld corresponds to what has been done. This sense does not require perfection. People do not expect exact symmetry. They do, however, expect recognizability. The response must make sense in relation to the event.

This recognizability is what anchors interpretation. When something happens, the person does not only ask what occurred, but whether what follows corresponds. If it does, even imperfectly, the event settles. It becomes part of a world that still holds together. If it does not, the event resists integration. It remains unsettled, not only because of what happened, but because of how it was answered.

Fairness operates at both a cognitive and an emotional level. Cognitively, it allows for evaluation. The person can say, "This response fits," or "This does not align." Emotionally, it produces a sense of stability. When fairness is present, there is a kind of quiet assurance. The person may not articulate it, but they feel that things are proceeding in a way that makes sense.

This emotional dimension is critical. Fairness is not only about rightness; it is about trust. It allows people to invest in the world with the expectation that their investment will be met in a way that corresponds. A person works, trusting that effort will connect to outcome. A person acts with integrity, trusting that integrity will be recognized. A person refrains from harm, trusting that harm, if it occurs, will be addressed.

These are not guarantees. They are expectations grounded in fairness. Without them, engagement becomes uncertain. The person does not know how to act because they do not know how their action will be held. Fairness provides the assurance that action and response are meaningfully connected.

This connection is not only individual; it is communal. Fairness operates within shared structures. It is not simply a private sense, but a collective expectation. Communities function because there is a shared understanding that responses will correspond to actions in recognizable ways. When this understanding holds, relationships are sustained. Trust is reinforced. Participation becomes possible.

Within this communal context, fairness takes on an additional dimension: consistency. It is not enough that a response corresponds in a single instance. It must also correspond across instances. Similar actions should lead to similar outcomes. Similar harms should receive similar responses. This consistency reinforces the perception that the system is stable, not arbitrary.

When consistency is present, fairness becomes more than a momentary experience. It becomes a pattern. The person begins to rely not only on individual instances of correspondence, but on the expectation that such correspondence will continue. This expectation deepens trust. It allows the person to move through the world with confidence that what happens will be met in ways that make sense.

This is why fairness functions as an anchor. It holds the structure of moral logic in place. Without it, the sequence of action and consequence may still exist conceptually, but it loses its credibility. The person may still believe that actions should lead to consequences, but they no longer trust that this will occur.

When fairness holds, even difficult outcomes can be accepted. A negative consequence, if it corresponds to an action, can be integrated. The person may not prefer the outcome, but they recognize its place within the sequence. This recognition allows for acceptance. It does not eliminate discomfort, but it prevents disorientation.

This is evident in everyday experiences. A person receives criticism that aligns with their behavior. It may be difficult to hear, but it makes sense. A consequence follows a decision. It may be unwelcome, but it is understandable. In these moments, fairness stabilizes the experience. The person can locate themselves within the sequence and respond accordingly.

By contrast, when fairness is absent, even neutral or positive outcomes can become destabilizing. A response that does not correspond introduces uncertainty. The person does not know how to interpret what has happened. The sequence remains intact conceptually, but it no longer holds experientially.

This distinction between conceptual and experiential fairness is important. A person may believe in fairness as a principle while experiencing its absence in practice. This creates tension. The belief remains, but the experience does not support it. Over time, this tension can erode trust.

Fairness, then, is not only about outcomes. It is about the reliability of the connection between outcomes and events. It is about whether the person can trust that what happens will be answered in ways that make sense.

This trust extends into identity. People understand themselves in relation to fairness. They see themselves as individuals who act within a system that responds. Their sense of agency is tied to the expectation that their actions matter. When fairness holds, agency is reinforced. The person experiences themselves as someone whose actions have meaning.

When fairness begins to falter, this sense of agency is affected. The person may still act, but they are less certain that their actions will connect to outcomes in recognizable ways. This uncertainty can lead to hesitation. Not because the person no longer believes in acting, but because the connection between action and consequence is no longer secure.

This hesitation is often subtle. It may appear as caution, as a slight delay in response, as a reconsideration of how much to invest. But over time, it can accumulate. The person begins to adjust their engagement with the world, not in response to a single event, but in response to a pattern of misalignment.

At its core, fairness is about proportion. It is the expectation that responses will reflect the weight of what has occurred. This reflection does not require exact equivalence, but it requires recognition. The response must carry some relationship to the event. It must signal that what happened has been seen, understood, and answered.

Proportion, then, becomes the language of fairness. It is how the person interprets whether a response fits. When proportion is present, the response feels appropriate. When it is absent, the response feels off—either excessive or insufficient.

This sense of proportion is deeply intuitive. People recognize it without needing to define it. They know when something fits and when it does not. This intuitive recognition is what gives fairness its power. It operates beneath explicit reasoning, shaping perception immediately.

Because of this, violations of fairness are often felt before they are understood. The person senses that something is wrong before they can articulate why. They experience misalignment, imbalance, a lack of correspondence. This experience prompts further evaluation, but the initial recognition is immediate.

This immediacy is part of what makes fairness so central to moral life. It is not something that must be constructed in each moment. It is already present as a framework through which events are interpreted.

And because it is so deeply embedded, its disruption is profoundly unsettling.

When fairness is violated, the person does not only question the event. They question the structure that allowed them to trust the event. The anchor begins to loosen. The sequence may still exist, but it is no longer held in place.

This loosening does not immediately lead to collapse. The person may continue to rely on fairness, to look for proportion, to assume correspondence. But the certainty is diminished. The anchor is still there, but it no longer holds with the same strength.

It is within this weakening that the next layer of moral disruption begins to emerge.

PART 2: THE MEANING OF WHAT IS EARNED

If fairness stabilizes the moral structure by anchoring response in proportion, it does so most powerfully through the idea of what is earned. The concept of earning is one of the primary ways people interpret their place within the sequence of action and consequence. It provides a framework through which outcomes are not only observed but justified. When something is earned, it is understood as belonging within the order of things. It fits.

To say that something is earned is to say that there is a recognizable connection between what was done and what has followed. The outcome is not random, not imposed from outside the sequence, but arising from within it. Effort leads to result. Harm leads to consequence. Integrity leads to trust. These connections are not merely functional; they are meaningful. They allow the person to see themselves as participants in a world that responds.

This participation is central to identity. People do not simply act; they understand themselves through the relationship between their actions and the outcomes that follow. A person sees themselves as responsible because their actions produce consequences. They see themselves as capable because their efforts lead to results. They see themselves as trustworthy because their behavior is met with corresponding trust.

In this way, earning is not only about outcomes. It is about self-understanding. It provides a mirror through which the person interprets who they are. When the connection between action and outcome holds, the reflection is stable. The person can locate themselves within the moral structure and understand their place within it.

This stability extends into trust. Trust is not only relational; it is structural. A person trusts others, but they also trust the system within which those relationships operate. They trust that actions will be recognized, that responses will correspond, that what is earned will be acknowledged. This trust allows for investment. It allows the person to engage fully, to act without constant calculation, to participate without needing to secure every outcome in advance.

When earning holds, trust deepens. The person begins to rely not only on individual instances of correspondence, but on the expectation that such correspondence will continue. This expectation reduces the need for vigilance. The person does not have to monitor every interaction, evaluate every response, or question every outcome. They can act with a degree of ease.

This ease is not the absence of effort, but the absence of constant uncertainty. The person still works, still makes decisions, still navigates complexity. But they do so within a framework that supports their engagement. Their actions are not disconnected from what follows. They carry forward into outcomes that make sense.

This is why the idea of earning carries such weight. It is not simply a cultural construct or a social preference. It is a mechanism through which meaning is stabilized. It allows people to interpret outcomes as connected, to see themselves as agents within a system that responds.

However, this same mechanism can also intensify disruption when it fails.

When outcomes do not align with what is earned, the effect is not only disappointment. It is disorientation. The person has acted within the structure, has followed the sequence, has participated as expected, and yet what follows does not correspond. The connection between action and outcome is weakened.

This weakening affects identity. The person can no longer rely on outcomes to reflect their actions in recognizable ways. They may begin to question whether their efforts matter, whether their integrity is meaningful, whether their actions are truly connected to what follows. This questioning is not abstract. It is grounded in experience.

The person may continue to act, but the meaning of their action shifts. They are no longer certain that what they do will be reflected in what happens. This uncertainty introduces hesitation. Not necessarily withdrawal, but a recalibration of engagement.

This recalibration often appears as a change in how the person invests. They may still participate, but with less expectation that their participation will lead to corresponding outcomes. They may limit their effort, not because they no longer care, but because the relationship between effort and result has become uncertain.

This shift can be subtle, but it is significant. It marks a change in how the person relates to the world. They are no longer fully oriented by the expectation of earning. They are adapting to a context in which earning does not consistently produce what it once did.

This adaptation has relational implications as well. Trust, which was built on the expectation of correspondence, begins to change. The person may still trust others, but more cautiously. They may still engage in relationships, but with an awareness that responses may not align as expected.

This awareness does not eliminate trust, but it alters its nature. Trust becomes more conditional, more dependent on ongoing evaluation. The person pays closer attention to how others respond, to whether actions are recognized, to whether outcomes correspond. Trust becomes something that must be continually assessed rather than assumed.

This ongoing assessment introduces effort. The person is no longer able to rely on the structure to hold automatically. They must monitor it. They must interpret each interaction, each outcome, each response. This monitoring can become exhausting. It adds a layer of complexity to what was previously straightforward.

Over time, this can affect how the person understands fairness itself. Fairness, which once felt like a stable anchor, begins to feel less certain. The person may still believe in fairness as a principle, but their experience does not consistently support that belief. This creates tension between conviction and reality.

This tension can lead to different responses. Some may double down on the expectation of earning, holding more tightly to the belief that outcomes should correspond, even in the face of contradiction. Others may begin to loosen that expectation, adjusting their understanding of how the world works. Neither response resolves the tension fully. Both are attempts to navigate it.

At the center of this tension is a question: what does it mean for something to be deserved?

Deserving is closely related to earning, but it introduces an additional layer of evaluation. It is not only about what has been done, but about what should follow from what has been done. It brings together action, outcome, and judgment.

When something is deserved, it carries a sense of rightness. The outcome is not only connected to the action, but appropriate to it. This appropriateness reinforces fairness. It affirms that the structure is not only functioning, but functioning well.

But when what is deserved does not occur—when outcomes do not align with what the person believes should follow—the disruption deepens. It is no longer only a question of correspondence, but of justice. The person experiences not only misalignment, but violation.

This is where fairness begins to take on a sharper edge. It is no longer only stabilizing; it becomes evaluative in a more intense way. The person begins to judge not only individual outcomes, but the system itself. They ask whether the structure can be trusted, whether it reflects what is right, whether it holds in the way it should.

This questioning prepares the ground for the next movement. Because when fairness begins to feel uncertain, and when earning no longer guarantees correspondence, the person is left with a structure that still exists but no longer stabilizes in the same way.

And it is within this instability that the deeper rupture begins to emerge.

PART 3: WHEN FAIRNESS BEGINS TO FRACTURE

Fairness stabilizes moral experience by anchoring events in proportion, reinforcing the connection between action and outcome, effort and result, harm and response. It allows the person to trust that what happens will be answered in ways that make sense. But this stability depends on more than isolated moments of alignment. It depends on continuity. Fairness must hold not only occasionally, but consistently enough to sustain belief in the structure itself.

When this continuity begins to weaken, the effect is not immediate collapse but gradual fracture. The person does not suddenly abandon fairness. They continue to rely on it, to look for it, to expect it. But they begin to notice that it does not hold in the same way across situations. Some responses align. Others do not. Some outcomes reflect what has been done. Others seem disconnected.

At first, these discrepancies are interpreted as exceptions. The person preserves the framework by treating misalignment as temporary or situational. They assume that additional information will restore coherence, that what appears inconsistent will eventually make sense. This is an attempt to protect the stability that fairness provides.

But when discrepancies accumulate—when multiple experiences resist integration—the interpretive effort increases. The person must work harder to maintain the belief that fairness still holds. They begin to track inconsistencies more closely, to compare outcomes across situations, to evaluate whether responses truly correspond.

This evaluation introduces a new layer of awareness. Fairness, which once operated as a background assumption, moves into the foreground. The person becomes conscious of it. They begin to observe not only what happens, but how what happens is being answered. They ask whether responses reflect events, whether outcomes align with effort, whether consequences correspond to harm.

This shift from assumption to observation is significant. It changes how fairness functions. It is no longer something the person simply relies on. It becomes something they monitor.

Monitoring fairness requires attention. It demands that the person continually assess whether the structure is holding. This assessment can become effortful. What was once immediate now requires evaluation. The person is no longer able to move through experience with the same level of ease.

This change affects emotional experience as well. When fairness holds, there is a quiet sense of stability. When it begins to fracture, that stability is replaced by tension. The person feels the misalignment, even before they can fully articulate it. Something is off. Something does not correspond.

This feeling often manifests as frustration. Not simply because outcomes are undesirable, but because they do not make sense in relation to what has occurred. The person experiences a gap between expectation and reality, and that gap produces discomfort.

Over time, this frustration can deepen into something more persistent. The person begins to anticipate misalignment. They no longer assume that responses will correspond. Instead, they watch for signs that fairness may not hold. This anticipation changes how they engage with the world.

They become more cautious. Not necessarily withdrawn, but attentive. They evaluate situations more carefully. They consider not only what should happen, but what might happen if fairness does not hold. This dual awareness requires effort. It introduces complexity into what was once straightforward.

This complexity can lead to a form of internal division. The person holds two orientations simultaneously. One continues to expect fairness—to believe that actions should lead to corresponding outcomes. The other prepares for its absence—to account for the possibility that this will not occur.

These orientations do not resolve into one another. They coexist, creating tension. The person moves between them, sometimes relying on expectation, sometimes anticipating disruption. This movement is not always conscious, but it is felt.

This internal division affects trust. Trust, which was once grounded in the expectation of fairness, becomes less certain. The person may still trust in some contexts, but not in others. They may extend trust cautiously, testing whether it will be met in ways that correspond.

This testing introduces a new dynamic into relationships. The person is no longer simply engaging. They are evaluating. They are observing how others respond, how outcomes unfold, whether fairness is present. This evaluation can create distance. Not because the person no longer desires connection, but because they are no longer certain that connection will be held in a stable way.

This distance can be subtle. It may appear as hesitation, as a reluctance to fully invest, as a carefulness in what is shared. The person remains present, but less exposed. They are managing engagement rather than inhabiting it fully.

At the same time, the person may experience a growing sense of disillusionment. Fairness, which once felt like an anchor, begins to feel unreliable. The person may still believe in fairness as an ideal, but their experience does not consistently support that belief. This creates a gap between conviction and reality.

This gap is difficult to hold. The person is faced with a choice, though it may not be experienced as such. They can attempt to maintain the belief in fairness despite contradictory experience, or they can begin to adjust their expectations to align with what they are encountering. Neither option is fully satisfying.

Maintaining belief without support can feel like denial. Adjusting expectation can feel like loss. The person may move back and forth between these positions, trying to find a way to reconcile them. But the tension remains.

This is where fairness begins to fracture internally. It is no longer only a matter of external misalignment. It becomes a matter of internal conflict. The person's understanding of how the world should work no longer aligns with how the world is experienced.

This internal fracture has implications for meaning. Fairness has provided a way to interpret events, to assign value, to understand outcomes. When it becomes unstable, interpretation itself becomes more difficult. The person is less certain about how to evaluate what happens.

This uncertainty can lead to a kind of interpretive fatigue. The person grows tired of trying to make sense of misalignment. They may begin to disengage from the effort, not because they no longer care, but because the effort no longer yields clarity.

This disengagement can take different forms. It may appear as resignation, as a sense that outcomes cannot be relied upon to reflect actions. It may appear as cynicism, as a belief that fairness is not a reliable feature of the world. It may appear as detachment, as a reduction in emotional investment.

Each of these responses reflects an attempt to cope with the instability of fairness. They are not final positions, but adaptations. The person is adjusting to a world in which the anchor no longer holds in the same way.

At this stage, fairness has not disappeared. It continues to exert influence. The person still recognizes misalignment, still feels the absence of proportion, still responds to violations. But fairness no longer stabilizes experience in the same way. It no longer provides the same level of assurance.

This weakening prepares the ground for a deeper shift. Because when fairness can no longer anchor interpretation, the person must find another way to make sense of what happens. They must develop new strategies for navigating a world in which proportion is not consistently present.

It is here that moral clarity begins to take on a different role—not as a reflection of stable structure, but as a means of survival within instability.

And it is into this space that the next chapter moves.

CHAPTER 3

How We Survive Through Moral Clarity

PART 1: NAMING WHAT IS WRONG

WHEN FAIRNESS BEGINS TO fracture and the connection between action and outcome no longer holds with consistency, the person does not simply abandon the need for coherence. The need remains. It intensifies. What changes is not the desire for meaning, but the way meaning is constructed. In the absence of stable correspondence, the person turns toward something more immediate, more controllable, more definitive. They turn toward moral clarity.

Moral clarity is the act of naming what is wrong in a way that restores a sense of order. It is not necessarily the same as understanding. It does not require full explanation, complete context, or nuanced interpretation. It requires identification. Something is wrong. Someone is responsible. Something should not have happened. This naming provides an anchor when fairness can no longer stabilize the structure.

The movement toward clarity is not accidental. It is adaptive. When the broader framework becomes unstable, the person narrows the field of interpretation. They focus on what can be known with certainty, or at least with confidence. They reduce complexity in order to regain orientation. This reduction is not a failure of thought. It is a response to disruption.

In moments of instability, ambiguity becomes difficult to hold. The person is already managing uncertainty at a structural level. To introduce additional uncertainty at the level of interpretation would compound the disorientation. Moral clarity offers a way to limit that expansion. It creates boundaries. It defines what is right and what is wrong, who is responsible and who is not. These definitions may not capture the full reality, but they provide something that can be held.

This is why moral clarity often emerges quickly in the aftermath of disruption. The person does not remain indefinitely in a state of open-ended questioning. They move toward conclusion. They name the event, assign responsibility, and establish a narrative that allows them to proceed. This movement is often experienced as necessary. Without it, the event would remain too diffuse, too unstable to engage.

Naming, then, becomes a form of survival. It allows the person to regain a sense of footing. When something is named, it can be located. When it is located, it can be responded to. The person is no longer suspended in uncertainty. They have something to stand on.

This process is evident in both individual and communal responses. An individual who has experienced harm may move quickly to define what has happened in clear terms. They identify the harm, the source, and the meaning of the event. A community may do the same, establishing shared language that clarifies what occurred and how it should be understood. These acts of naming create cohesion. They align interpretation across individuals, reducing the fragmentation that disruption can produce.

However, the clarity that emerges in these moments is often simplified. Complexity is reduced in order to achieve stability. Nuance is set aside in favor of definiteness. The goal is not to capture every dimension of the situation, but to establish enough coherence to move forward.

This simplification has both strengths and limitations. On one hand, it allows for decisive response. When something is clearly named as wrong, action can follow. Accountability can be pursued. Boundaries can be set. The person or community can respond in ways that reassert order.

On the other hand, simplification can obscure aspects of reality that do not fit neatly within the established categories. Situations that are morally complex may be reduced to binary distinctions. Individuals may be categorized in ways that do not fully reflect their actions or motivations. Context may be minimized in favor of clarity.

These limitations are often accepted, at least temporarily, because of the function clarity serves. In the aftermath of disruption, the priority is not exhaustive understanding but regained orientation. The person needs to know where they stand, what has happened, and how to proceed. Moral clarity provides that direction.

It is important to recognize that this movement toward clarity is not inherently problematic. It is a necessary response to instability. Without it, the person would remain in a state of ongoing disorientation, unable to act or respond. Clarity allows for engagement. It makes participation possible in a context that has become uncertain.

At the same time, the reliance on clarity introduces a particular kind of rigidity. Once something has been named, it becomes more difficult to revisit. The categories established in the moment of disruption tend to hold. They provide stability, and stability is not easily relinquished.

This rigidity can be reinforced by repetition. As the person or community continues to refer to the event in the same terms, the interpretation becomes solidified. Alternative perspectives become less accessible. The initial naming takes on the weight of truth, not only because it was accurate in the moment, but because it has been consistently reinforced.

Over time, this can shape how future events are interpreted. The person carries forward the categories established in previous moments of disruption. They apply them to new situations, using familiar patterns to make sense of what is occurring. This can create continuity, but it can also limit perception. The person may see what fits the established framework and overlook what does not.

This pattern reflects the deeper function of moral clarity. It is not only a response to a single event, but a strategy for navigating a world that no longer feels fully stable. It allows the person to maintain a sense of order by defining what can be known and acted upon, even when broader coherence is uncertain.

At its core, moral clarity answers a fundamental question: What is this? It provides a definitive response where uncertainty would otherwise prevail. It allows the person to say, "This is wrong," or "This is unjust," or "This should not have happened." These statements may not capture every nuance, but they provide a starting point for response.

This starting point is crucial. Without it, the person would remain suspended in ambiguity. They would be unable to move from interpretation to action. Clarity bridges that gap. It translates experience into something that can be addressed.

Yet even as clarity stabilizes, it carries within it the seeds of future tension. Because the reality it simplifies does not disappear. The aspects of the situation that were set aside remain present, even if they are not fully acknowledged. Over time, these unresolved elements may reemerge, challenging the clarity that was established.

For now, however, clarity serves its purpose. It allows the person to survive the initial disruption. It provides a framework within which the event can be held, responded to, and integrated—at least partially—into the ongoing experience of life.

This is the first movement in the survival strategy that emerges when moral coherence begins to break down. It is not the final answer. It is the immediate response.

The person names what is wrong.

And in doing so, they regain just enough stability to continue.

PART 2: DIVIDING THE WORLD TO MAKE IT HOLD

Once something has been named as wrong, the next movement is to organize that naming into a structure that can be maintained. Clarity does not remain at the level of isolated identification. It extends outward, shaping how the person categorizes the world around them. What was once a single event becomes part of a broader pattern. What was once experienced as disruption begins to be organized into a system of meaning that can be relied upon.

This organizing process is essential. Naming alone stabilizes the immediate moment, but it does not provide long-term orientation. The person must be able to carry that clarity forward. They must be able to apply it beyond the initial event. This is where categorization emerges as a necessary extension of moral clarity.

Categorization divides experience into recognizable groupings. It establishes boundaries between what is right and what is wrong, what is safe and what is dangerous, what can be trusted and what cannot. These divisions are not arbitrary. They are constructed in response to disruption, shaped by the need to prevent further disorientation.

The act of dividing the world in this way allows the person to reduce uncertainty. Instead of encountering each new situation as entirely open, they approach it with a framework already in place. They do not need to begin from nothing. They have categories that guide their interpretation.

This guidance is stabilizing. It allows the person to move more quickly from perception to judgment. They see something, recognize its alignment with an existing category, and respond accordingly. This reduces the cognitive and emotional effort required to navigate each moment.

However, the efficiency of categorization comes with a cost. The categories that are formed in response to disruption are often shaped by the intensity of the initial experience. They are not neutral. They carry the weight of what has happened. As a result, they may be broader, more rigid, or more definitive than the situation would otherwise require.

For example, a single instance of betrayal may lead to a category that encompasses a wider range of behaviors or individuals. The person, seeking to prevent further harm, expands the boundary of what is considered untrustworthy. This expansion provides protection, but it can also limit perception. Not everything within the category may warrant the same response, but the category itself does not easily allow for distinction.

This is one of the central tensions of moral clarity. It stabilizes by simplifying, but in doing so, it can obscure complexity. The person is aware, at some level, that reality is more nuanced than the categories they have established. But returning to that nuance would require reentering a space of uncertainty that they have worked to avoid.

As a result, the categories are maintained. They become part of how the person interprets not only the original event, but subsequent experiences. The world is filtered through them. New information is evaluated in relation to what has already been defined.

This filtering process reinforces the categories over time. Each instance that appears to confirm the category strengthens it. Instances that do not fit may be set aside, minimized, or reinterpreted to align with the existing framework. This is not necessarily a conscious act of distortion. It is a way of preserving coherence.

In this way, categorization becomes self-sustaining. The framework that was created to respond to disruption begins to shape perception in a way that perpetuates itself. The person continues to encounter the world through the lens they have established, and that lens continues to confirm the necessity of its own existence.

This process extends beyond individual perception into relational and communal dynamics. Groups also engage in categorization as a way of maintaining stability. They define who belongs and who does not, what actions are acceptable and what are not, what narratives are affirmed and which are rejected. These collective categories provide a shared framework that aligns interpretation across individuals.

When these categories are shared, they create cohesion. Members of the group understand one another more easily because they are operating within the same system of meaning. This alignment reduces internal conflict and strengthens collective identity.

However, this cohesion can also lead to exclusion. Those who do not fit within the established categories may be seen as outside the structure. Their perspectives may be dismissed, their experiences minimized, their presence questioned. This is not always intentional. It is often a byproduct of the need to maintain clarity.

The more the group depends on these categories for stability, the more resistant it becomes to challenges that would introduce complexity. Alternative interpretations are not simply evaluated; they are often experienced as threats to coherence. To entertain them would require loosening the structure that has been built to withstand disruption.

This resistance reinforces the rigidity of the categories. Over time, what began as a response to a specific event becomes a fixed framework through which all events are interpreted. The categories become less responsive to new information and more protective of the stability they provide.

At the individual level, this rigidity can manifest as decisiveness. The person appears certain, clear, confident in their judgments. They know what is right and what is wrong, who can be trusted and who cannot, what actions are acceptable and what are not. This certainty can be reassuring, both to the person and to those around them.

But beneath this certainty is often a recognition that the clarity has come at a cost. The person may sense that something has been simplified, that aspects of reality have been set aside in order to maintain stability. They may not always be able to articulate what has been lost, but they feel the limitation.

This feeling does not necessarily lead to immediate change. The cost of reintroducing complexity is high. It would require revisiting the instability that gave rise to the categories in the first place. It would mean loosening the structure that has allowed the person to function.

And so the categories remain.

This is where the process of deciding becomes central. Categorization provides the framework, but decisions enact it. The person does not only interpret the world through categories; they act on those interpretations. They make choices based on the distinctions they have established.

These decisions reinforce the structure further. Each action taken in alignment with the categories strengthens their authority. The person experiences the outcome of their decision as confirmation that the framework is valid. This feedback loop deepens the reliance on moral clarity as a survival strategy.

At the same time, decision-making becomes more constrained. The range of possible responses narrows. The person is less likely to consider options that fall outside the established categories. They act within the boundaries they have set, even when alternative responses might be possible.

This narrowing is not necessarily experienced as limitation. It often feels like clarity. The person knows what to do. They do not have to deliberate extensively. The categories provide direction, and the decision follows.

Yet this clarity is maintained by the exclusion of complexity. It depends on the continuation of the divisions that were created in response to disruption. It requires that the world remain organized in ways that support the framework.

As long as this organization holds, the person can continue to function with a sense of stability. They have a way of interpreting events, a method for making decisions, a structure that allows them to engage with the world.

But this stability is contingent.

Because the world does not always conform to the categories that have been established.

And when it does not, the tension that was held at bay begins to return.

PART 3: THE NEED FOR CLOSURE—AND ITS COST

Once something has been named and the world has been divided into categories that restore a sense of order, the next movement is toward closure. Naming provides orientation. Categorizing provides structure. Closure provides finality. It answers not only what has happened and how it should be understood, but whether the matter is settled. It marks the point at which the person can stop returning to the event, stop reinterpreting it, stop holding it open as an unresolved question.

Closure is deeply compelling because it promises relief. It offers the possibility that the instability introduced by disruption can be contained. The person can draw a line around what has happened and say: this is finished. This has been addressed. This no longer requires my attention. In this way, closure functions as a release from the ongoing effort of interpretation.

The need for this release should not be underestimated. When moral coherence has been disrupted, the person has already expended significant energy attempting to restore it. They have named what is wrong, established categories to organize their experience, and made decisions that align with those categories. Each of these steps requires effort. Closure appears as the final step in that process—a way of consolidating what has been established and bringing the matter to rest.

Without closure, the process remains open. The event continues to demand attention. It resists being placed fully in the past. It interrupts thought, returns in memory, influences how new situations are perceived. This ongoing presence can be exhausting. The person is drawn back into the work of interpretation again and again, without resolution.

Closure offers a way out of this cycle. It allows the person to disengage from the constant need to revisit the event. It provides a sense that the work has been completed. The person can move forward without carrying the same level of interpretive burden.

This is why closure is often pursued with urgency. It is not merely a preference; it is a response to fatigue. The person has been living within tension, managing uncertainty, holding together competing interpretations. Closure promises an end to that strain.

However, the very qualities that make closure appealing also introduce risk. Because closure requires that the complexity of the situation be resolved into a definitive form. It requires that ambiguity be reduced, that competing interpretations be set aside, that the event be understood in a way that allows it to be considered finished.

This reduction is rarely complete. The aspects of the situation that do not fit neatly within the established narrative do not disappear. They are set aside, minimized, or excluded in order to achieve finality. Closure, then, is not only an act of resolution; it is an act of selection. It determines which elements of the experience will be carried forward and which will be left behind.

This selective process can stabilize the person in the short term. It provides a clear narrative that can be relied upon. It allows the person to say, with confidence, what has happened and what it means. But it can also create tension over time. The elements that were excluded do not cease to exist. They remain, often at the edges of awareness, influencing perception in subtle ways.

This is why closure can sometimes feel incomplete, even when it appears definitive. The person may declare that the matter is settled, yet still experience moments in which the unresolved aspects resurface. A memory returns. A question emerges. A feeling that had been set aside becomes present again. These moments do not necessarily overturn the closure, but they challenge its completeness.

The presence of these unresolved elements can create a sense of instability within the closure itself. The person may begin to question whether the resolution they have reached is sufficient. They may revisit the event, reconsider the narrative, reengage the process they had hoped to conclude.

At this point, the person faces a tension between the desire for closure and the persistence of complexity. To maintain closure, they must continue to hold the simplified narrative. To engage the complexity, they must reopen what they have attempted to close. Neither option is without cost.

Maintaining closure can require the ongoing exclusion of aspects of the experience that do not fit. This can lead to rigidity. The person may become resistant to new information or alternative perspectives that would challenge the established narrative. They may defend the closure, not only because it is accurate, but because it is necessary for their stability.

Reopening the experience, on the other hand, reintroduces uncertainty. It requires the person to reengage the interpretive process, to hold ambiguity, to reconsider what has been settled. This can be destabilizing, particularly if the original disruption was significant.

This tension reveals the dual nature of closure. It is both necessary and limited. It provides relief from the ongoing work of interpretation, but it does so by simplifying a reality that may not be fully resolvable. It allows the person to move forward, but it does not eliminate the presence of what remains unresolved.

In this sense, closure is not an absolute state, but a provisional one. It represents a point at which the person has achieved enough stability to continue, even if that stability is not complete. It is a functional resolution rather than a final one.

This provisional nature of closure becomes more apparent over time. As the person encounters new experiences, the framework they have established may be tested. Situations may arise that do not fit within the categories they have created. Responses may occur that challenge the narrative they have constructed. In these moments, the limits of closure are exposed.

The person may respond by reinforcing the existing framework, doubling down on the clarity they have established. They may interpret new experiences in ways that preserve the closure, even if this requires further simplification. This response maintains stability, but at the cost of flexibility.

Alternatively, the person may begin to allow the framework to shift. They may reintroduce complexity, reconsider previous conclusions, and adjust their understanding of what has happened. This response increases adaptability, but it also reopens the tension that closure was meant to resolve.

Neither response fully eliminates the tension. Both represent different ways of navigating the limits of closure.

At a deeper level, the need for closure reflects a fundamental aspect of human experience: the desire for completion. People seek to resolve what has been disrupted, to restore what has been broken, to bring events into a form that can be integrated into their understanding of the world. This desire is not misguided. It is part of how people make meaning.

But not all experiences can be fully resolved. Some resist closure. They do not lend themselves to definitive interpretation. They remain open, not because the person has failed to understand them, but because they exceed the frameworks available to contain them.

When this is the case, the pursuit of closure can become a source of further strain. The person may continue to seek resolution that cannot be achieved, revisiting the event in an attempt to bring it into a form that will finally settle. This ongoing effort can be exhausting, reinforcing the very instability that closure was meant to address.

It is here that the limits of moral clarity become most evident. Naming, categorizing, and deciding provide essential tools for navigating disruption, but they do not fully resolve it. Closure offers a way to consolidate these tools into a stable narrative, but it cannot eliminate the presence of what does not fit.

This realization marks a turning point. The person begins to recognize that the strategies they have used to survive—while necessary—are not sufficient to account for everything they encounter. The clarity they have constructed holds, but not completely. The closure they have achieved provides relief, but not finality.

This does not render these strategies invalid. It reveals their scope. They are ways of managing disruption, not of eliminating it.

And it is at this point—when the limits of clarity and closure become apparent—that a different kind of question begins to emerge. Not how to restore the structure that has been disrupted, or how to finalize what has been unsettled, but how to live within a reality that does not fully conform to either.

This question does not yet have a clear answer.

But it prepares the way for what follows.

CHAPTER 4

Moral Injury as Violation of Justice

PART 1: WHEN SOMETHING WRONG HAPPENS

UP TO THIS POINT, we have traced how people rely on moral logic to make sense of the world, how fairness stabilizes that logic through proportion, and how moral clarity emerges as a way of surviving when that stability begins to fracture. Naming, categorizing, and deciding provide a means of regaining orientation when coherence is threatened. These strategies allow the person to continue functioning within a world that no longer aligns as it once did. But these responses, while necessary, are reactive. They arise after disruption has already occurred. To understand moral injury more fully, we must return to the moment of disruption itself—the point at which something wrong happens and cannot be easily integrated into the structure that gives events their meaning.

Moral injury begins with violation. Not simply the occurrence of harm, but the recognition that what has occurred should not have happened. This distinction matters. Harm, in a general sense, can be incorporated into the moral structure if it is followed by response—if it is acknowledged, addressed, and situated within a sequence that restores proportion. Moral injury emerges when that sequence breaks. The event is not only harmful; it is misaligned with the expectations that allow harm to be understood.

The phrase "something wrong has happened" carries more weight than it initially suggests. It is not merely descriptive. It is evaluative. It signals that the event has been measured against a standard and found lacking. That standard may be explicit or implicit, personal or communal, but it is real. It reflects a set of expectations about how the world should function—expectations that have been shaped by experience, reinforced by culture, and sustained by the moral logic that undergirds daily life.

When those expectations are violated, the response is immediate. The person recognizes that what has occurred does not belong within the structure as it is understood. There is a sense of dissonance, a feeling that the event is out of place. This recognition is not always fully articulated, but it is felt. It is the moment in which the person says, internally or aloud, "This should not have happened."

This statement marks the beginning of moral injury. It identifies the event as a violation, not only of personal preference, but of the moral order itself. It asserts that the sequence has been broken, that the relationship between action and consequence, harm and response, has been disrupted in a way that cannot be easily reconciled.

At this stage, the person often attempts to interpret the event within the existing framework. They look for explanations that might restore coherence. They consider context, intention, circumstance. They ask whether there is something they have misunderstood, something that, if clarified, would allow the event to be placed within the sequence.

This effort reflects the strength of the underlying structure. The person does not immediately abandon the framework that has guided their understanding. They attempt to preserve it. They seek to reintegrate the event into the system that has previously made sense of experience.

But when this reintegration fails—when the event resists placement despite repeated attempts—the nature of the disruption becomes clear. The issue isnot a lack of information. It is a failure of alignment. The event does not correspond to the expectations that define what should happen. It cannot be made to fit without distorting those expectations.

This is the point at which the violation deepens. The person is no longer dealing with a single event, but with a challenge to the structure that gives events their meaning. The question shifts from "What happened?" to "How can this happen in a world that is supposed to work this way?" The disruption extends beyond the event into the person's understanding of the world itself.

This extension is what gives moral injury its distinctive character. It is not confined to the immediate harm. It alters the conditions under which harm is interpreted. The person's framework for making sense of experience is no longer fully reliable. The sequence that once held events in place has been compromised.

This compromise affects more than cognition. It reaches into emotional and relational domains. The person may experience anger, not only at the harm itself, but at the violation of expectation. They may feel betrayed, not only by the individual or system responsible for the harm, but by the structure that was supposed to prevent or address it.

Betrayal is a key dimension of moral injury. It reflects the relational aspect of the violation. The person has relied on others—individuals, institutions, communities—to act within the moral structure, to uphold the expectations that make trust possible. When those expectations are violated, the person experiences not only harm, but a breakdown of trust.

This breakdown is not easily repaired. Trust is built over time through consistent alignment between expectation and response. When that alignment fails in a significant way, the person cannot simply return to the previous state of trust. The conditions that made trust possible have been altered.

This is why moral injury often persists even after the immediate harm has been addressed. The issue is not only what happened, but what the event revealed about the reliability of the structure. The person has learned something about the world that cannot be unlearned. They have seen that the sequence can break, that the expectations they depended on are not guaranteed.

This realization introduces a lasting tension. The person continues to need the moral structure. They still rely on it to interpret events, to make decisions, to engage with others. But they no longer trust it in the same way. They are aware of its limits, of its potential to fail.

This awareness reshapes how they move through the world. They may become more cautious, more attentive to potential violations. They may rely more heavily on the survival strategies described in the previous chapter—naming, categorizing, deciding—in order to maintain a sense of stability.

At the same time, the experience of violation can lead to a heightened sensitivity to injustice. The person becomes more attuned to instances where the sequence does not hold, where harm is not addressed, where expectations are violated. This sensitivity can be both protective and burdensome. It allows the person to recognize potential threats, but it also makes it more difficult to ignore misalignment.

This heightened awareness can extend beyond personal experience. The person may begin to see patterns of violation in broader contexts—within communities, institutions, or systems. They may recognize that the disruption they experienced is not isolated, but part of a larger pattern. This recognition can deepen the sense of moral injury, as it suggests that the issue is not limited to a single event, but reflects a more pervasive instability.

At this point, the person is faced with a complex reality. They have experienced something that violates their understanding of how the world should work. They have attempted to reintegrate the event into their framework and have found that it does not fit. They have recognized that the structure itself is not as stable as they believed.

This recognition does not eliminate the need for the structure. The person still depends on it. But it changes how they relate to it. They are no longer able to rely on it without question. They must engage with it more consciously, more critically, more cautiously.

This shift marks the transition from stability to vulnerability within the moral framework. The structure still exists, but it no longer provides the same level of assurance. The person must navigate a world in which the expectations that once held are now uncertain.

It is here that the full weight of moral injury becomes apparent. It is not only about what has happened, but about what can no longer be assumed. It is about the loss of a reliable framework for interpreting experience, the breakdown of trust in the structures that sustain meaning, and the ongoing effort required to navigate a world that no longer aligns as it once did.

This is the first movement in understanding moral injury as violation of justice. It begins with the recognition that something wrong has happened. It deepens as that recognition extends into the structure that gives meaning to what is right and wrong. And it persists as the person continues to live within the tension created by that disruption.

From here, the question becomes more specific. Not only that something wrong has happened, but how that wrong is understood in relation to justice itself—how the absence, failure, or distortion of justice shapes the experience of moral injury.

That is where we turn next.

PART 2: BETRAYAL, FAILURE, AND THE WEIGHT OF HARM

If moral injury begins with the recognition that something wrong has happened, it deepens as that wrong is understood in relation to those who were expected to prevent it, address it, or bear responsibility for it. The violation is not experienced in isolation. It is situated within a network of relationships—individual, institutional, and communal—that give structure to moral expectation. When those relationships fail, the injury takes on a different quality. It becomes not only a matter of harm, but of betrayal.

Betrayal is not simply the presence of wrongdoing. It is the failure of trust within a relationship that was expected to uphold the moral order. It occurs when someone who should have acted differently does not, when someone who was relied upon to respond does not respond, or when someone who holds authority uses it in ways that violate the expectations attached to that authority. The harm is intensified by the relationship in which it occurs.

This relational dimension is central to moral injury. People do not form expectations in a vacuum. They develop them within contexts that shape what they believe is possible, appropriate, and necessary. These contexts include families, communities, professions, institutions, and systems. Each of these carries its own set of expectations about how individuals and groups should act, how harm should be addressed, and how justice should be maintained.

When these expectations are violated, the impact extends beyond the immediate event. The person experiences not only the harm itself, but the failure of the structure that was meant to prevent or respond to that harm. The question is no longer only "What happened?" but "How could this happen within a system that is supposed to function differently?"

This question introduces a second layer to the injury. The first layer is the harm. The second is the failure of the system. These layers do not exist independently. They interact. The harm is interpreted through the lens of the failure, and the failure amplifies the harm. What might have been experienced as a difficult but understandable event becomes something else when it occurs within a context that should have prevented it.

This is particularly evident in situations involving authority. Authority carries with it an expectation of responsibility. Those in positions of authority are entrusted with maintaining the structures that allow fairness and justice to function. When they fail to do so, the violation is not only of the specific action, but of the role itself.

The person who experiences this kind of violation is not only responding to what was done, but to what was not done. They are responding to the absence of action where action was expected, to the misuse of power where responsibility was assumed, to the silence or indifference of those who were supposed to respond. This absence is not neutral. It is experienced as a form of harm.

In this way, moral injury often involves multiple points of failure. There is the initial harm, and there is the failure of response. There may also be a failure of acknowledgment, a failure to recognize what has occurred in a way that reflects its significance. Each of these failures adds a layer to the injury.

These layers accumulate. The person is not only carrying the original event, but the subsequent responses—or lack of responses—that have shaped how the event is understood. The injury becomes more complex, more difficult to integrate, because it is not confined to a single moment. It unfolds over time.

This unfolding can be particularly disorienting. The person may initially interpret the harm within the existing framework, expecting that it will be addressed in ways that restore coherence. When that response does not come, or comes in a way that does not correspond, the interpretation shifts. The person must account not only for the harm, but for the failure of the system to respond as expected.

This shift often introduces a sense of isolation. The person may feel that their experience is not being recognized in the way it should be. They may question whether others see what they see, whether the significance of the event is understood, whether the expectations they hold are shared. This questioning can lead to a sense of disconnection from the community or system in which the injury occurred.

At the same time, the person may continue to rely on that system. They may remain within the institution, the profession, the community that has failed them, because it still provides structure in other ways. This creates a tension between dependence and disillusionment. The person needs the system, but no longer trusts it in the same way.

This tension is difficult to navigate. It requires the person to hold conflicting realities simultaneously. The system is both necessary and unreliable. The relationships within it are both meaningful and compromised. The expectations that once guided engagement are still present, but no longer secure.

In response to this tension, the person may intensify their reliance on moral clarity. They may name the failure in definitive terms, assign responsibility clearly, and establish boundaries that protect them from further harm. These actions provide a sense of control in a situation that has become unpredictable.

However, the complexity of the injury often resists this kind of simplification. The person may recognize that the individuals or systems involved are not entirely reducible to the categories they have established. There may be elements of good within the same context that produced harm, or moments of integrity within a broader pattern of failure. These contradictions complicate the process of naming and categorizing.

This complication does not eliminate the need for clarity, but it does make it more difficult to sustain. The person is aware that the reality they are attempting to organize is not entirely captured by the categories they have created. This awareness can create additional tension, as the person must choose whether to maintain the clarity that provides stability or to engage the complexity that introduces uncertainty.

At the same time, the weight of harm itself continues to exert pressure. Harm is not only an event; it is an experience that affects the person's sense of self, their relationships, and their understanding of the world. It carries emotional, relational, and often physical consequences. These consequences do not disappear simply because the event has been named or categorized.

The person must find a way to live with what has occurred. They must integrate the experience into their ongoing life, even if it does not fully make sense. This integration is complicated by the layers of betrayal and failure that surround the harm. The person is not only processing what was done, but how it was responded to.

In many cases, the absence of appropriate response becomes as significant as the harm itself. The person may find that what remains most difficult is not the initial event, but the way it was handled—or not handled—by those who were expected to respond. The lack of acknowledgment, the minimization of the event, the failure to take responsibility—these responses shape the experience in ways that are difficult to undo.

This is why moral injury often persists even when the immediate circumstances have changed. The person may no longer be in the same situation, but the impact of the violation remains. It continues to influence how they interpret new experiences, how they relate to others, how they understand themselves.

This persistence reflects the depth of the injury. It is not confined to a single moment. It is embedded in the person's ongoing experience of the world. It affects how they perceive fairness, how they engage with systems, how they extend trust.

At this stage, the person is navigating a complex landscape. They are holding the reality of harm, the experience of betrayal, the recognition of systemic failure, and the need to continue living within a world that still requires engagement. They are using the tools available to them—naming, categorizing, deciding—to maintain some level of stability.

But these tools, while necessary, do not fully resolve the tension. The injury remains. The questions remain. The sense of misalignment between what has happened and what should have happened continues to shape the person's experience.

This is where the understanding of moral injury as violation of justice becomes more precise. It is not only that something wrong has happened, but that the structures responsible for addressing what is wrong have failed to do so in ways that restore coherence. The injury is located not only in the event, but in the absence or distortion of justice.

And it is from within this absence—this failure of justice to function as expected—that the next and most disruptive movement begins to emerge.

PART 3: WHEN JUSTICE DOES NOT CLOSE THE GAP

If moral injury emerges when something wrong happens and deepens through betrayal, failure, and the absence of response, it would seem that justice is the natural resolution. Justice, as it is commonly understood, restores proportion. It reconnects action and consequence. It answers harm with accountability. It closes the gap between what has occurred and what should follow. Within the moral structure we depend on, justice is what repairs the sequence when it has been broken.

This expectation is not incidental. It is foundational. The belief that justice can restore coherence is what allows people to endure disruption without losing their orientation entirely. Even when harm is significant, the possibility of justice provides a future point at which the imbalance will be addressed. It allows the person to say, "This is not how it should be, but it will be answered." This anticipated response stabilizes the present by projecting resolution into the future.

However, the experience of moral injury often complicates this expectation. Justice does not always arrive. When it does, it does not always function in ways that restore coherence. The person may encounter situations in which accountability is partial, delayed, or absent altogether. They may see responses that do not reflect the weight of what has occurred. They may witness systems that are unable or unwilling to act in ways that correspond to the harm.

In these cases, the anticipated closure does not take place. The gap remains open. The person continues to carry the misalignment between what has happened and what should have followed. The sequence is not restored. The structure remains unstable.

Even when justice does occur, it may not fully resolve the disruption. A consequence may be enacted. Responsibility may be assigned. But the experience of harm may not be fully addressed by these responses. The person may find that the outcome, while technically aligned with the structure, does not correspond to the depth of what was experienced.

This reveals a limitation within the concept of justice as it is often understood. Justice operates within the same moral logic that has been disrupted. It seeks to restore proportion by aligning response with event. But when the event itself has fractured the person's ability to trust that structure, the restoration of proportion may not be sufficient to reestablish coherence.

The person may recognize that justice has been done, and yet still feel that something remains unsettled. The response fits the framework, but the framework itself no longer holds in the same way. The sequence has been repaired, but the confidence in the sequence has not been restored.

This creates a secondary tension. The person is confronted with a form of resolution that does not fully resolve. They are told, explicitly or implicitly, that the matter has been addressed, that the appropriate response has been given. But their experience does not align with that conclusion. The sense of closure that justice is meant to provide does not fully take hold.

At this point, the person is left with a complex reality. The moral structure has been reaffirmed through the enactment of justice, but their trust in that structure remains compromised. They are asked to accept that the sequence has been restored, even as they continue to feel its instability.

This disjunction can be difficult to navigate. The person may question their own response. They may wonder why the resolution does not feel sufficient, why the closure that has been provided does not fully settle the experience. They may feel out of alignment with the system that has declared the matter resolved.

This sense of misalignment is not necessarily a rejection of justice. It is a recognition of its limits. Justice addresses the relationship between action and consequence, but it does not always address the deeper disruption of meaning that moral injury produces. It restores proportion, but it does not always restore trust.

This distinction is critical. Trust is not rebuilt solely through the enactment of appropriate responses. It is rebuilt through the reestablishment of reliable correspondence over time. A single act of justice, even if it is significant, may not be enough to restore the person's confidence in the structure. The memory of the violation remains. The awareness that the sequence can break is not undone.

In this context, justice becomes one element within a larger process of navigating disruption. It is necessary, but not sufficient. It provides a response, but not a complete resolution. It closes certain aspects of the gap, but not all of them.

This incomplete closure creates a space that remains open. The person continues to live within the tension between what has been addressed and what has not. They may move forward, but they carry with them the knowledge that the resolution was partial, that the structure has limits.

It is within this open space that a different kind of response begins to appear.

Not as a continuation of the sequence.

Not as an extension of justice.

But as something that enters from outside the expected order.

This is where grace begins to emerge.

Grace does not operate within the same logic as justice. It does not seek to restore proportion by aligning response with event. It does not follow the sequence of action and consequence in the same way. Instead, it introduces a response that is not determined by what has occurred.

At first, this may appear as an alternative form ofresolution. If justice has not fully closed the gap, perhaps grace will. If accountability has not restored coherence, perhaps mercy will complete what justice has begun.

But this expectation quickly encounters difficulty.

Because grace does not simply supplement justice.

It disrupts it.

Grace does not complete the sequence.

It interrupts it.

Where justice seeks to align response with event, grace introduces a response that is not proportionate to the event. It gives where nothing has been earned. It forgives where accountability has not been fully enacted. It extends beyond the boundaries that justice establishes.

This extension is not easily integrated into the moral structure that has already been strained by the experience of moral injury. The person, already navigating the limits of justice, is now confronted with a response that does not align with the logic that justice attempts to restore.

At this point, the tension shifts.

The question is no longer only about the absence or inadequacy of justice.

It becomes a question about the presence of something that does not follow justice at all.

The person must now interpret not only what has happened and how it has been addressed, but what it means for a response to occur that is not governed by the expectations they have relied upon.

This introduces a new kind of instability.

If justice was meant to close the gap and has not fully done so, and if grace enters in a way that does not correspond to the event, then the structure itself is called into question at a deeper level.

The person is no longer only dealing with a failure of the system.

They are encountering something that does not operate according to the system.

This is where the experience of grace begins to intersect with moral injury in a way that is not immediately comforting.

It does not simply offer relief.

It introduces further disruption.

The person who has been seeking coherence—through moral logic, through fairness, through clarity, through justice—now encounters a response that does not align with any of these frameworks.

Grace does not restore the sequence.

It reframes it.

And in doing so, it destabilizes the very structures that the person has been using to survive.

This is the pivot.

Up to this point, the movement of the book has been toward understanding how people make sense of disruption within the moral structure they depend on. From this point forward, the focus shifts to what happens when something enters that cannot be fully understood within that structure.

Grace is not simply another response.

It is a different kind of reality.

And before it can be received as good, it must be encountered as something that does not fit.

PART II

When Grace Disrupts

(The Offense of Mercy)

CHAPTER 5

Grace Violates Moral Logic

PART 1: WHEN THE SEQUENCE NO LONGER HOLDS

UP TO THIS POINT, the movement has followed a recognizable arc. Moral logic establishes the structure through which events are understood. Fairness stabilizes that structure through proportion. Moral clarity emerges as a way of surviving when that stability begins to fracture. Justice is expected to restore what has been disrupted, to reconnect action and consequence, harm and response. Each of these elements operates within a shared assumption: that the world, while imperfect, can be made intelligible through the alignment of what happens with what should follow.

Grace enters that structure, but it does not reinforce it. It does not stabilize it. It does not restore it in the ways that have been assumed. Instead, grace introduces a response that is not governed by the sequence that has organized moral experience. It does not align with the expectation that actions lead to proportionate consequences. It does not wait for accountability before extending forgiveness. It does not require that what has been broken be repaired before something is given.

In this sense, grace does not simply fail to follow moral logic. It violates it.

This violation is not always immediately recognized as such. Grace is often framed in language that suggests continuity with the moral structure: restoration, reconciliation, renewal. These terms imply that grace completes what has been disrupted, that it brings the sequence to its proper conclusion. But when grace is encountered in lived experience, particularly in contexts shaped by moral injury, it does not always function this way.

Instead, it interrupts.

The sequence that has been relied upon—wrong leading to consequence, harm to accountability, guilt to cost—is broken, not by failure, but by response. Something is given that does not correspond to what has occurred. The person who expects alignment encounters misalignment of a different kind. Not the absence of response, but the presence of a response that does not fit.

This is where the experience becomes disorienting. The person has already navigated the instability introduced by harm and the incomplete restoration offered by justice. They have relied on moral clarity to regain orientation. They have constructed categories, made decisions, and sought closure where possible. These strategies have allowed them to continue within a structure that, while weakened, still provides a framework for understanding.

Grace does not operate within that framework.

It introduces something that cannot be easily placed within the categories that have been established. It does not correspond to the distinctions between right and wrong in the way those distinctions have been used to stabilize experience. It does not reinforce the boundaries that have been drawn to protect against further disruption.

Instead, it crosses them.

This crossing is not neutral. It carries implications that extend beyond the immediate moment. If grace is given where it is not earned, if forgiveness is extended where accountability has not been completed, if restoration is offered without the sequence being fulfilled, then the logic that has governed interpretation is called into question.

The person is faced with a difficult reality. The structure that has been used to make sense of the world is not only incomplete. It is being actively disrupted by something that is presented as good.

This is the beginning of the offense.

The person does not reject grace because they misunderstand it. They resist it because they understand, at least implicitly, what it does to the structure they depend on. Grace does not simply add something new to the system. It alters the system itself.

This alteration affects how events are interpreted. If outcomes are no longer tied to actions in predictable ways, if responses are not determined by what has occurred, then the ability to anticipate what will happen is diminished. The person can no longer rely on the sequence to guide their understanding.

This loss of predictability is not trivial. It affects how the person engages with the world. Anticipation is a key component of participation. People act not only based on what is, but based on what they expect will follow. When that expectation is disrupted, action becomes more uncertain.

Grace introduces that uncertainty.

It does not provide a new sequence that can replace the old one. It does not establish a different set of rules that can be relied upon in the same way. It resists systematization. It cannot be reduced to a predictable pattern. It appears in ways that are not consistent, not proportional, not easily explained.

This resistance to systematization is part of what makes grace what it is. But it is also what makes it difficult to receive. The person who has relied on moral logic to navigate the world is now confronted with something that cannot be navigated in the same way.

They must decide how to interpret what they are encountering.

One possibility is to attempt to incorporate grace into the existing framework. The person may try to reinterpret grace as a delayed form of justice, or as a hidden form of proportion. They may assume that what appears unearned will eventually be balanced, that what appears misaligned will be accounted for in ways that are not immediately visible.

This approach preserves the structure. It allows the person to maintain the belief that the sequence still holds, even if it is not fully apparent. But it does so at the cost of distorting grace. It forces grace into a pattern it does not follow.

Another possibility is to reject grace as inconsistent with the moral structure. The person may conclude that what they are witnessing is not good, not just, not appropriate. They may interpret grace as a failure to uphold the standards that should govern response. This approach preserves the integrity of the structure, but it does so by excluding grace from it.

Both responses reflect an attempt to resolve the tension. They seek to bring grace into alignment with the moral logic that has been disrupted. But grace resists both incorporation and exclusion. It remains present as something that does not fit.

This is where the experience becomes most acute. The person is not only dealing with a violation of expectation. They are dealing with the presence of something that cannot be easily categorized within their existing framework. They must hold together two realities: that grace is being presented as good, and that it does not align with the structure that defines what is good.

This tension cannot be resolved through explanation alone. It is not a problem of information. It is a problem of alignment. The categories that have been used to interpret experience are no longer sufficient to account for what is being encountered.

At this point, the person may return to the strategies of moral clarity. They may attempt to name grace in definitive terms, to categorize it in ways that allow it to be managed. They may describe it as inappropriate, premature, or unjust. These descriptions provide a way of responding to the disruption.

But they do not eliminate it.

Grace continues to appear.

And each time it does, it reintroduces the same tension. The sequence does not hold. The response does not correspond. The structure is not restored.

This repetition can be unsettling. The person may begin to recognize that the disruption is not temporary. It is not a single instance that can be resolved and set aside. It is a recurring feature of how grace operates.

This recognition deepens the sense of instability. The person is no longer dealing with an isolated anomaly. They are confronting a pattern that does not conform to the expectations that have guided their understanding.

The question becomes more urgent.

Not only how to interpret grace, but how to live in a world where grace operates in this way.

This is the beginning of a new kind of inquiry. It moves beyond the attempt to restore the sequence or to reconcile grace with existing categories. It asks what it means to inhabit a reality in which the sequence itself is no longer the final measure of meaning.

That question does not yet have an answer.

But it defines the movement that follows.

PART 2: WHY GRACE FEELS LIKE INSTABILITY

If grace violates moral logic by interrupting the sequence that connects action and consequence, its effect is not limited to intellectual confusion. It produces a more immediate and embodied response: instability. The person does not only struggle to interpret grace. They feel unsettled by it. What has been relied upon to navigate the world no longer holds in the same way, and the absence of that stability is experienced not as freedom, but as exposure.

Moral logic provides more than a way of understanding events. It provides a sense of containment. When actions lead to consequences and responses correspond to what has occurred, the world feels bounded. Even when those consequences are difficult, they are located within a structure that can be anticipated. The person knows, at least in general terms, how things will unfold. This knowledge allows for a sense of security.

Grace disrupts that containment. It introduces responses that are not tied to what has occurred, and in doing so, it removes the boundaries that have made the world feel navigable. The person is no longer able to rely on the sequence to determine what will follow. Outcomes are no longer contained within the limits of expectation.

This lack of containment is experienced as instability. The person does not know where the edges are. They do not know how far the response will extend, or what will govern it. The familiar markers that have indicated where one thing ends and another begins are no longer clear. The world feels less defined.

This experience can be particularly acute in situations shaped by moral injury. The person has already encountered a breakdown in the expected sequence. They have already experienced the instability that comes when harm is not followed by appropriate response. They have worked to regain orientation through clarity and categorization. They have sought closure where possible, or at least a way of moving forward.

Grace reopens that instability.

But it does so in a different way. The instability introduced by harm is experienced as a failure of the structure. The instability introduced by grace is experienced as a challenge to the structure itself. It does not simply reveal that the sequence has failed in a particular instance. It suggests that the sequence is not the final measure of how responses occur.

This suggestion is difficult to absorb. The person has depended on the sequence not only to interpret events, but to regulate emotional and relational engagement. They have learned to anticipate responses, to manage expectations, to protect themselves within the boundaries that moral logic provides. Grace disrupts those regulatory mechanisms.

Without predictable correspondence, the person cannot easily determine how to respond. They do not know what to expect from others, or even from themselves. The categories that have been used to guide action become less reliable. The clarity that has been constructed begins to loosen.

This loosening is not experienced as openness. It is experienced as vulnerability.

The person is exposed to a range of possibilities that are not easily contained. Responses may come that do not align with expectation. Outcomes may occur that cannot be anticipated. The person must engage with a level of uncertainty that extends beyond what they have previously managed.

This uncertainty can produce a range of emotional responses. Confusion is often the first. The person attempts to understand what is happening, to locate grace within the framework they know. When that effort fails, the confusion deepens. It is not only about what is occurring, but about how to interpret it.

Alongside confusion, there is often resistance. The person pushes back against what they are encountering, not necessarily because they reject grace in principle, but because they experience its effects as destabilizing. They seek to reassert the boundaries that have been disrupted, to restore the sequence that has been interrupted.

This resistance can take many forms. It may appear as critique, as an attempt to redefine grace in ways that align with moral logic. It may appear as rejection, as a refusal to accept responses that do not correspond to what has occurred. It may appear as withdrawal, as a decision to disengage from situations where grace is operating in ways that feel unsafe.

Underlying these responses is a common concern: the loss of predictability.

Predictability is not simply a convenience. It is a condition of trust. The person trusts that actions will lead to consequences, that responses will correspond to events, that the world will function in ways that make sense. This trust allows them to act, to invest, to participate without needing to secure every outcome.

Grace disrupts that trust.

It does not provide a new form of predictability that can replace the old one. It does not establish a different sequence that can be relied upon in the same way. It operates in ways that are not consistent, not proportional, not easily anticipated. The person cannot form expectations about grace in the same way they form expectations about justice.

This lack of predictability makes it difficult to engage with grace confidently. The person may hesitate to accept it, not because they do not desire what it offers, but because they do not know what accepting it will mean. They cannot anticipate how it will unfold, what it will require, or how it will affect the structures they depend on.

This hesitation is often accompanied by a sense of dissonance. The person is told, or has learned, that grace is good. It is presented as something to be welcomed, something that brings relief and restoration. But their experience does not align with that description. They feel unsettled, exposed, uncertain.

This dissonance creates tension between belief and experience. The person may affirm the goodness of grace at a conceptual level while resisting it at an experiential level. They may feel that they should receive grace, even as they find themselves unable to do so.

This tension can be difficult to articulate. It may not be expressed directly. Instead, it may appear as frustration, as discomfort, as a reluctance to engage with situations where grace is present. The person may struggle to explain why something that is described as good does not feel that way.

Part of the difficulty lies in the way grace interacts with the strategies that have been used to survive disruption. Moral clarity, categorization, and closure all depend on the ability to define, to distinguish, to finalize. Grace resists these processes. It does not conform to clear categories. It blurs distinctions. It reopens what has been closed.

This reopening can be particularly unsettling. The person may have worked hard to establish a sense of resolution, to bring an event into a form that can be carried forward. Grace, by introducing a response that does not align with that resolution, can destabilize what has been achieved.

The person may feel as though they are being asked to relinquish the stability they have constructed. They may experience grace as a demand rather than a gift—a demand to reconsider what has been settled, to reopen what has been closed, to engage with complexity they have already worked to manage.

This experience can lead to a sense of loss. The person is not only losing predictability. They are losing the structures that have allowed them to navigate a difficult reality. The clarity they have achieved, the categories they have established, the closure they have reached—these are not trivial accomplishments. They are the result of significant effort.

Grace does not necessarily remove these structures, but it calls them into question. It introduces a different way of responding that does not depend on them. This introduction can feel like a destabilization of the very tools the person has used to survive.

It is important to recognize that this response is not irrational. It is grounded in the person's experience. They have learned, through disruption, that stability is fragile. They have worked to reconstruct that stability through moral clarity. Grace appears to unsettle that reconstruction.

This is why grace does not always feel like comfort. Comfort would reinforce the structures that have been established. It would align with the expectations that have been formed. It would provide a sense of continuity.

Grace does not always do this.

It introduces discontinuity.

It creates a break, not only in the sequence of action and consequence, but in the way the person has learned to manage that sequence. It asks the person to engage with a form of response that does not follow the patterns they have relied upon.

This engagement requires a different kind of orientation. It cannot be based solely on moral logic, fairness, or clarity. It requires the person to hold together the reality of disruption and the presence of something that does not fit within the structures that have been used to navigate it.

This holding is not easy. It involves living within tension, without immediate resolution. It requires the person to remain present to an experience that is both unsettling and, in some sense, presented as good.

This is where the emotional intensity of grace becomes most apparent. It is not simply an idea to be understood. It is an experience that affects how the person feels, how they relate to others, how they engage with the world.

And it is within this emotional landscape—marked by confusion, resistance, vulnerability, and dissonance—that the deeper question begins to emerge.

Not whether grace is good.

But how it is to be received when it does not feel that way.

PART 3: WHY GRACE PROVOKES PROTEST

If grace disrupts the moral sequence and produces instability rather than comfort, the next movement is not quiet confusion but active response. The person does not remain neutral in the face of disruption. They react. And one of the most consistent forms that reaction takes is protest.

This protest is not always loud or public. It may be internal, expressed as resistance, discomfort, or refusal. But it is real. It reflects the person's attempt to defend the moral structure that has been relied upon to make sense of the world. When grace violates that structure, the person does not simply adjust. They push back.

This pushback often takes the form of anger.

Anger, in this context, is not merely an emotional outburst. It is a moral response. It arises from the perception that something is wrong—not only in what has happened, but in how it is being responded to. The person experiences grace not as a correction of injustice, but as a further distortion of it.

This perception is grounded in the expectations that have shaped moral understanding. If harm should be followed by accountability, if wrongdoing should be met with consequence, then a response that bypasses these expectations appears unjust. Grace, when it is extended without proportion, can be experienced as a violation of justice rather than its fulfillment.

The person's anger, then, is not directed at grace as an abstract concept. It is directed at what grace appears to do within a specific context. It is a reaction to the way grace interrupts the sequence that has been used to interpret events.

This is why the protest of grace often sounds like a defense of fairness. The person insists that what has happened should be answered in a way that corresponds. They appeal to proportion, to accountability, to the structures that have provided stability. They argue that something is being overlooked, minimized, or bypassed.

These arguments are not without merit. They reflect a deeply held commitment to justice. They express the person's understanding of how the world should work. They are rooted in the same moral logic that has been explored throughout this book.

But grace does not operate within that logic.

It does not deny it entirely, but it does not conform to it. It introduces a response that is not determined by what has been done. It gives where something has not been earned. It forgives where accountability has not been completed. It restores where the sequence has not been fulfilled.

This creates a conflict between two ways of understanding what is right.

On one side is the logic of justice: action should lead to consequence, harm to accountability, guilt to cost. On the other side is the logic of grace: response is not limited by what has been done, and what is given is not determined by what has been earned.

These logics do not easily align. They operate according to different principles. When they are brought into contact, the tension becomes apparent.

The person who protests grace is often standing within the logic of justice. They are defending the structure that has allowed them to make sense of harm, to pursue accountability, to seek restoration. From within that structure, grace appears to undermine the very conditions that make justice possible.

This is why grace can be experienced as a threat.

It threatens the connection between action and consequence. It disrupts the expectation that wrongdoing will be addressed in proportion to its impact. It introduces the possibility that outcomes are not determined by what has occurred.

For the person who has relied on that connection to navigate the world, this threat is significant. It calls into question the reliability of the structure they depend on. It suggests that the categories they have used to interpret experience are not final.

This suggestion can be difficult to accept.

The person may respond by reinforcing the logic of justice more strongly. They may insist on the necessity of accountability, the importance of consequence, the need for proportion. They may view grace as premature, inappropriate, or even harmful in the context in which it is being extended.

This response is not simply resistance. It is an attempt to preserve coherence. The person is trying to maintain a framework that allows them to understand and respond to the world. They are protecting the structure that has made meaning possible.

At the same time, this protest reveals something important about grace itself.

Grace does not simply invite acceptance.

It provokes response.

It exposes the underlying commitments that shape how people understand what is right. It brings to the surface the assumptions that have been operating beneath the level of conscious awareness. It reveals the extent to which moral logic has been relied upon to define meaning.

In this way, the protest of grace becomes a form of disclosure. It shows what the person believes about justice, fairness, and responsibility. It makes visible the structure that has been used to interpret experience.

This disclosure is not comfortable. It requires the person to confront the possibility that the framework they have relied upon is not complete. It raises questions about whether the logic of justice, while necessary, is sufficient to account for the full range of human experience.

These questions do not immediately lead to resolution. They often deepen the tension. The person may feel pulled between two competing realities: the need for justice and the presence of grace.

This pull can create a sense of internal conflict. The person may affirm the importance of grace in principle while resisting its application in practice. They may believe that grace is good, but not here, not now, not in this way.

This qualification reflects the difficulty of integrating grace into the moral structure. The person is attempting to limit grace to contexts where it does not disrupt the sequence too severely. They are trying to preserve the stability of the structure while allowing for the presence of grace in a controlled way.

But grace resists this limitation.

It does not remain within the boundaries that are set for it. It appears in places where it is not expected, in ways that do not align with the established categories. It continues to disrupt the sequence.

This persistence intensifies the protest.

The person may feel that grace is being imposed upon them, that it is demanding a response that they are not prepared to give. They may experience it as an intrusion, as something that enters their experience without regard for the structures they have relied upon.

This experience can be particularly sharp in situations of moral injury. The person who has been harmed, who has sought accountability, who has worked to make sense of what has happened, may encounter grace extended toward the one who caused harm. In that moment, grace is not experienced as a gift. It is experienced as a violation.

It appears to bypass the process that the person has depended on to restore coherence. It seems to offer resolution without proportion, to extend forgiveness without acknowledgment, to move forward without addressing what has been broken.

This perception can generate intense anger.

The person may feel that their experience is being minimized, that the harm they have endured is being overlooked, that the structures that should have protected them are being disregarded. They may interpret grace as a denial of justice rather than its fulfillment.

This interpretation is not easily dismissed. It reflects a genuine tension within the experience of grace. It highlights the ways in which grace, when encountered within a framework shaped by moral injury, can feel like an extension of the disruption rather than its resolution.

At this point, the offense of grace is fully visible.

It is not a minor discomfort or a temporary confusion. It is a profound challenge to the way the person understands the world. It calls into question the structures that have provided stability, the strategies that have enabled survival, and the expectations that have guided interpretation.

The person stands at a crossroads.

They can continue to resist grace, to defend the moral logic that has sustained them, to insist on the necessity of proportion and accountability. Or they can begin to consider the possibility that grace, while disruptive, may be pointing to something beyond the structures they have relied upon.

This consideration is not immediate. It cannot be forced. It requires time, reflection, and a willingness to remain within the tension without resolving it prematurely.

For now, the protest remains.

And it is from within that protest—not beyond it—that the next movement of this book begins.

CHAPTER 6

The Offense of Unearned Mercy

PART 1: WHEN NOTHING HAS BEEN PAID

IF GRACE VIOLATES MORAL logic and provokes protest, the offense becomes sharper when it is encountered not as an abstract idea but as an unearned reality. The question is no longer only how grace disrupts the sequence of action and consequence, but how it is experienced when something is given without cost. The disruption becomes personal. It enters the space where harm has been carried, where accountability has been expected, where the weight of what has happened has not yet been answered.

Unearned mercy is not difficult to define. It is mercy given where no payment has been made, no repair completed, no proportion established between what has occurred and what follows. It is the extension of forgiveness, restoration, or acceptance in the absence of the conditions that would normally justify it within the moral structure. What makes it offensive is not that it is incomprehensible, but that it is intelligible enough to be recognized as a departure from what should have happened.

The person encountering unearned mercy does not struggle to see what is being offered. They recognize it immediately. They understand that something is being given that has not been earned. And it is precisely this recognition that creates the tension. The clarity of the gift does not resolve the disruption; it intensifies it.

Within the framework that has been established throughout this book, earning plays a central role in stabilizing meaning. Actions are connected to outcomes. Effort leads to result. Harm leads to consequence. These connections allow the person to interpret events in ways that preserve coherence. When something is earned, it fits within that structure. It can be located, understood, and integrated.

Unearned mercy does not fit.

It breaks the connection between action and outcome. It introduces a response that cannot be traced back to what has occurred. The person is left without a clear way to account for what they are seeing. The sequence that has guided interpretation is interrupted, not by absence, but by presence. Something is there that should not be there, at least not according to the logic that has been relied upon.

This interruption is not neutral. It carries implications that extend into how the person understands justice, fairness, and responsibility. If mercy can be given without being earned, then the relationship between action and outcome is not as stable as it has been assumed to be. The categories that have been used to define what is deserved and what is not begin to loosen.

For the person who has been harmed, this loosening can feel like a direct threat. The expectation that harm will be followed by accountability is not only a moral preference. It is a way of preserving the significance of what has occurred. It ensures that the harm is recognized, that it is not minimized or overlooked. It affirms that what has happened matters.

Unearned mercy appears to bypass that affirmation.

When mercy is extended without cost, it can seem as though the harm has been set aside, as though the weight of what has occurred has not been fully acknowledged. The person may feel that the sequence has been interrupted before it has had the opportunity to complete. Accountability has not been realized, and yet the process moves forward.

This experience can be deeply unsettling. The person is not only witnessing a disruption of moral logic; they are experiencing a disruption of meaning. The connection between what has happened and what should follow is no longer intact. The event has not been carried through the sequence in the way that would allow it to be resolved.

This is where the offense begins to take on a relational dimension. Unearned mercy is not simply a structural disruption. It affects how the person relates to others, to the one who caused harm, to the community that extends mercy, and to themselves.

When mercy is extended toward the one who has caused harm, the person who has been harmed may experience this as a form of displacement. The focus shifts from the harm to the one who has done the harm. The attention that was expected to remain on what has occurred moves elsewhere. The person may feel that their experience is being overshadowed, that the significance of what they have endured is being diminished.

This perception is not necessarily a reflection of intention. Those who extend mercy may not be seeking to minimize harm. They may be acting ךותמ a commitment to forgiveness, to restoration, to a vision of reconciliation that transcends the sequence of justice. But the effect, from the perspective of the one who has been harmed, can be experienced differently.

The shift in focus creates a sense of imbalance. The person may feel that the structure that should hold their experience in place has been altered. The harm has not been carried through the sequence, and yet the process has moved forward. This movement can feel premature, as though something essential has been left unfinished.

This sense of incompletion is central to the offense of unearned mercy. The person is not only reacting to what has been given; they are responding to what has not been done. The absence of accountability, the lack of proportion, the incomplete acknowledgment of harm—these elements remain present, even as mercy is extended.

The coexistence of these realities creates tension. Mercy is present, but the conditions that would make it intelligible within the moral structure are not. The person must hold together two experiences: the recognition that something is being offered, and the awareness that something remains unaddressed.

This tension is not easily resolved. It cannot be dismissed by appealing to the goodness of mercy, because the experience is not only about the value of what is given. It is about the relationship between what is given and what has occurred. The person is not rejecting mercy as such; they are questioning how it is being applied.

This questioning often takes the form of moral protest. The person may ask whether mercy is appropriate in this context, whether it has come too soon, whether it has bypassed necessary steps. They may insist that something must be done before mercy can be meaningfully extended. These questions reflect an attempt to restore the sequence, to reestablish the connection between action and response.

At the same time, the person may experience a more internal conflict. They may recognize, at some level, that mercy is being offered in good faith, that it carries a kind of goodness that they cannot entirely dismiss. But this recognition does not eliminate the discomfort. It intensifies it.

The person is caught between two competing perceptions. On one hand, mercy is something that is understood as good, as valuable, as central to the moral and spiritual life. On the other hand, the way it is being encountered does not align with the structures that have been used to define what is good.

This conflict can produce a sense of disorientation. The person does not know how to respond. To accept the mercy feels like a betrayal of the structure that affirms the significance of harm. To reject it feels like a denial of something that is, in some sense, good.

This is the space in which the offense of unearned mercy is most acutely felt. It is not simply a rejection of mercy, nor is it an unqualified acceptance. It is a struggle to hold together two realities that do not easily align.

This struggle is not a sign of failure. It is a reflection of the depth of the disruption that unearned mercy introduces. It reveals the extent to which the moral structure has been relied upon to make sense of the world, and the difficulty of encountering something that does not conform to that structure.

At this stage, the person is not yet ready to resolve the tension. They remain within it, experiencing the pull of competing interpretations, the weight of what has been done, and the presence of something that does not fit.

This is where the exploration must continue.

Because the offense of unearned mercy is not only about what is given.

It is about how that gift is received—and what it does to the person who receives it.

PART 2: WHY UNDESERVED MERCY FEELS WRONG

If unearned mercy destabilizes the moral structure by breaking the connection between action and outcome, its emotional impact becomes most visible in the response it provokes. The disruption is not experienced only as confusion or uncertainty. It produces a more immediate and often more intense reaction: the sense that something is wrong. This sense is not merely discomfort. It is moral dissonance—the experience of encountering a response that conflicts with deeply held convictions about how the world should work.

At the center of this dissonance is the idea of deserving. Deserving is one of the primary ways people organize moral experience. It provides a link between what has been done and what should follow. When something is deserved, it carries a sense of rightness. The outcome is not only connected to the action, but appropriate to it. This appropriateness reinforces the stability of the moral structure. It confirms that the sequence holds.

Undeserved mercy disrupts this connection. It introduces an outcome that is not appropriate in the way the person understands appropriateness. It gives where giving is not justified. It forgives where forgiveness has not been earned. It restores where restoration has not been secured through the sequence of accountability and repair.

This disruption is not easily absorbed because deserving is not a peripheral concept. It is central to how people interpret justice, fairness, and responsibility. It shapes expectations, guides responses, and stabilizes meaning. When the connection between action and deserved outcome is broken, the person experiences not only a challenge to a specific event, but to the framework that gives events their significance.

The emotional response to this disruption often takes the form of anger. This anger is not arbitrary. It is rooted in the perception that the moral order has been violated. The person experiences undeserved mercy as a form of injustice—not because mercy itself is harmful, but because it appears to override the principles that ensure that harm is taken seriously.

This is particularly evident in situations where the person has been directly affected by harm. The expectation that wrongdoing will be followed by consequence is not abstract. It is tied to the need for acknowledgment, for validation, for the recognition that what has been experienced matters. When mercy is extended without that sequence being completed, it can feel as though the significance of the harm has been diminished.

The anger that emerges in this context is often protective. It seeks to defend the meaning of what has occurred. It insists that the harm should not be bypassed, that the process of accountability should not be interrupted. It asserts that the structure that connects action and consequence must be maintained in order for the experience to be honored.

This protective function of anger is important to recognize. It is not simply resistance to mercy. It is a response to the perceived erosion of justice. The person is attempting to preserve a framework that affirms the reality of harm and the necessity of response.

At the same time, this anger can extend beyond the specific event. It can shape how the person relates to mercy more generally. Undeserved mercy becomes associated with instability, with the breakdown of proportion, with the possibility that outcomes are not governed by what has occurred. The person may begin to view mercy with suspicion, questioning its appropriateness, its timing, its impact.

This suspicion is often accompanied by a sense of resentment. Resentment, in this context, is not simply a lingering negative feeling. It is a response to perceived imbalance. The person sees something being given that does not correspond to what has been done, and this perceived imbalance creates tension.

This tension is not only about the recipient of mercy. It also involves the person who is witnessing or experiencing the extension of mercy. They may feel that something has been taken from them—that the recognition they expected, the response they anticipated, has been displaced by a response that does not align with their experience.

This sense of displacement can be difficult to articulate. It is not always clear what has been lost, but the person feels the absence of something that should have been present. The sequence has been interrupted, and with it, the assurance that what has happened will be answered in a way that makes sense.

This is where moral dissonance becomes most pronounced. The person is holding two conflicting understandings simultaneously. On one hand, they may believe that mercy is good, that it is a value to be upheld, that it plays a necessary role in human and spiritual life. On the other hand, they experience the specific instance of mercy as misaligned, as inappropriate, as undermining the structure that gives meaning to what has occurred.

These two understandings do not easily reconcile. The person may attempt to resolve the tension by adjusting their interpretation of mercy, by limiting its application, or by redefining its meaning. They may conclude that mercy is good in general, but not in this case, or not at this time, or not in this way.

This qualification allows the person to maintain their broader belief in mercy while preserving the integrity of the moral structure in the specific context. But it does not eliminate the underlying tension. The dissonance remains, even if it is managed.

Over time, this dissonance can affect how the person engages with moral and spiritual concepts more broadly. They may become more cautious in their acceptance of ideas that do not align with their experience. They may prioritize consistency and proportion over other values, seeking to maintain a sense of stability in their understanding.

This prioritization reflects the depth of the disruption that undeserved mercy introduces. It is not simply a matter of disagreement. It is a challenge to the way the person has learned to make sense of the world. It calls into question the reliability of the structures that have been used to interpret experience.

At the same time, the person may remain aware that their response to mercy is not entirely comfortable. They may recognize that their anger and resentment, while understandable, do not fully resolve the tension. They may feel that something is unresolved, that their reaction does not fully account for what they are encountering.

This awareness can create a secondary layer of conflict. The person is not only struggling with the dissonance between justice and mercy, but also with their own response to that dissonance. They may question whether their anger is justified, whether their resistance is appropriate, whether there is something they are not seeing.

This questioning does not necessarily lead to resolution. It often deepens the complexity of the experience. The person becomes more aware of the layers of their response, the multiple factors that are shaping how they interpret what is happening.

This layered experience reflects the full weight of undeserved mercy as an offense. It is not a simple rejection or acceptance. It is a complex engagement with something that both affirms and disrupts the person's understanding of what is right.

At this stage, the person is still operating within the framework of moral logic, even as that framework is being challenged. They are evaluating mercy in terms of deserving, proportion, and fairness. They are attempting to make sense of it within the categories they have relied upon.

But these categories are beginning to strain under the weight of what they are encountering.

The question is no longer only whether mercy is deserved.

It becomes whether the concept of deserving is sufficient to account for what mercy is.

That question does not yet have an answer.

But it marks the beginning of a shift.

PART 3: THE FRACTURE WITHIN

If unearned mercy destabilizes moral logic and provokes anger and resentment, its most profound effect is not only external but internal. The disruption does not remain at the level of interpretation or reaction. It moves inward. It begins to reshape how the person understands themselves, their moral commitments, and their place within the world they are trying to navigate.

The person who encounters unearned mercy is not only evaluating what is happening around them. They are also confronting their own response to it. They are aware of their resistance, their anger, their dissonance. They recognize that something in them is pushing back against what is being presented as good. This recognition can be as unsettling as the experience of mercy itself.

At one level, the person may feel justified in their response. Their resistance is grounded in a coherent moral framework. It reflects their commitment to justice, to fairness, to the idea that actions should correspond to outcomes. Their anger is not arbitrary. It arises from a deeply held conviction that what has happened should be answered in a way that acknowledges its weight.

But at another level, the person may sense that their response is incomplete. They may recognize that their framework, while necessary, is not fully accounting for what they are encountering. They may feel the tension between their commitment to justice and the presence of something that does not fit within that commitment.

This tension creates a fracture within the self.

The person is no longer unified in their response. They are divided. One part of them insists on the necessity of proportion, accountability, and earned response. Another part is aware—however faintly—that what they are encountering cannot be entirely dismissed. These parts do not easily reconcile. They exist alongside one another, creating a sense of internal instability.

This instability is not merely cognitive. It is emotional and, for many, spiritual. The person may feel unsettled in ways that are difficult to name. They may experience a sense of unease that does not resolve through analysis or argument. They may find themselves returning to the moment of mercy, not because they accept it, but because it continues to disrupt their understanding.

This return is significant. It indicates that the experience has not been fully integrated. It remains active, influencing how the person thinks and feels, even if they have attempted to resolve it. The fracture is not something that can be easily closed. It persists.

At the same time, the person may attempt to manage this fracture through familiar strategies. They may double down on moral clarity, reinforcing their commitment to justice and dismissing the experience of mercy as misaligned. They may seek to stabilize their understanding by excluding what does not fit.

This approach can provide temporary relief. It allows the person to regain a sense of coherence, to reestablish a unified position from which to interpret the world. But it does so by narrowing the field of experience. It requires the person to set aside aspects of what they have encountered in order to maintain stability.

Alternatively, the person may begin to engage the fracture more directly. They may allow the tension to remain, resisting the urge to resolve it immediately. This does not mean they accept mercy without question. It means they acknowledge that their existing framework does not fully account for what they are experiencing.

This acknowledgment can be difficult. It requires the person to tolerate uncertainty, to hold together conflicting perceptions without forcing them into alignment. It challenges the desire for closure that has been explored in previous chapters. It asks the person to remain within an open question.

This openness is not comfortable. It exposes the limits of the structures that have been relied upon to make sense of the world. It reveals that moral logic, fairness, clarity, and even justice—while necessary—do not fully contain the range of human experience.

For some, this realization may lead to a reevaluation of their moral framework. They may begin to consider whether the categories they have used to interpret events are sufficient, whether the logic they have depended on can account for what they are encountering. This reevaluation is not immediate. It unfolds over time, often in small shifts rather than dramatic changes.

For others, the response may be more resistant. The person may hold firmly to their existing framework, interpreting the fracture as something to be resolved rather than explored. They may seek to restore unity by reaffirming the principles that have guided them, even if those principles do not fully account for the experience.

Both responses reflect the difficulty of living within the fracture. It is not an easy space to inhabit. It challenges the person's sense of stability, their confidence in their understanding, their ability to interpret what is happening around them.

At the heart of this fracture is a deeper question about identity. The person must confront not only what they believe, but who they are in relation to what they believe. If their moral framework is challenged, what does that mean for their sense of self? If the structures they have relied upon are not complete, how do they understand their place within the world?

These questions do not have immediate answers. They cannot be resolved through analysis alone. They must be lived.

This is where the experience of unearned mercy becomes most profound. It is not only a challenge to external structures. It is an invitation—though not one that is easily accepted—to reconsider the foundations of meaning. It asks whether the person is willing to engage with a reality that does not conform to the categories they have established.

This engagement does not require immediate acceptance. It does not demand that the person abandon their commitment to justice or their concern for fairness. It requires only that they remain present to the tension, that they allow the fracture to exist without closing it prematurely.

This is a difficult posture to maintain. It runs counter to the impulse toward clarity, categorization, and closure that has been described throughout this book. It requires a different kind of endurance—one that does not resolve the tension, but holds it.

In this sense, the fracture becomes a space of possibility.

Not because it is comfortable, but because it opens the possibility that the person's understanding of the world may expand. It creates room for something that does not fit within the existing framework to be considered, not as an error, but as a reality that requires attention.

This possibility is not yet fully realized. It remains tentative, fragile, easily set aside in favor of more familiar structures. But it is present.

And it marks the beginning of a shift.

The person is no longer only reacting to unearned mercy.

They are beginning to consider what it might mean to live in relation to it.

This movement is not complete. It will be developed further in the chapters that follow. But it begins here, within the fracture—within the space where the person's understanding has been disrupted and has not yet been reformed.

It is from this space that the next question emerges.

Not whether unearned mercy is right or wrong.

But what it reveals about the limits of the structures we have used to determine what those categories mean.

CHAPTER 7

When Mercy Feels Like Injustice

PART 1: THE VIEW FROM THE WOUND

Up to this point, the argument has traced how moral logic structures experience, how fairness stabilizes that structure, how moral clarity emerges as a survival strategy, how justice attempts to restore what has been broken, and how grace disrupts that entire sequence. These movements have been examined primarily at the level of structure, interpretation, and response. But the experience of grace changes when it is encountered from within the wound itself. What appears as mercy from a distance can feel like something else entirely when viewed from the place where harm has been carried.

The perspective of the harmed is not simply another angle on the same event. It is a different reality. It is shaped not only by what has happened, but by what it has cost, what it has altered, and what it continues to affect. The person who has been harmed does not encounter grace as a neutral observer. They encounter it as someone whose understanding of the world has already been disrupted, whose expectations have already been violated, whose sense of stability has already been compromised.

From within this perspective, the extension of mercy is not experienced first as generosity. It is experienced in relation to what has been endured. The person measures what is being given against what has been taken, what has been lost, what has not been restored. This measurement is not a calculation in the abstract. It is an attempt to locate the response within the reality of the wound.

When mercy is extended toward the one who has caused harm, the person who has been harmed often experiences a shift in focus. Attention moves away from the wound and toward the one who created it. The narrative changes. The question is no longer only what has happened and how it has affected those who were harmed, but how the one who caused harm will be treated, restored, or forgiven.

This shift can feel like displacement. The person may experience it as a movement away from their reality toward something that does not fully account for it. The harm has not disappeared, but it is no longer the central point of reference. Something else has taken its place.

This is where mercy begins to feel like injustice.

The person does not necessarily reject the idea of mercy in itself. They may believe in its value, affirm its importance, even desire it in other contexts. But in this moment, in this situation, the extension of mercy appears to contradict the expectations that have been relied upon to preserve the meaning of what has happened.

If harm should be followed by accountability, if wrongdoing should be addressed in proportion to its impact, then mercy extended without that sequence being completed appears misaligned. It seems to interrupt the process before it has reached a point that would allow the event to be integrated.

This interruption is not experienced as neutral. It is experienced as a failure to carry the weight of the event through the sequence that would affirm its significance. The person may feel that something essential has been bypassed, that the process has moved forward without fully engaging what has occurred.

This perception is intensified by the relational nature of harm. The person who has been harmed is not only dealing with an event, but with the ongoing effects of that event. These effects may include loss, change in identity, altered relationships, or a diminished sense of safety. They are not confined to a single moment. They continue to shape the person's experience.

When mercy is extended toward the one who caused harm, the person may feel that these ongoing effects are not being adequately considered. The focus on forgiveness or restoration can appear to overlook the persistence of the wound. It may seem as though the response is oriented toward moving forward rather than fully engaging what remains.

This creates a sense of imbalance. The person may feel that the response does not correspond to the reality of their experience. The extension of mercy, rather than restoring proportion, appears to distort it. The sequence that would connect what has happened to what should follow is not completed in a way that aligns with the depth of the harm.

This is why mercy can feel like a second injury.

The first injury is the harm itself—the violation, the loss, the disruption of expectation. The second injury occurs when the response to that harm does not align with what is needed to acknowledge and address it. The person experiences not only the original event, but the way that event is handled.

When mercy is perceived as bypassing accountability or minimizing the significance of the harm, it can be experienced as an extension of the disruption rather than its resolution. The person may feel that their reality is being overridden by a response that does not fully engage it.

This experience is not simply emotional. It is moral. The person is evaluating what is happening in relation to their understanding of justice. They are asking whether the response corresponds to the event, whether it affirms the significance of what has occurred, whether it maintains the integrity of the moral structure.

When the answer to these questions is no, the person experiences the response as unjust, even if it is described as merciful.

This tension reveals the limits of viewing mercy solely as a positive good. It shows that the experience of mercy is shaped by context, by timing, by the relationship between what has been done and what is being offered. Mercy that is abstractly good can be concretely disruptive when it is encountered within the lived reality of harm.

The person who experiences mercy as injustice is not necessarily rejecting mercy itself. They are responding to the way it is being applied. They are questioning whether it has been extended in a way that corresponds to the situation, whether it has accounted for the reality of the wound.

This questioning often takes the form of protest. The person may speak against the extension of mercy, argue for the necessity of accountability, insist that something must be addressed before forgiveness can be meaningful. These responses reflect a desire to restore the sequence, to ensure that the event is carried through the process that would allow it to be integrated.

At the same time, the person may feel isolated in their response. Others may view mercy as inherently good, as something that should be welcomed and affirmed. The person who resists may be seen asunwilling to forgive, as holding on to the past, as failing to embrace what is offered.

This perception can deepen the sense of disconnection. The person is not only navigating the experience of harm and the disruption of mercy. They are also navigating how their response is understood by others. They may feel misunderstood, mischaracterized, or pressured to respond in ways that do not align with their experience.

This social dimension adds another layer to the experience. The person must negotiate not only their own response, but the expectations of those around them. They may feel caught between their own sense of what is right and the pressure to conform to a narrative that emphasizes mercy without fully engaging the complexity of the situation.

This tension is not easily resolved. It reflects the depth of the conflict between justice and mercy as they are experienced in the context of moral injury. It shows that the extension of mercy, while intended as a good, can be experienced as a disruption when it does not align with the structures that have been relied upon to make sense of harm.

From within the wound, the question is not abstract.

It is immediate.

Does this response honor what has happened?

Does it carry the weight of what has been endured?

Does it make sense in relation to the reality of the harm?

When the answer to these questions is uncertain or negative, mercy does not feel like relief.

It feels like something else.

And it is from within this experience that the next layer of the argument begins to unfold.

PART 2: WHEN MERCY FEELS LIKE BETRAYAL

If mercy, from within the wound, can feel like injustice, it deepens further when it is experienced as betrayal. The shift from misalignment to betrayal is not simply a matter of intensity. It reflects a change in how the person interprets the relationship between themselves, the one who caused harm, and those who respond to that harm. What was initially perceived as a disruption of sequence becomes, at this stage, a violation of trust.

Betrayal is not only about what is done. It is about who does it and within what relationship it occurs. It arises when those who are expected to uphold the moral structure instead act in ways that undermine it. In the context of unearned mercy, betrayal is experienced when those who are expected to carry the weight of harm—whether individuals, communities, or institutions—extend mercy in ways that appear to bypass that weight.

The person who has been harmed often carries an implicit expectation: that others will recognize what has happened, that they will respond in ways that affirm the significance of the harm, that they will participate in maintaining the moral structure that has been violated. This expectation is not always stated, but it is deeply felt. It reflects a reliance on others to help hold the reality of what has occurred.

When mercy is extended without that recognition being fully expressed, the person may experience it as a withdrawal of that support. The response shifts away from the harmed and toward the one who caused harm. The person may feel that those they relied upon to stand with them have instead aligned themselves with someone else.

This perceived shift in alignment is what gives the experience its quality of betrayal.

The person is not only reacting to the content of the response. They are responding to what the response communicates about relationship. Mercy, in this context, can be interpreted as a signal that the harm is not being held in the way it should be, that the expectations of justice are not being upheld, that the person's experience is not being fully recognized.

This interpretation is not necessarily what those extending mercy intend. They may believe they are acting rightly, that they are embodying a form of goodness that transcends the sequence of justice. But intention does not eliminate perception. The person who has been harmed experiences the response through the lens of what they have endured and what they expected would follow.

From that perspective, mercy can feel like a reordering of priorities. The focus appears to move away from addressing the harm toward restoring the one who caused it. The person may feel that the process has shifted before it has been completed, that the attention required to carry the weight of the event has been redirected.

This redirection can feel like abandonment.

The person may experience it as being left alone with the reality of the harm while others move toward resolution. The structures that were expected to hold the experience in place no longer function in the same way. The person must now carry the weight of the event without the support they anticipated.

This sense of abandonment intensifies the injury. It adds a relational layer to the disruption that has already occurred. The person is not only dealing with the original harm, but with the way that harm is being responded to by others.

At this stage, the response to mercy often becomes more pronounced. The person may articulate their resistance more clearly. They may express anger not only at the one who caused harm, but at those who extend mercy. They may question the appropriateness of the response, challenge its timing, or reject it altogether.

These reactions are often interpreted by others as a refusal to forgive or a lack of openness to grace. But from within the experience of the person, they are not primarily about forgiveness. They are about trust. They are about whether the relationships and structures that were relied upon can still be depended on to uphold the moral order.

This is why the language of betrayal is so significant. It names not only the disruption of expectation, but the rupture of relationship. It acknowledges that something has shifted in how the person understands their connection to others.

This rupture can have lasting effects. The person may become more guarded in their relationships, less willing to rely on others to uphold shared expectations. They may question whether the structures that once provided stability can be trusted. They may withdraw, not as a rejection of relationship, but as a way of protecting themselves from further disruption.

At the same time, the person may continue to desire what has been lost. They may long for a response that affirms their experience, that carries the weight of what has occurred, that restores a sense of alignment between expectation and response. This longing can exist alongside their resistance, creating a complex emotional landscape.

This complexity is often difficult for others to see. The person's protest may be visible, but the underlying desire for recognition and support may be less apparent. As a result, the person may be misunderstood, their response interpreted in ways that do not fully account for the depth of what they are experiencing.

This misunderstanding can deepen the sense of isolation. The person is not only navigating the original harm and the disruption of mercy. They are also navigating how their response is perceived by others. They may feel that their experience is being simplified or mischaracterized, that the nuance of their position is not being acknowledged.

This adds another layer to the sense of betrayal. The person may feel that they are not only being asked to accept a response that does not align with their experience, but that their resistance to that response is not being understood. They are left without a clear place within the shared narrative.

In this context, mercy is not experienced as a bridge toward reconciliation. It is experienced as a point of fracture. It highlights the difference between how the person understands the situation and how others are responding to it. It brings the tension into sharper focus.

This does not mean that mercy is inherently a form of betrayal. It means that, when encountered within the context of moral injury, it can be experienced that way. The perception of betrayal arises from the interaction between the response of mercy and the expectations that have been shaped by the experience of harm.

Understanding this perception is critical. It allows us to take seriously the response of the person who experiences mercy as betrayal, rather than dismissing it as a misunderstanding or a failure to embrace what is good. It acknowledges that the response is grounded in a coherent framework, even if that framework is being challenged.

At the same time, it reveals the depth of the tension that grace introduces. Grace does not simply challenge the logic of justice at an abstract level. It enters into relationships, into communities, into lived experiences, and it interacts with the expectations that have been formed there.

When those expectations have been shaped by harm, by betrayal, by the failure of structures to hold, the introduction of grace does not occur in a neutral space. It enters into a context already marked by disruption, and it interacts with that disruption in ways that are not easily resolved.

This is where the experience of grace becomes most complex.

It is not only a matter of what grace is.

It is a matter of how it is encountered within the realities that people are living.

And when it is encountered as betrayal, the response is not simply resistance.

It is an attempt to make sense of a world in which the structures that once held have been altered in ways that are difficult to reconcile.

PART 3: REMAINING WITHOUT RESOLUTION

If mercy, from within the wound, can feel like injustice and even betrayal, the natural impulse is to resolve that tension as quickly as possible. The person seeks a way to restore coherence, to bring the experience into alignment with a structure that makes sense. This impulse is not misguided. It reflects the deep human need for stability, for closure, for a way of moving forward without carrying unresolved conflict.

But the experience of grace, particularly in the context of moral injury, does not lend itself easily to resolution. The tension between justice and mercy, between what has happened and what is being offered, resists the kinds of conclusions that would allow it to be neatly integrated. The person is left with a reality that does not fully align with the frameworks they have relied upon.

At this point, the question is not only how to resolve the tension, but whether it is possible—or even appropriate—to do so.

The impulse toward resolution often takes familiar forms. The person may attempt to reassert the primacy of justice, to insist that the sequence must be completed before mercy can be meaningfully extended. They may reject the mercy that is offered, viewing it as premature or inappropriate. This response restores a sense of coherence, but it does so by excluding the presence of grace.

Alternatively, the person may attempt to embrace mercy by reframing it in ways that align with their existing structure. They may interpret it as a form of delayed justice, or as a hidden process that will eventually restore proportion. This approach allows mercy to be accepted, but it does so by reshaping it to fit within the moral logic that has been disrupted.

Both responses aim to resolve the tension. Both seek to bring the experience into alignment with a framework that can be relied upon. But in doing so, both risk overlooking the significance of the disruption itself.

What if the tension is not something to be resolved, but something to be inhabited?

This question marks a turning point. It shifts the focus from finding an answer to remaining present within the experience. It suggests that the discomfort, the dissonance, the sense of misalignment are not problems to be eliminated, but realities to be engaged.

Remaining within tension is not passive. It requires a different kind of effort than resolution. It involves resisting the urge to simplify, to categorize, to finalize. It asks the person to hold together competing realities without forcing them into agreement.

This is not how people are typically taught to navigate moral experience. The frameworks that have been explored throughout this book—moral logic, fairness, clarity, justice—are all oriented toward resolution. They aim to bring events into a form that can be understood, acted upon, and ultimately settled.

Grace disrupts that orientation.

It introduces a reality that does not move toward closure in the same way. It resists being reduced to a set of principles that can be applied consistently. It appears in ways that do not align with the expectations that have guided interpretation.

To remain within this reality requires a shift in posture.

The person must learn to live with questions that do not have immediate answers. They must tolerate the presence of conflicting interpretations, the coexistence of justice and mercy in ways that do not resolve into a single framework. They must accept that the structures they have relied upon are not sufficient to account for everything they encounter.

This acceptance is not resignation. It is not a surrender of moral conviction. The person does not abandon their commitment to justice or their concern for fairness. These remain important. They continue to shape how the person understands the world and responds to it.

What changes is the recognition that these commitments do not exhaust the reality they are trying to engage.

The person begins to see that there is more to the situation than what can be captured within the categories they have established. They recognize that the tension they are experiencing is not a sign that something has gone wrong, but an indication that they are encountering something that exceeds their current framework.

This recognition does not eliminate the discomfort. The tension remains. The person may continue to feel the pull of competing interpretations, the desire to resolve what is unresolved. They may continue to experience moments of anger, resistance, or confusion.

But alongside these responses, there is the possibility of a different kind of engagement.

Instead of seeking to eliminate the tension, the person may begin to explore it. They may ask what the tension reveals about the limits of their understanding, about the assumptions that have shaped their expectations, about the ways in which their framework has both enabled and constrained their experience.

This exploration is not straightforward. It requires patience, reflection, and a willingness to remain with what is uncomfortable. It may involve revisiting moments of harm, reconsidering responses, reengaging questions that have not been resolved.

It may also involve a reexamination of what it means to receive grace.

If grace does not fit within the existing moral structure, then receiving it cannot be reduced to an act of agreement or acceptance. It is not simply a matter of deciding that grace is good and embracing it accordingly. It involves a transformation in how the person understands what it means for something to be good.

This transformation does not occur all at once. It unfolds over time, often in ways that are difficult to trace. The person may begin to notice shifts in how they interpret certain experiences, in how they respond to others, in how they understand their own reactions.

These shifts may be subtle. They may not immediately resolve the tension, but they indicate that something is changing. The person is beginning to engage with grace in a way that is not fully determined by the structures they have relied upon.

This does not mean that the tension disappears. It means that the person's relationship to the tension begins to change.

Instead of seeing it solely as a problem to be solved, they begin to see it as a space in which something is unfolding. They recognize that the discomfort they feel is part of the process of encountering something that does not fit within their existing framework.

This recognition can create a different kind of stability. Not the stability that comes from resolution, but the stability that comes from being able to remain within uncertainty without being overwhelmed by it.

This is a more fragile form of stability. It does not provide clear answers or definitive conclusions. It does not eliminate the need for moral judgment or the desire for justice. But it allows the person to continue engaging with a reality that is more complex than their previous understanding allowed.

In this sense, remaining without resolution becomes a form of endurance.

It is a way of continuing to live, to think, to respond, even when the structures that once provided certainty are no longer sufficient. It is a refusal to collapse the tension prematurely, to force an answer where one has not yet emerged.

This endurance is not without cost. It requires the person to carry the weight of unresolved questions, to live with the ongoing presence of dissonance. It can be exhausting. It can feel uncertain.

But it also creates the possibility for a deeper kind of understanding.

Not one that eliminates tension, but one that holds it in a way that allows for new forms of meaning to emerge.

This is where the chapter leaves us.

Not with a resolution, but with a posture.

A way of remaining within the tension between justice and mercy, between what has happened and what is being offered, without forcing them into alignment before they are ready.

And it is from within this posture that the next movement of the book begins.

CHAPTER 8

The Uneven Distribution of Grace

PART 1: WHY THEM?

If grace violates moral logic and unsettles the structures that connect action to outcome, its disruptive power intensifies when it does not appear evenly. The difficulty is not only that grace is unearned, but that it is not distributed in ways that correspond to any recognizable pattern of deserving. Some receive it. Others do not. Some are restored quickly, even unexpectedly, while others remain within the consequences of what has happened, waiting for a resolution that does not come.

This unevenness introduces a new dimension to the offense of grace. It is no longer only about the interruption of sequence, or the bypassing of proportion, or the destabilization of moral clarity. It becomes a question of distribution. Who receives grace, and why? Why does mercy appear in one place and not in another? Why is restoration extended here, while elsewhere the effects of harm continue without relief?

These questions are not abstract. They emerge from lived experience. The person who has already encountered moral injury and the dissonance of unearned mercy now observes that grace does not operate consistently across situations. They see differences. They notice disparities. They compare outcomes.

Comparison is a natural response to uneven distribution. It is a way of making sense of difference. When two situations appear similar but result in different outcomes, the person seeks an explanation. They look for variables that might account for the difference—intent, severity, context, effort, repentance. They attempt to locate a pattern that would restore coherence.

But grace resists pattern.

It does not align with the variables that would normally explain difference. It does not correspond reliably to effort, to sincerity, to degree of harm, or to visible change. It appears in ways that are not easily traced to the factors that would justify it within the moral structure.

This resistance to pattern deepens the sense of instability. The person cannot easily explain why one outcome occurs instead of another. The categories they have used to interpret events do not account for what they are observing. The unevenness remains.

This is where the question "Why them?" begins to take on moral weight.

It is not simply curiosity. It is not a neutral inquiry. It is a question that carries within it an implicit expectation: that there should be a reason, that the difference in outcome should correspond to some identifiable factor. When that expectation is not met, the question becomes more pointed.

Why them?

Why is grace extended in this case, and not in another?

Why is restoration possible here, while elsewhere the consequences remain?

Why is forgiveness given to this person, while another continues to bear the weight of what has been done?

These questions are not easily dismissed. They reflect a genuine attempt to reconcile what is being observed with what is believed about how the world should function. They arise from the same moral logic that has been explored throughout this book—the expectation that outcomes correspond to actions, that responses align with events, that fairness governs distribution.

When grace appears to violate these expectations unevenly, the person is left without a clear way to account for what they are seeing.

This lack of explanation creates space for interpretation.

One possible interpretation is that the distribution of grace reflects hidden factors that are not immediately visible. The person may assume that there is something they do not know, some aspect of the situation that justifies the difference. This assumption preserves the possibility that the moral structure still holds, even if it is not fully apparent.

Another interpretation is that the distribution of grace is arbitrary. It is not governed by discernible criteria. It does not correspond to what has been done. It appears in ways that are unpredictable, inconsistent, and, from the perspective of moral logic, unjustified.

This interpretation is more difficult to accept.

If grace is arbitrary, then it cannot be relied upon. It cannot be anticipated or understood in ways that align with the structures that have been used to navigate the world. It introduces a level of unpredictability that extends beyond individual events into the broader understanding of how outcomes occur.

This unpredictability can be deeply unsettling.

The person who has already experienced the instability of moral injury and the dissonance of unearned mercy now faces an additional layer of disruption. Not only does grace break the sequence, it does so unevenly. It does not offer a consistent alternative to the moral logic it disrupts. It introduces variation without clear explanation.

This variation intensifies comparison.

The person begins to place their own experience alongside the experiences of others. They measure what has happened to them against what has happened to someone else. They ask whether the outcomes correspond in ways that make sense. They look for alignment, for proportion, for fairness.

When that alignment is not present, the comparison produces tension.

The person may feel that something is lacking in their own experience. They may perceive that grace has been extended to others in ways that have not been extended to them. This perception can create a sense of absence, of being left out of a process that appears to benefit others.

This absence is not only about what has not been received. It is about what that absence implies. The person may begin to question whether there is something about them or their situation that accounts for the difference. They may wonder whether they have failed in some way, whether they have not met conditions that, while not explicit, seem to govern the distribution of grace.

These questions can lead to a form of internalization. The person turns the question inward.

Why not me?

Why has grace appeared there and not here?

What is different about my situation?

What does this difference say about me?

This internalization can be difficult to navigate. The person is attempting to make sense of disparity by locating its source within themselves or their circumstances. They are seeking an explanation that restores coherence, even if that explanation introduces new forms of discomfort.

At the same time, the person may resist this internalization. They may reject the idea that the difference reflects something about them. They may instead interpret the uneven distribution of grace as a problem within the system itself. They may see it as evidence that grace, as it is operating, is not aligned with the principles of fairness they have relied upon.

This interpretation can lead to resentment.

Resentment, in this context, is not simply jealousy. It is a response to perceived injustice. The person sees a disparity that cannot be explained within the moral structure and interprets that disparity as a failure of fairness. They may feel that something has been given to others that has not been given to them, and that this difference is not justified.

This feeling can be intensified when the outcomes are visible. When the restoration of another person is apparent, when their situation changes in ways that suggest grace has been extended, the comparison becomes more concrete. The person is not only imagining disparity. They are witnessing it.

This witnessing can be painful.

It confronts the person with a reality that does not align with their expectations. It challenges their understanding of how outcomes should be distributed. It raises questions that do not have clear answers.

Why them?

Why not me?

Why this outcome here, and a different outcome there?

These questions are not easily resolved.

They do not yield to simple explanations or straightforward interpretations. They remain open, pressing against the structures that have been used to make sense of experience.

At this stage, the person is not yet moving toward resolution.

They are still within the tension.

They are observing the unevenness of grace, experiencing the dissonance it creates, and attempting to make sense of it within a framework that is no longer fully sufficient.

This is where the exploration must continue.

Because the uneven distribution of grace does not only raise questions about fairness.

It reveals something about the limits of the structures we use to ask those questions in the first place.

PART 2: THE WEIGHT OF COMPARISON

If the uneven distribution of grace raises the question "Why them?" the next movement carries that question inward and outward at the same time. It becomes not only an inquiry about others, but a comparison that reshapes how the person understands themselves. The presence of grace in one place and its absence in another does not remain an isolated observation. It becomes a lens through which identity, worth, and belonging are interpreted.

Comparison is not a peripheral response. It is a primary way people orient themselves within a shared world. Individuals understand their own experience in relation to the experiences of others. They measure outcomes, not only to evaluate fairness, but to locate themselves within a broader moral landscape. When outcomes appear uneven, comparison intensifies.

This intensification is particularly pronounced in contexts where grace is perceived to be operating. The person does not simply observe that grace has been extended elsewhere. They place that extension alongside their own experience and begin to interpret the difference. The comparison becomes a means of making sense of disparity.

At first, this process may appear analytical. The person considers the variables that might account for the difference. They examine the actions, the circumstances, the responses of those involved. They look for distinctions that would justify the different outcomes. This effort reflects the continued reliance on moral logic as a means of interpretation.

But as the comparison persists without yielding a clear explanation, it begins to take on a different character. It becomes less about identifying external factors and more about evaluating internal ones. The person shifts from asking "What is different about the situation?" to "What is different about me?"

This shift is significant.

It marks the movement from structural analysis to identity formation. The uneven distribution of grace is no longer only a problem to be solved. It becomes a mirror in which the person sees themselves.

Why them, and not me?

What accounts for the difference?

Is there something in me that explains the absence of grace?

This line of questioning can lead to a form of self-assessment that is difficult to navigate. The person begins to evaluate their own actions, their own responses, their own worth, in relation to what they observe in others. They may search for deficiencies, for failures, for aspects of themselves that might account for the disparity.

This search is not always explicit. It may occur beneath the level of conscious awareness, shaping how the person feels about themselves without being fully articulated. It may manifest as a sense of inadequacy, as a perception that something is lacking, even if that lack cannot be clearly defined.

At the same time, the person may resist this internalization. They may recognize that the comparison is not yielding a fair or accurate assessment of their situation. They may reject the idea that the absence of grace reflects a deficiency within themselves. They may insist that the disparity is not justified by differences in worth or action.

This resistance, however, does not eliminate the impact of comparison. The tension remains. The person is aware of the difference, even if they reject the conclusions that might be drawn from it. The unevenness continues to press against their understanding of themselves.

This is where resentment often begins to take shape.

Resentment, in this context, is not merely an emotional reaction to another's good fortune. It is a response to perceived imbalance in the distribution of what is understood to be good. The person sees grace being extended in one place and withheld in another, and this disparity creates a sense of injustice.

This sense of injustice is not abstract. It is felt. It affects how the person relates to others, how they interpret events, how they understand their own experience. The presence of grace in another's life becomes a point of tension rather than celebration.

This tension can be difficult to acknowledge. The person may feel that they should respond differently, that they should be able to affirm the goodness of what is happening for someone else. They may believe that resentment is not an appropriate response, that it reflects a failure to align with values they hold.

But the feeling persists.

It arises from the same moral logic that has been explored throughout this book—the expectation that outcomes should correspond to actions, that distribution should reflect fairness. When this expectation is not met, the response is not neutral.

Resentment, then, is not simply a personal failing. It is a signal. It indicates that the person is encountering a disparity that does not fit within their understanding of how the world should function. It reflects the tension between what is observed and what is expected.

This tension can extend into spiritual domains as well.

In many contexts, grace is not only a moral concept but a spiritual one. It is associated with divine action, with the presence of something that transcends human effort. When grace is understood in this way, its uneven distribution can raise questions not only about fairness, but about the nature of the divine.

The person may begin to ask whether grace is governed by criteria that are not visible or understandable. They may wonder whether there is a logic to its distribution that lies beyond human comprehension. They may question whether the disparity reflects something about divine intention or purpose.

These questions can be unsettling.

They introduce a level of uncertainty that extends beyond the moral structure into the spiritual framework that supports it. The person is not only questioning how events are distributed. They are questioning how meaning itself is structured.

This questioning can lead to a sense of distance.

The person may feel removed from the source of grace, uncertain of their place within a system that does not appear to operate in ways that align with their expectations. They may feel disconnected, not only from others, but from the broader framework that has provided a sense of orientation.

This sense of distance can affect how the person engages with their own experience. They may become more guarded, less willing to expect or anticipate grace. They may lower their expectations, not as a form of humility, but as a way of protecting themselves from disappointment.

At the same time, the person may continue to desire what they observe in others. The presence of grace elsewhere does not eliminate the longing for it. It may intensify it. The person is aware of what is possible, even if it is not present in their own experience.

This awareness creates a complex emotional landscape.

The person holds together desire and resentment, recognition and resistance, longing and frustration. These elements do not easily resolve into a single response. They coexist, shaping how the person interprets what is happening around them.

This coexistence is not stable.

It produces ongoing tension. The person may move between different responses, at times emphasizing one and at times another. They may feel resentment in one moment and empathy in another, frustration in one instance and understanding in the next.

This fluctuation reflects the difficulty of integrating the uneven distribution of grace into a coherent framework.

The person is attempting to hold together realities that do not align: the belief that grace is good, the observation that it is unevenly distributed, the experience of its absence in their own life, and the presence of it in others.

These realities do not easily reconcile.

They challenge the categories that have been used to interpret experience. They reveal the limits of moral logic as a means of accounting for what is observed.

At this stage, the person is not yet moving beyond comparison.

They are still within it, still measuring, still interpreting, still attempting to make sense of disparity through the frameworks they have relied upon.

But those frameworks are beginning to strain.

The comparison is no longer yielding clarity.

It is revealing complexity.

And it is from within this complexity that the next movement begins.

PART 3: WHEN FAIRNESS IS NO LONGER ENOUGH

If the uneven distribution of grace provokes comparison, resentment, and questions of identity, it ultimately presses more deeply into the structure that has been used to interpret all of these responses: fairness itself. The person who has been measuring outcomes, asking why grace appears in one place and not another, begins to encounter a more difficult realization. The issue is not only that grace is uneven. It is that fairness, as it has been understood, may not be sufficient to account for what grace is.

This realization does not arrive easily. It emerges gradually, often through repeated encounters with disparity that cannot be resolved within the existing framework. The person continues to compare, to evaluate, to seek explanation. But the explanations do not hold. The patterns that would restore coherence do not emerge. The unevenness remains resistant to interpretation.

At this point, the question shifts.

It is no longer only "Why them?" or "Why not me?" It becomes "What kind of reality is this, in which outcomes do not align with fairness as I understand it?" The focus moves from individual instances to the structure that governs them. The person begins to examine not only the distribution of grace, but the assumptions they have been using to evaluate that distribution.

Fairness, within the moral logic that has been explored throughout this book, functions as a stabilizing principle. It connects action to outcome in ways that preserve proportion. It ensures that responses correspond to events, that what is given aligns with what has been done. It provides a sense of order that allows people to interpret and navigate their experience.

This function of fairness is not trivial. It is essential for the maintenance of social and moral life. Without some sense of proportion and correspondence, the world would become difficult to navigate. Expectations would be unclear. Responses would be unpredictable. The structures that allow for trust and accountability would weaken.

The person does not easily relinquish this understanding.

Even as they encounter the uneven distribution of grace, they continue to rely on fairness as a means of interpretation. They attempt to bring grace into alignment with fairness, to understand it as a variation within the same structure. They look for ways in which grace might still correspond to action, even if the correspondence is not immediately visible.

But this effort encounters limits.

Grace does not consistently align with fairness in this way. It does not distribute itself according to proportion. It does not correspond to effort, to merit, or to visible criteria that would justify its presence in one place and its absence in another. The person's attempts to reconcile grace with fairness begin to falter.

This faltering creates a moment of tension.

The person is faced with a choice, though it may not be immediately recognized as such. They can continue to insist that fairness is the final measure, interpreting the uneven distribution of grace as a problem to be corrected or explained. Or they can begin to consider the possibility that fairness, while necessary, is not exhaustive.

This consideration does not require the abandonment of fairness. It does not suggest that fairness is irrelevant or unimportant. It suggests that fairness may not be the only principle at work.

This suggestion is difficult to accept.

Fairness has been the foundation upon which moral understanding has been built. It has provided a way of making sense of harm, of distributing responsibility, of ensuring that outcomes correspond to actions. To consider that it may not be sufficient is to question the stability of that foundation.

The person may resist this questioning.

They may reaffirm their commitment to fairness, emphasizing its importance, its necessity, its role in maintaining order. They may view the uneven distribution of grace as an anomaly, as something that should be brought into alignment with fairness rather than something that challenges it.

This response preserves stability.

It allows the person to maintain a coherent framework, to continue interpreting events in ways that align with their expectations. But it does so by limiting the scope of what is considered. It sets aside the aspects of grace that do not fit within the structure of fairness.

Alternatively, the person may begin to engage the tension more directly.

They may allow the possibility that fairness does not fully account for what they are encountering. They may consider that there are dimensions of reality that operate according to different principles, that the distribution of grace reflects something that cannot be reduced to proportion.

This engagement is not comfortable.

It requires the person to hold together two realities that do not easily align: the necessity of fairness and the presence of something that does not conform to it. It challenges the assumption that the moral structure is complete.

At this stage, the person is not yet abandoning fairness.

They are recognizing its limits.

They begin to see that fairness provides a way of organizing certain aspects of experience, but not all of them. It is effective within its domain, but it does not extend to every dimension of reality.

This recognition opens a new space.

It allows the person to consider that the uneven distribution of grace may not be a failure of fairness, but an indication that fairness is not the only framework through which events can be understood. It suggests that there may be other principles at work, other ways of interpreting what is occurring.

This does not immediately resolve the tension.

The person may still feel the pull of comparison, the presence of resentment, the desire for outcomes to align with expectation. These responses do not disappear simply because the person recognizes the limits of fairness.

But the recognition changes how these responses are held.

The person may begin to see their reactions not only as responses to disparity, but as reflections of the framework they have been using to interpret that disparity. They may become more aware of the assumptions that underlie their sense of what is right.

This awareness introduces a different kind of question.

Not only "Why is grace distributed this way?" but "What does my response to this distribution reveal about how I understand what is good?"

This question moves the inquiry inward in a new way.

It is no longer focused solely on external events or outcomes. It is concerned with the structure of interpretation itself. It asks how the person's understanding of fairness shapes their response to what they are encountering.

This movement does not provide immediate answers.

It deepens the complexity of the experience. The person is now engaging not only with the uneven distribution of grace, but with the limits of the framework they have been using to evaluate it.

This engagement can feel destabilizing.

The person is no longer able to rely on fairness as a comprehensive guide. They must navigate a space in which fairness is necessary but not sufficient, in which other principles may be at work but are not yet fully understood.

This is a difficult place to remain.

It requires the person to tolerate uncertainty, to hold questions that do not have clear answers, to resist the urge to resolve the tension by collapsing it into a familiar structure.

But it is also a necessary place.

Because it creates the possibility for a different kind of understanding to emerge.

Not one that replaces fairness, but one that expands the framework within which fairness operates. Not one that eliminates the desire for proportion, but one that recognizes that proportion is not the only measure of what is good.

This expansion is not yet complete.

It is only beginning.

The person has moved from asking why grace is uneven to questioning the adequacy of the structures they have used to interpret that unevenness. They have begun to see that the offense of grace is not only about what is given or withheld, but about what those realities reveal about the limits of moral logic.

This realization does not resolve the tension.

It intensifies it.

But it also prepares the way for the next movement.

Because once fairness is no longer sufficient, the question becomes unavoidable:

If not fairness alone, then what?

And it is toward that question that the book now turns.

CHAPTER 9

Grace and the Loss of Control

PART 1: WHEN GRACE CANNOT BE MANAGED

If the uneven distribution of grace reveals the limits of fairness, it also exposes a deeper and more unsettling reality: grace cannot be controlled. It cannot be managed, predicted, or organized within the systems that have been constructed to regulate moral and social life. This loss of control is not a secondary feature of grace. It is central to its nature. And it is one of the primary reasons grace is experienced as destabilizing rather than comforting.

Up to this point, much of the moral structure described in this book has depended on the ability to anticipate outcomes. Moral logic connects action to consequence. Fairness stabilizes that connection through proportion. Moral clarity allows for decisive interpretation. Justice restores alignment when it is broken. Each of these elements contributes to a world that, while imperfect, remains navigable because it is, to some degree, predictable.

Predictability is not only about knowledge. It is about control.

When outcomes can be anticipated, they can be influenced. When responses correspond to actions, behavior can be adjusted to produce desired results. Individuals and communities can act with a sense of agency, shaping their engagement with the world based on expectations that are, if not certain, at least reliable.

Grace disrupts this dynamic.

It introduces responses that are not determined by what has been done. It appears in ways that are not governed by consistent criteria. It does not follow patterns that can be mapped or rules that can be applied. As a result, it cannot be managed in the same way as the structures that have been explored throughout this book.

This inability to manage grace creates a profound sense of loss.

The person who has relied on moral logic to navigate the world finds that one of the central elements of their framework no longer holds. They cannot predict when grace will appear, to whom it will be extended, or how it will operate. They cannot ensure that it will align with their expectations or their understanding of what should happen.

This unpredictability undermines a key aspect of control.

Control, in this context, is not about domination or manipulation. It is about the ability to act within a system that responds in recognizable ways. It is about the confidence that one's actions will have consequences that can be understood and, to some extent, anticipated.

Grace removes that confidence.

It introduces outcomes that are not tied to action in predictable ways. It breaks the link between behavior and response that has allowed for a sense of agency. The person can no longer rely on the system to produce outcomes that correspond to what they do.

This can be deeply unsettling.

The loss of control is experienced not only as uncertainty, but as exposure. The person is no longer able to secure outcomes through adherence to the structures they have relied upon. They must engage with a reality in which outcomes are not fully determined by their actions.

This engagement requires a different kind of posture.

The person must move from managing outcomes to receiving them. They must shift from controlling the sequence to encountering it. This shift is not easily made. It runs counter to the ways in which people have learned to navigate the world.

In many contexts, control is associated with responsibility. To act responsibly is to understand the consequences of one's actions and to act in ways that produce desired outcomes. This understanding is reinforced by systems that reward alignment between action and consequence.

Grace does not operate within this system.

It does not reward in proportion to action. It does not follow the patterns that would allow for strategic engagement. It appears as a gift, not as a result. This distinction is critical.

A system can be managed.

A gift cannot.

A system operates according to rules that can be understood and applied. It produces outcomes that correspond to inputs. It allows for planning, for adjustment, for control.

A gift operates differently.

It is given, not produced. It is received, not earned. It does not follow from what has been done. It is not guaranteed by adherence to a set of conditions. It cannot be secured through effort or strategy.

This difference between system and gift is at the heart of the loss of control that grace introduces.

The person who has been operating within systems—moral, social, institutional—encounters something that does not function according to those systems. They must confront the possibility that not everything can be organized in ways that allow for control.

This confrontation can be resisted.

The person may attempt to reframe grace as a system. They may look for patterns, for principles, for conditions that govern its distribution. They may seek to identify what leads to grace, to determine how it can be accessed or secured.

This effort reflects a desire to restore control.

If grace can be understood as operating according to certain rules, then it can be managed. It can be integrated into the existing framework. It can be anticipated and responded to in ways that align with the structures that have been relied upon.

But this effort encounters limits.

Grace does not consistently conform to the patterns that would allow it to be systematized. Attempts to reduce it to a set of principles often fail to account for its variability, its unpredictability, its resistance to proportion.

This failure reinforces the sense of loss.

The person realizes that the strategies they have used to navigate other aspects of the world are not effective here. They cannot secure grace through effort. They cannot predict it through analysis. They cannot control it through adherence to a system.

This realization can lead to frustration.

The person may feel that something essential has been taken from them—the ability to influence outcomes, to act with confidence, to engage with a world that responds in predictable ways. They may experience grace as a removal of agency rather than an extension of it.

At the same time, the loss of control introduces a different possibility.

If grace cannot be managed, then it cannot be restricted by the limitations of the systems that have been constructed. It is not bound by the criteria that govern fairness or the rules that define proportion. It is free to operate in ways that exceed those structures.

This freedom is part of what makes grace what it is.

But it is also what makes it difficult to receive.

The person must learn to engage with something that does not conform to their expectations, that does not respond to their efforts, that cannot be secured or controlled. They must encounter grace not as something to be managed, but as something to be received.

This encounter requires a reorientation.

The person must shift from a posture of control to a posture of openness. They must move from attempting to secure outcomes to being present to what is given. This shift is not immediate. It unfolds over time, often through repeated experiences of encountering grace in ways that cannot be anticipated or explained.

During this process, the person may continue to struggle.

They may move back and forth between attempts to control and moments of openness. They may experience frustration when grace does not appear as expected, and surprise when it appears where it was not anticipated. They may feel the tension between their desire for predictability and the reality of unpredictability.

This tension is not easily resolved.

It reflects the fundamental difference between systems and gifts, between structures that can be managed and realities that must be received. It highlights the limits of control as a framework for engaging with certain aspects of experience.

At this stage, the person is not yet fully oriented toward receiving grace.

They are still grappling with the loss of control. They are still attempting to make sense of a reality that does not conform to the patterns they have relied upon. They are still negotiating the tension between managing and receiving.

But something has shifted.

The recognition that grace cannot be controlled has introduced a new question.

Not how to manage grace.
But how to live in relation to it.

PART 2: WHY SYSTEMS RESIST GRACE

If grace cannot be managed at the individual level, its incompatibility with institutional life becomes even more pronounced. Institutions are, by their nature, structured around predictability, consistency, and control. They exist to organize behavior, to establish expectations, to regulate outcomes in ways that sustain coherence over time. Where individuals may tolerate a degree of uncertainty, institutions cannot function without some level of stability. They require patterns that can be relied upon, rules that can be applied, and processes that produce consistent results.

Grace does not fit easily within this environment.

It does not operate according to predictable patterns. It does not conform to standardized procedures. It does not produce outcomes that can be replicated across situations. It resists codification. It cannot be reduced to policy. As a result, it introduces a form of instability that institutions are not designed to absorb.

This mismatch creates tension.

Institutions are built to manage complexity by reducing it. They establish categories, define roles, set boundaries, and create systems of accountability that allow for coordinated action. These structures are necessary. Without them, institutions would not be able to function. They would lack the coherence required to sustain collective life.

Grace, however, does not reduce complexity in this way.

It introduces responses that are not governed by the categories that institutions rely upon. It blurs boundaries rather than reinforcing them. It disrupts the distinctions that allow institutions to operate effectively. It cannot be easily integrated into systems that depend on clarity and consistency.

This is why institutions often attempt to translate grace into something more manageable.

They develop frameworks for forgiveness, guidelines for restoration, processes for reconciliation. They seek to create structures that allow grace to be applied in ways that align with institutional needs. These efforts are not necessarily misguided. They reflect a genuine attempt to hold together the values associated with grace and the requirements of organizational life.

But in translating grace into system, something changes.

What was originally given becomes administered. What was once unpredictable becomes regulated. What was experienced as a gift becomes part of a process. The language of grace remains, but its operation is altered. It begins to function within the parameters of the system rather than outside of it.

This transformation allows institutions to maintain control.

By incorporating grace into structured processes, institutions can manage its effects. They can determine when it is appropriate, how it should be applied, and what outcomes it should produce. They can ensure that it aligns with broader goals and does not undermine the stability of the system.

But this control comes at a cost.

The more grace is systematized, the less it retains the qualities that made it disruptive in the first place. Its unpredictability is reduced. Its capacity to interrupt established patterns is diminished. It becomes one element among others within a larger framework, rather than something that challenges the framework itself.

This creates a paradox,

Institutions may claim to value grace, to uphold it as an important principle, to incorporate it into their practices. But in doing so, they often reshape it into something that no longer functions as grace in its original sense. They preserve the language while altering the reality.

This paradox is not always recognized.

From within the institution, the processes that have been established may appear to reflect grace. They provide mechanisms for forgiveness, opportunities for restoration, pathways for reintegration. These are meaningful and often necessary. They address real needs and contribute to the functioning of the system.

But they do so within limits.

The application of grace is conditioned by institutional priorities. It must align with policies, with procedures, with the need to maintain order. It cannot be allowed to disrupt the system in ways that would compromise its ability to function.

As a result, grace is often applied selectively.

It is extended in ways that can be contained, in situations where its impact can be managed. It is withheld in contexts where it would introduce too much instability, where it would challenge established structures or undermine authority. The distribution of grace becomes shaped by the needs of the institution rather than by the logic of grace itself.

This selective application reinforces the unevenness that was explored in the previous chapter.

Grace does not appear consistently across contexts, and the reasons for its distribution are not always transparent. Within institutions, these disparities can be particularly pronounced. Decisions about when and how to extend grace may be influenced by factors that are not visible to those affected by them.

This lack of transparency can create additional tension.

The person who experiences the uneven distribution of grace within an institutional context may not only question the disparity, but also the processes that produced it. They may perceive the application of grace as inconsistent, as influenced by considerations that do not align with fairness or justice.

This perception can lead to distrust.

The institution, which is expected to uphold standards and provide stability, appears to operate in ways that are not fully coherent. The introduction of grace, rather than resolving tension, becomes another point of instability. The person may question whether the institution can be relied upon to act consistently, whether its processes are aligned with its stated values.

At the same time, the institution faces its own challenges.

It must navigate the tension between maintaining order and responding to situations that call for something beyond established procedures. It must balance the need for consistency with the recognition that not all situations can be addressed through uniform application of rules. It must decide how to incorporate values associated with grace without undermining its ability to function.

These decisions are not simple.

They involve competing priorities, limited information, and the need to act within constraints. The institution cannot simply abandon its structures in order to allow grace to operate freely. To do so would risk creating a level of instability that could compromise its purpose.

And yet, in maintaining its structures, the institution may limit the presence of grace.

It may find itself unable to respond in ways that reflect the full disruptive potential of grace. It may default to processes that preserve order at the expense of responding to the particularities of a situation. It may prioritize consistency over responsiveness, predictability over openness.

This tension reveals something fundamental about the relationship between systems and gifts.

Systems are designed to produce consistent outcomes. They rely on rules that can be applied across situations. They aim to minimize variability in order to maintain stability.

Gifts, by contrast, are not governed by rules in the same way. They are given, not produced. They do not follow from inputs. They are not guaranteed by adherence to conditions. They introduce variability rather than reducing it.

When a gift enters a system, the system must decide how to respond.

It can attempt to incorporate the gift into its processes, reshaping it to fit within its structures. Or it can allow the gift to remain outside those structures, accepting the instability that it introduces.

Neither option is without cost.

Incorporation preserves stability but alters the nature of the gift. Allowing the gift to remain outside preserves its character but challenges the system's ability to function.

This dilemma is at the heart of the institutional struggle with grace.

It is not simply a matter of resistance or acceptance. It is a matter of navigating the tension between two fundamentally different ways of organizing reality.

At this stage, the person observing or participating in institutional life may begin to see this tension more clearly.

They may recognize that the uneven distribution of grace is not only a feature of individual experience, but of systems that attempt to manage what cannot be fully controlled. They may see that the limitations they have encountered are not only personal, but structural.

This recognition does not resolve the tension.

But it deepens the understanding of it.

It shows that the difficulty of receiving grace is not only about individual response, but about the contexts in which grace is encountered. It reveals that the structures designed to provide stability may also limit the presence of what disrupts that stability.

And it raises a new question.

If grace cannot be fully contained within systems, and if systems cannot function without some form of control, then how are we to understand the relationship between them?

That question remains open.

But it prepares the way for what comes next.

PART 3: LEARNING TO LIVE WITHOUT MANAGING GRACE

If grace cannot be managed at the personal level and cannot be fully contained within institutional systems, the question that remains is not how to control it, but how to live in relation to it. This question marks a decisive shift. It moves the focus away from structuring grace toward responding to it, away from securing outcomes toward inhabiting a reality in which outcomes are no longer governed by predictable sequence.

This shift is not merely conceptual. It is existential. The person who has relied on moral logic, fairness, clarity, and even justice as ways of navigating the world now encounters a reality that does not conform to those structures. The loss of control is not an abstract idea. It is a lived experience that affects how the person understands agency, responsibility, and participation.

To live without managing grace is to relinquish a particular form of control—the belief that outcomes can be secured through alignment with a system. It is to recognize that not everything can be organized according to principles that ensure predictability. This recognition does not eliminate the need for action or responsibility, but it changes how those are understood.

Action, within a system, is often oriented toward producing a desired result. The person acts in ways that are expected to lead to specific outcomes. Responsibility is tied to the ability to influence those outcomes, to act in ways that align with the structure that governs them.

Grace disrupts this orientation.

It introduces outcomes that are not tied to action in predictable ways. It breaks the link between behavior and response that has allowed for a sense of control. The person must now act without the assurance that their actions will produce the outcomes they expect.

This can feel like a loss of agency.

The person may wonder what it means to act if outcomes are not determined by action, how to take responsibility if the connection between effort and result is no longer reliable. They may experience a sense of uncertainty about how to engage with the world, unsure of how their actions will be received or what they will produce.

This uncertainty is not easily resolved.

It cannot be addressed by simply adjusting expectations or refining strategies. It reflects a deeper shift in how reality is understood. The person is no longer operating within a framework that guarantees correspondence between action and outcome.

At the same time, this loss of control does not eliminate the possibility of meaningful action.

It reframes it.

Action becomes less about producing a specific result and more about participating in a reality that cannot be fully controlled. The person acts not to secure an outcome, but to engage with what is present. Responsibility is no longer tied solely to results, but to the integrity of the action itself.

This reframing is difficult.

It runs counter to the ways in which people have been taught to understand responsibility and agency. It requires the person to act without the assurance that their actions will be effective in the ways they expect. It asks them to remain engaged even when outcomes are uncertain.

This is where the experience of grace becomes particularly significant.

Grace does not eliminate the need for action. It does not remove the importance of responsibility. But it changes the relationship between action and outcome. It introduces a space in which the person must act without control, respond without certainty, and remain present without guarantee.

This space is not comfortable.

It exposes the limits of the structures that have been relied upon to provide stability. It reveals that control, while useful in many contexts, is not absolute. It cannot account for all aspects of experience. There are dimensions of reality that exceed its reach.

To live within these dimensions requires a different kind of posture.

It involves openness rather than control, receptivity rather than management, attentiveness rather than prediction. The person must learn to encounter what is given without immediately attempting to organize it within a system that ensures stability.

This learning process is gradual.

It often involves moments of resistance, where the person returns to familiar strategies in an attempt to regain control. They may seek to interpret grace in ways that align with their expectations, to incorporate it into a framework that can be managed. These attempts are understandable. They reflect the difficulty of relinquishing control.

But over time, the limitations of these strategies become apparent.

The person begins to see that grace does not conform to the structures they are attempting to impose. It continues to appear in ways that resist systematization. It continues to disrupt the patterns they have relied upon.

This repetition can lead to a shift.

The person may begin to experiment with a different way of engaging. Instead of attempting to control grace, they may begin to receive it. This does not mean passive acceptance or uncritical agreement. It means allowing grace to be what it is, without immediately reducing it to something that can be managed.

Receiving, in this sense, is an active posture.

It involves attention, awareness, and a willingness to engage with what is present. It requires the person to remain open to outcomes that are not determined by their actions, to responses that do not align with their expectations. It asks them to participate in a reality that cannot be fully predicted.

This participation is not without risk.

The person is no longer able to rely on control as a means of ensuring stability. They must navigate uncertainty, tolerate unpredictability, and remain engaged without guarantee. This can feel vulnerable. It can create a sense of exposure.

But it also creates a different kind of possibility.

When control is relinquished, the person is no longer limited by the constraints of the system they have been operating within. They are able to encounter realities that exceed those constraints, to engage with responses that are not determined by the logic of proportion or fairness.

This does not eliminate the tension between justice and grace.

That tension remains. The person may continue to experience moments of dissonance, to question how grace operates, to struggle with its implications. But their relationship to that tension begins to change.

Instead of seeking to resolve it through control, they begin to inhabit it.

They learn to live within a space where outcomes are not fully determined, where responses are not entirely predictable, where the structures they have relied upon are not sufficient to account for everything they encounter.

This way of living is not easily defined.

It does not lend itself to clear rules or consistent patterns. It is shaped by responsiveness rather than control, by engagement rather than management. It requires the person to remain attentive to what is present, to respond in ways that are appropriate to the situation, even when those responses cannot be secured in advance.

This attentiveness is not passive.

It involves discernment, judgment, and a willingness to act without full assurance. The person must continue to make decisions, to evaluate situations, to respond to what is happening around them. But they do so with an awareness that their actions do not fully determine the outcome.

This awareness can be both unsettling and freeing.

It is unsettling because it removes the guarantee of control. It is freeing because it releases the person from the burden of having to secure outcomes through their own effort. They are no longer responsible for managing what cannot be controlled.

This release does not eliminate responsibility.

It redefines it.

The person is responsible for how they act, for how they respond, for how they engage with what is given. But they are not responsible for ensuring that outcomes align with their expectations. They participate in a reality that includes both action and gift, both effort and grace.

At this stage, the person is beginning to live in relation to grace in a new way.

They are no longer attempting to manage it. They are learning to receive it, to engage with it, to respond to it without reducing it to a system they can control.

This learning is ongoing.

It does not reach a point of completion. The tension between control and openness, between system and gift, continues to shape the person's experience. They may move between different postures, at times returning to control, at times embracing openness.

But something has shifted.

The loss of control is no longer experienced solely as a deficit.

It is recognized as part of what makes grace what it is.

And it is from within this recognition that the next movement of the book begins.

PART III

The Human Response to Grace

(Resistance, Anger, and Moral Disorientation)

CHAPTER 10

The Right to Be Offended

PART 1: OFFENSE AS AN HONEST RESPONSE

IF GRACE DISRUPTS MORAL logic, destabilizes fairness, resists control, and appears unevenly in ways that defy expectation, then the offense it provokes must be taken seriously. It cannot be dismissed as misunderstanding, reduced to immaturity, or corrected through simple explanation. Offense, in this context, is not an error in perception. It is a response that emerges from the collision between what is encountered and the structures that have been relied upon to make sense of the world.

To be offended by grace is to recognize that something does not align.

This recognition is not superficial. It arises from a deeply formed moral framework—one that connects action to consequence, harm to accountability, and responsibility to response. When grace interrupts that framework, the person does not simply adjust. They experience a rupture. Offense is the name we give to that rupture when it is felt as a contradiction rather than a resolution.

This is why offense must be understood before it is evaluated.

Too often, offense is treated as a problem to be solved. It is seen as a barrier to acceptance, a resistance that must be overcome in order for grace to be received. The offended person is encouraged to move past their reaction, to adopt a different perspective, to align their response with what is presented as good.

But this approach assumes that the offense is misplaced.

It assumes that the problem lies in the person's response rather than in the disruption they are encountering. It treats offense as a failure of understanding rather than as a legitimate reaction to something that does not fit within the structures that have been used to interpret reality.

This assumption needs to be challenged.

Offense, in the context of grace, is not a failure of faith or a deficiency of character. It is an honest response to disruption. It reflects the person's engagement with a reality that contradicts their expectations in ways that cannot be easily reconciled.

The person who is offended is not refusing to see what is good.

They are responding to what appears, from within their framework, to be wrong.

This distinction is critical.

It allows us to take offense seriously as a form of moral perception rather than dismissing it as resistance. It recognizes that the offended person is not simply reacting emotionally, but is interpreting what they are encountering through a coherent, if challenged, understanding of how the world should function.

This understanding has been developed over time.

It has been shaped by experience, reinforced by social and institutional structures, and sustained by the need for stability in a world that can otherwise feel unpredictable. The person has learned to rely on connections between action and outcome, to expect proportion in response, to trust that the structures they inhabit will uphold certain standards.

When grace disrupts these connections, the offense that emerges is rooted in the perceived violation of those standards.

It is not arbitrary.

It is grounded in a commitment to a particular vision of what is right.

This is why offense often carries a moral tone.

The person does not simply say, "I do not like this." They say, "This is not right." The language reflects a judgment, an evaluation of what is being encountered. It indicates that the response is not only emotional, but moral.

To acknowledge this is to grant offense a certain legitimacy.

It is to recognize that the person's reaction is not without basis. It is to affirm that there is something real being perceived, even if that perception does not fully account for the reality of grace.

This affirmation does not resolve the tension.

It does not mean that the offense is the final word. But it does mean that the offense is not something to be dismissed or bypassed on the way to resolution. It must be engaged.

Engaging offense requires a shift in posture.

Instead of moving immediately to correct or reinterpret the offended response, the focus turns toward understanding it. What is being perceived? What expectations are being violated? What structures are being challenged?

These questions do not aim to justify the offense in an absolute sense.

They aim to locate it.

They seek to understand how the offense emerges from within a coherent framework, how it reflects the person's attempt to make sense of what they are encountering.

This process of understanding is essential.

Without it, any attempt to move beyond offense will be superficial. It will address the response without engaging the underlying structure that produced it. It will offer solutions that do not account for the depth of the disruption.

To remain with offense, then, is not to endorse it uncritically.

It is to recognize that it has something to reveal.

Offense exposes the points at which grace collides with moral logic. It highlights the assumptions that have been operating beneath the surface. It brings into view the expectations that shape how the person interprets what is good.

In this way, offense becomes a form of insight.

It shows where the tension lies, where the framework is being stretched, where the limits of understanding are being encountered. It provides a map of the disruption, indicating the areas where the person's interpretation of reality is being challenged.

This does not make offense comfortable.

It remains difficult, often accompanied by anger, confusion, or resistance. But it does make offense meaningful. It transforms it from a problem to be eliminated into a response that can be explored.

This exploration requires patience.

The person cannot be rushed through their offense without losing something important. The process of engaging with the disruption takes time. It involves revisiting assumptions, reconsidering interpretations, and allowing the tension to remain present.

This is not how offense is typically treated.

In many contexts, offense is seen as something to be overcome quickly. The goal is to move toward agreement, to resolve conflict, to restore alignment. The discomfort of offense is minimized in favor of a more immediate sense of coherence.

But in the context of grace, this approach can be counterproductive.

To rush past offense is to bypass the very point at which grace is doing its work. It is to avoid the disruption that reveals the limits of the existing framework. It is to move toward resolution without fully engaging what has been unsettled.

This does not mean that offense should be preserved indefinitely.

It means that it should be taken seriously as part of the process.

The person must be allowed to remain within the experience of offense long enough for its implications to become clear. They must be given space to articulate their response, to explore the reasons behind it, to understand what is being challenged.

This space is not always available.

In many environments, the expectation is that offense will be resolved quickly, that the person will adjust their perspective, that they will align with the response that is being presented as correct. This expectation can create pressure, making it difficult for the person to remain within the tension.

When this pressure is present, the person may feel that their response is not valid, that their offense is a problem to be fixed rather than a reality to be engaged. They may suppress their reaction, move toward premature resolution, or withdraw from the situation altogether.

These responses do not resolve the tension.

They conceal it.

The underlying disruption remains, even if it is not fully acknowledged. The person may appear to have moved past their offense, but the questions and uncertainties that gave rise to it continue to shape their experience.

To validate offense, then, is to create space for honesty.

It is to allow the person to acknowledge what they are experiencing without fear of dismissal or correction. It is to affirm that their response, while not final, is real and significant.

This validation does not settle the question of how to respond to grace.

It does not determine whether the offense is ultimately justified or how it will be resolved. But it establishes a starting point—a place from which the person can begin to engage with the disruption in a way that is both honest and open.

From this starting point, a different kind of movement becomes possible.

Not one that bypasses offense, but one that moves through it.

Not one that resolves tension immediately, but one that allows tension to shape understanding.

Not one that demands agreement, but one that invites deeper engagement.

This movement has not yet begun.

But it will.

And it begins here—with the recognition that to be offended by grace is not, in itself, a failure.

It is an honest response to a reality that does not fit.

PART 2: WHAT OFFENSE IS TRYING TO PROTECT

If offense is an honest response to disruption, then it is not random. It arises from something that the person is attempting to preserve. It reflects a perceived threat to structures that have been relied upon to make sense of the world, to navigate experience, and to sustain a coherent sense of self. To understand offense, then, is not only to acknowledge its presence, but to ask what it is defending.

Offense protects.

It emerges at the point where something valued is perceived to be at risk. The intensity of the response often corresponds to the significance of what is being threatened. When the disruption is minor, the offense is limited. When the disruption touches something foundational, the offense deepens.

In the context of grace, what is being protected is not superficial.

It is the moral structure that connects action to consequence, the sense of fairness that stabilizes interpretation, and the identity that has been formed within that structure. Offense arises when these elements are unsettled in ways that cannot be easily reconciled.

At one level, offense protects justice.

Justice, as it has been explored throughout this book, is not only a system of rules. It is a way of affirming that what happens matters, that actions have consequences, that harm is not ignored. It provides a framework within which experiences can be interpreted and addressed. It ensures that events are carried through a sequence that acknowledges their significance.

When grace interrupts that sequence, the person may experience it as a threat to justice.

If mercy is extended without accountability, if forgiveness is offered without repair, if restoration is initiated without proportion, then the connection between action and consequence appears to weaken. The person may feel that what has happened is not being fully addressed, that the process that would affirm its significance has been bypassed.

Offense, in this case, functions as a defense of that process.

It insists that the sequence must be maintained, that the event must be carried through the structures that ensure it is properly recognized. It resists responses that appear to undermine this recognition. It seeks to preserve the integrity of the moral order.

This defense is not misplaced.

It reflects a genuine concern that harm be taken seriously, that justice not be compromised. It expresses a commitment to a framework that has provided stability and meaning. To dismiss this defense as unnecessary or misguided is to overlook the role that justice plays in sustaining moral life.

At the same time, offense also protects meaning.

Meaning, in this context, is not abstract. It is the coherence that allows the person to interpret their experience in ways that make sense. It is the ability to locate events within a structure that explains what has happened and why it matters. It is what allows the person to move forward without being overwhelmed by uncertainty.

The moral logic described in earlier chapters contributes to this sense of meaning.

It provides a way of organizing experience, connecting events, and establishing expectations. It allows the person to anticipate outcomes, to understand responses, and to situate themselves within a broader narrative.

When grace disrupts this logic, the coherence of that narrative is challenged.

The person is no longer able to rely on the same connections to interpret what is happening. The sequence that has provided meaning is interrupted. Events do not lead to the outcomes that would make sense within the established framework.

Offense arises as a response to this disruption of meaning.

It seeks to restore coherence, to reestablish the connections that have been broken. It resists interpretations that do not align with the narrative that has been used to make sense of experience. It attempts to preserve a structure within which events can be understood.

This preservation is essential.

Without some form of coherence, the person would struggle to interpret their experience at all. The disruption introduced by grace does not only challenge specific expectations. It challenges the broader framework that gives those expectations their meaning.

Offense, then, is not only about defending justice.

It is about defending the possibility of understanding.

In addition to justice and meaning, offense also protects identity.

Identity is formed within the structures that have been described throughout this book. It is shaped by how the person understands their actions, their responsibilities, and their place within the moral order. It is reinforced by the consistency of the framework that connects action to outcome.

The person knows who they are, in part, because they understand how their actions relate to the world around them.

They act, and they see the results. They respond, and they observe the consequences. They develop a sense of themselves as agents within a system that is, to some degree, predictable.

When grace disrupts this system, the foundations of identity are affected.

If outcomes are no longer tied to actions in predictable ways, then the person's understanding of themselves as an agent within that system becomes less stable. They can no longer rely on the same connections to interpret their role, their responsibility, or their impact.

This destabilization can be deeply unsettling.

The person is not only losing a way of interpreting events. They are losing a way of understanding themselves. The structures that have supported their identity are no longer fully reliable.

Offense arises as a defense of that identity.

It resists changes that would undermine the coherence of the self. It seeks to preserve the connections that have allowed the person to understand who they are. It pushes back against responses that introduce uncertainty into that understanding.

This defense can take many forms.

The person may insist on the necessity of fairness, emphasizing its role in maintaining a stable identity. They may reject interpretations that challenge the connection between action and outcome. They may resist responses that introduce unpredictability into the system they rely on.

These responses are not merely stubbornness.

They are attempts to preserve a sense of self within a changing framework. They reflect the difficulty of adapting to a reality that does not conform to the structures that have supported identity.

At this point, it becomes clear that offense is not a simple reaction.

It is a complex response that protects multiple dimensions of experience—justice, meaning, and identity. It emerges from a coherent framework that is being challenged by something that does not fit within it.

To validate offense, then, is not to endorse everything that follows from it.

It is to recognize what it is trying to protect.

This recognition changes how offense is engaged.

Instead of viewing it as an obstacle to be removed, it is understood as a signal that something significant is at stake. It indicates that the person is encountering a disruption that affects fundamental aspects of their experience.

This understanding allows for a different kind of response.

Rather than attempting to eliminate offense, the focus shifts to exploring it. What is being defended? Why does it matter? How has it been formed? What would it mean for these structures to be altered or expanded?

These questions do not immediately resolve the tension.

They deepen it.

The person becomes more aware of the layers of their response, the multiple elements that are involved in their reaction. They see that their offense is not only about the specific situation, but about the broader framework that gives that situation meaning.

This awareness can be both clarifying and unsettling.

It clarifies the source of the response, making it more intelligible. But it also reveals the extent of the disruption, showing that what is at stake is not limited to a single event.

At this stage, the person is still within the protective function of offense.

They are still defending the structures that have supported their understanding. They are still resisting the full implications of the disruption introduced by grace.

But the recognition of what offense is protecting introduces a new possibility.

If these structures are being defended so strongly, what would it mean for them to be reexamined?

Not abandoned, but reconsidered.

Not dismissed, but expanded.

This possibility is not yet realized.

It remains a question.

But it is a question that will shape what comes next.

PART 3: REMAINING OPEN WITHIN OFFENSE

If offense is an honest response and a form of protection—guarding justice, meaning, and identity—then the question that follows is not how to eliminate offense, but how to remain within it without becoming closed. The danger is not that offense exists. The danger is what offense becomes when it is no longer engaged but fixed, when it shifts from a response to a position, from a moment of disruption to a settled stance.

To be offended is to recognize that something does not align. To remain offended is to continue holding that recognition. But to become closed within offense is to turn that recognition into a boundary that cannot be crossed, a final judgment that no longer allows for movement.

This distinction is subtle but significant.

Offense, in its initial form, is dynamic. It arises in response to an encounter, reflecting the tension between expectation and reality. It is part of a process of interpretation, an attempt to make sense of what has been experienced. It is open to development, capable of being explored, questioned, and, over time, transformed.

Closure within offense halts that process.

It fixes the response in place, solidifying it into a conclusion that resists further engagement. The person no longer asks what the offense reveals. They assert what it proves. The disruption is no longer a question. It becomes an answer.

This shift provides a certain kind of stability.

The person no longer needs to navigate uncertainty. They no longer need to hold conflicting interpretations or remain within tension. They have reached a conclusion that allows them to move forward without revisiting the disruption.

But this stability comes at a cost.

By closing within offense, the person limits their engagement with what has been encountered. They reduce the complexity of the situation to a single interpretation, one that aligns with the framework they have been defending. They preserve coherence, but they do so by excluding the possibility that their framework may not fully account for what they have experienced.

This exclusion can be protective.

It maintains the integrity of the structures that have provided meaning and identity. It shields the person from the discomfort of uncertainty and the vulnerability of not knowing. It allows them to continue operating within a familiar system.

But it also prevents movement.

The person remains within the limits of their existing framework, unable to engage with the aspects of reality that do not fit within it. The disruption that gave rise to offense is contained rather than explored. Its implications remain unexamined.

To remain open within offense is to resist this closure.

It is to continue engaging with the disruption, even when it is uncomfortable, even when it challenges the structures that have provided stability. It is to allow the offense to remain a question rather than forcing it into an answer.

This does not mean abandoning judgment.

The person does not suspend their sense of right and wrong. They do not relinquish their commitment to justice or their concern for fairness. These remain active. They continue to shape how the person interprets what is happening.

What changes is how these commitments are held.

They are no longer treated as final measures that resolve every situation. They are recognized as part of a larger framework that may not be complete. The person allows for the possibility that there are dimensions of the situation that their current understanding does not fully capture.

This allowance creates space.

It opens the possibility for new interpretations, for different ways of understanding what has been encountered. It does not guarantee that these interpretations will emerge, but it makes them possible.

Remaining open within offense requires a particular kind of discipline.

It involves resisting the impulse to resolve tension prematurely. It means tolerating uncertainty, holding questions that do not have immediate answers, and continuing to engage with a reality that does not fit within established categories.

This discipline is not easy.

It runs counter to the desire for closure that has been described throughout this book. It asks the person to remain within a state that feels unresolved, to continue engaging with discomfort rather than moving past it.

But this discipline is also generative.

It allows offense to function as more than a defensive reaction. It becomes a site of inquiry, a place where the limits of the current framework are exposed and where new understanding can begin to emerge.

This does not happen automatically.

The person must choose to remain open. They must actively resist the tendency to close, to settle, to finalize. They must return to the questions that offense raises, even when those questions are difficult.

What is being disrupted?

What assumptions are being challenged?

What does this reveal about how I understand justice, meaning, and identity?

These questions do not resolve offense.

They deepen it.

They move the person from reacting to reflecting, from defending to exploring. They create a different relationship to the disruption, one that allows for movement rather than closure.

At the same time, remaining open within offense does not eliminate the protective function of offense.

The person still cares about justice. They still seek coherence. They still hold to a sense of identity that has been formed within the structures they have relied upon. These concerns do not disappear.

What changes is how they are integrated into the response.

Instead of using offense to defend these structures at all costs, the person begins to hold them alongside the possibility that those structures may need to be expanded. They recognize that what they are protecting is important, but not necessarily complete.

This recognition introduces humility.

The person acknowledges that their understanding, while coherent, is limited. They accept that there may be aspects of reality that they do not yet see, dimensions of grace that do not fit within their current framework.

This humility is not self-negation.

It does not require the person to abandon their convictions. It requires them to hold those convictions in a way that allows for growth, for change, for the possibility that their understanding may be deepened.

This posture creates a different kind of engagement with grace.

Instead of encountering it as something that must be accepted or rejected, the person engages with it as something that must be understood. They remain within the tension, allowing the offense to shape their inquiry rather than determine their conclusion.

This engagement is ongoing.

It does not reach a point of final resolution. The tension between justice and grace, between fairness and gift, between control and openness, continues to shape the person's experience. They may move between different responses, at times leaning toward closure, at times toward openness.

But the choice to remain open within offense changes the trajectory.

It prevents the person from becoming fixed within a single interpretation. It allows for movement, for development, for the possibility that the disruption they have encountered is not only a challenge, but an invitation.

An invitation not to abandon what they have known.

But to see beyond it.

This invitation is not yet fully realized.

It is only beginning to take shape.

The person is still within offense, still holding the tension, still navigating the uncertainty. But they are doing so in a way that allows for something new to emerge.

And it is from within this openness that the next movement of the book begins.

CHAPTER 11

When Grace Threatens Identity

PART 1: "I AM THE ONE WHO WAS WRONGED"

IF OFFENSE PROTECTS IDENTITY, then the introduction of grace does not only disrupt moral logic or challenge fairness. It reaches into the structure of the self. It unsettles the narratives through which a person understands who they are, what has happened to them, and how they are situated within the moral order. This disruption is not incidental. It is central to the experience of grace as offense.

Identity is not formed in abstraction. It is constructed through experience, interpreted through narrative, and stabilized through the frameworks that give those narratives coherence. The person understands themselves by locating their actions, their relationships, and their experiences within a sequence that makes sense. They know who they are, in part, because they know what has happened and how it has been interpreted.

In situations of harm, one of the most powerful and stabilizing identities is that of the wronged.

"I am the one who was wronged."

This statement is not merely descriptive. It is interpretive. It locates the person within a moral framework that affirms the significance of what has happened. It acknowledges that harm has occurred, that it was not deserved, and that it matters. It connects the person's experience to a broader understanding of justice, in which wrongdoing is recognized and response is expected.

This identity can be deeply stabilizing.

In the aftermath of disruption, it provides clarity. It offers a way of making sense of what has happened. It allows the person to interpret their experience in terms that are coherent and morally grounded. It affirms that they have been acted upon in ways that are significant, that their experience is not arbitrary or meaningless.

This affirmation is not trivial.

It can be essential for survival.

When harm disrupts the expected order, the ability to name oneself as the one who was wronged provides a point of orientation. It restores a sense of coherence, allowing the person to understand their experience within a framework that recognizes the reality of what has occurred.

This identity is often reinforced by others.

Communities, institutions, and relationships may affirm the person's experience, acknowledging the harm and supporting the interpretation that the person has been wronged. This external validation strengthens the identity, embedding it within a network of recognition that further stabilizes it.

Over time, this identity can become integrated into the person's broader sense of self.

It may not define them entirely, but it becomes a significant part of how they understand their story. It shapes how they interpret new experiences, how they relate to others, how they navigate the world. It provides a reference point for understanding what has been done and what should follow.

It is within this context that grace begins to threaten identity.

When grace is introduced into a situation where harm has occurred, it does not simply offer a different response. It alters the narrative structure within which the identity of the wronged has been formed. It introduces a possibility that does not align with the sequence that has supported that identity.

If the one who caused harm is forgiven before accountability is completed, if restoration is extended without proportion, if the narrative shifts toward reconciliation without fully carrying the weight of what has happened, then the identity of the wronged is affected.

The person may begin to experience a loss of clarity.

The narrative that has provided coherence is no longer stable. The sequence that connected the event to its interpretation is interrupted. The person is left without the same assurance that their understanding of what has happened will be carried through in the way they expected.

This does not mean that the harm is erased.

The event remains.

But its place within the narrative is altered.

The person who has been wronged may find that their identity is no longer supported in the same way by the structures around them. The recognition that once affirmed their position may become less certain, less central, or redirected toward other aspects of the situation.

This redirection can be disorienting.

The person may feel that something essential is being taken from them—not the experience itself, but the clarity with which it has been understood. They may struggle to locate themselves within a narrative that no longer aligns with the structure they have relied upon.

This is where the threat to identity becomes most apparent.

The person is not only reacting to a change in how events are interpreted. They are confronting a shift in how they understand themselves in relation to those events. The identity that has provided stability is no longer fully secure.

This insecurity can produce resistance.

The person may reassert their identity more strongly, emphasizing the reality of the harm, the necessity of justice, the importance of maintaining the narrative that affirms their experience. They may resist interpretations that challenge this narrative, viewing them as attempts to minimize or overlook what has occurred.

This resistance is not arbitrary.

It is an effort to preserve coherence.

The person is defending a way of understanding themselves that has been essential for making sense of their experience. They are protecting a narrative that has allowed them to navigate disruption and maintain a sense of identity.

At the same time, the introduction of grace creates a tension that cannot be easily resolved within that narrative.

The person is aware that something is being offered that does not fit within the structure they have relied upon. They may recognize that grace is being presented as good, even as it disrupts their understanding of what is right. They are caught between competing interpretations, unable to fully integrate them.

This tension is not only intellectual.

It is deeply personal.

The person must confront the possibility that their identity, as it has been formed, is not sufficient to account for the reality they are encountering. They must consider whether there are aspects of their experience that are not fully captured by the narrative they have constructed.

This consideration is difficult.

It requires the person to question something that has provided stability and meaning. It asks them to hold their identity more loosely, to allow for the possibility that it may be expanded or altered in ways that are not immediately clear.

This does not mean abandoning the identity of the wronged.

The harm remains real. The need for justice does not disappear. The person's experience continues to matter. But it does mean recognizing that this identity, while important, may not be the whole story.

Grace introduces the possibility that the narrative is not complete.

It suggests that there may be dimensions of the situation that extend beyond the categories that have been used to interpret it. It invites the person to consider that their identity, while grounded in real experience, may be part of a larger and more complex reality.

This invitation is not easily accepted.

It requires the person to remain within uncertainty, to hold together competing interpretations, to resist the impulse to resolve the tension by retreating into the familiar narrative. It asks them to engage with a disruption that affects not only how they understand events, but how they understand themselves.

At this stage, the person is not yet ready to reconstruct identity.

They are still within the experience of threat, still navigating the loss of narrative clarity, still responding to the destabilization that grace introduces. They are aware that something has shifted, but they do not yet know what that shift will mean.

This is where the chapter begins.

Within the recognition that grace does not only challenge what we believe.

It challenges who we believe ourselves to be.

PART 2: WHEN THE ROLES NO LONGER HOLD

If the identity of the wronged provides stability, it does so in part because it is supported by a set of moral roles that organize how people understand themselves and others. These roles are not arbitrary. They arise from the same moral logic that connects action to consequence and assigns responsibility in ways that make experience intelligible. Within this framework, distinctions are drawn—between right and wrong, between those who act and those who are acted upon, between those who cause harm and those who endure it. These distinctions do more than categorize events. They structure relationships. They define positions. They allow individuals to locate themselves within a shared moral landscape.

In situations of harm, these roles often become sharply defined.

There is the one who has caused harm and the one who has been harmed. There is the agent and the recipient, the offender and the victim. These roles are not interchangeable. They carry with them different expectations, different responsibilities, and different moral weight. The one who causes harm is expected to be held accountable. The one who has been harmed is expected to be recognized, supported, and, where possible, restored.

This differentiation is essential for clarity.

It allows the person to interpret what has happened without confusion. It provides a way of assigning meaning that aligns with the experience of the event. It ensures that the moral structure remains intact, that the sequence of action and consequence can be followed and understood.

These roles also contribute to identity.

The person who has been harmed understands themselves in relation to the one who caused harm. Their identity is not only personal but relational. It is defined, in part, by their position within this structure. They are the one who was acted upon, the one who endured, the one who carries the impact of what has occurred.

This relational identity is reinforced by the clarity of the roles.

The distinction between good and bad, right and wrong, victim and offender, provides a stable framework within which the person can understand their place. It affirms that the roles are not ambiguous, that the positions are not interchangeable, that the moral order is clear.

Grace disrupts this clarity.

When grace enters the situation, it does not simply offer a different response. It alters the way roles are understood. It introduces a possibility that the distinctions, while still real, are not as fixed as they appeared to be.

If the one who caused harm is forgiven, restored, or reintroduced into the community without completing the expected sequence of accountability, the role of offender begins to shift. The person is no longer located solely within that category. They are no longer defined only by what they have done. Something else is being said about them.

At the same time, the role of the one who was harmed is affected.

If the narrative begins to move toward reconciliation, if the focus shifts from harm to restoration, if the attention is directed toward the possibility of a future that includes both parties, then the identity of the wronged is no longer the sole organizing category. It remains present, but it is no longer sufficient to account for the direction of the narrative.

This shift creates ambiguity.

The roles that once provided clarity are no longer as stable. The person may find that the distinctions they have relied upon are being blurred, not erased, but complicated. The categories that once allowed for straightforward interpretation now require more nuanced understanding.

This ambiguity can be deeply unsettling.

The person is not only losing clarity about the situation. They are losing clarity about how to understand themselves and others within it. The roles that structured their experience are no longer fully reliable.

This can lead to a sense of disorientation.

The person may ask: Who is this other now? Are they still the one who caused harm, or something else? And who am I, if the narrative is no longer centered on what was done to me? What happens to my place within this structure if the roles are no longer fixed?

These questions do not have immediate answers.

They reflect the tension between the established moral logic and the disruption introduced by grace. The person is attempting to navigate a reality in which the categories that have been used to organize experience are no longer sufficient.

In response, the person may attempt to reassert the roles more strongly.

They may emphasize the distinction between offender and victim, insisting that the categories remain clear and that the narrative should not move beyond them prematurely. They may resist any interpretation that blurs these distinctions, viewing it as a threat to the moral order.

This response is understandable.

It reflects a desire to preserve clarity, to maintain a framework that allows for coherent interpretation. The person is defending the structure that has made sense of their experience and affirmed the reality of what has occurred.

At the same time, this reassertion can limit engagement with what grace is introducing.

By insisting on fixed roles, the person may close off the possibility of recognizing dimensions of the situation that do not fit within those roles. They may reduce the complexity of the experience to a binary that no longer fully accounts for what is happening.

This reduction can provide temporary stability.

But it does so by narrowing the scope of interpretation.

Alternatively, the person may begin to engage with the ambiguity.

They may acknowledge that the roles are not as fixed as they once appeared, that the categories they have relied upon are being stretched. They may allow for the possibility that both the one who caused harm and the one who was harmed cannot be fully understood within a single, static role.

This engagement does not eliminate the distinction between right and wrong.

It does not deny that harm has occurred or that responsibility remains. But it introduces a recognition that identity cannot be entirely contained within these categories. It suggests that the person is more than the role they occupy within a particular event.

This recognition is difficult to hold.

It requires the person to tolerate complexity, to resist the urge to simplify, to remain within a space where clarity is not immediately available. It challenges the desire for fixed roles that provide stability and coherence.

It also raises questions about how to relate to others.

If the one who caused harm is not only the offender, but also something else, how should they be understood? If the one who was harmed is not only the victim, but also something more, how should they understand themselves? These questions complicate relationships, introducing layers that are not easily navigated.

This complexity can be resisted.

The person may prefer the clarity of fixed roles, even if that clarity does not fully account for the situation. They may choose to maintain a framework that allows for straightforward interpretation, even if it limits engagement with the reality they are encountering.

But the presence of grace continues to challenge this preference.

It does not allow the roles to remain entirely fixed. It introduces a dynamic that cannot be fully contained within the existing categories. It keeps the tension active, preventing the person from settling into a stable but incomplete understanding.

At this stage, the person is not yet resolving this tension.

They are still navigating it.

They are aware that the roles they have relied upon are being destabilized, but they do not yet know how to reconfigure them. They are experiencing the loss of clarity without having a new framework to replace it.

This is where the chapter deepens.

The disruption of identity is no longer only about the self.

It extends into how the person understands others, how they interpret relationships, how they navigate a world in which the roles that once provided stability no longer fully hold.

And it is from within this destabilization that the next movement begins.

PART 3: BECOMING WITHOUT FIXED ROLES

If grace destabilizes the identity of the wronged and unsettles the moral roles that once provided clarity, the person is left in a space that is difficult to inhabit. The narratives that once structured their understanding are no longer sufficient. The roles that once defined their position are no longer fixed. The coherence that once held their identity together has been disrupted.

This disruption is not simply a loss.

It is a transition.

But it does not feel like one.

From within the experience, the person does not yet perceive movement. They perceive absence. The clarity that once allowed them to say, "I am the one who was wronged," is no longer as stable. The roles that once allowed them to distinguish between themselves and others are no longer as clearly defined. The narrative that once provided direction is no longer fully intact.

This can feel like disintegration.

The person may experience a sense of fragmentation, as though the elements that once formed a coherent identity are no longer aligned. They may struggle to answer questions that once felt straightforward: Who am I in this situation? What does this mean about me? How do I understand what has happened now?

These questions do not have immediate answers.

They cannot be resolved by returning to the previous framework, because that framework has already been disrupted. The person cannot simply reassert the identity that once provided stability without ignoring the presence of grace and the changes it has introduced.

At the same time, the person does not yet have a new framework to replace the old one.

They are between.

Between clarity and ambiguity, between fixed roles and emerging complexity, between a narrative that once made sense and a reality that no longer fits within it.

This "between" is difficult.

It lacks the stability of the former structure and the coherence of a new one. It requires the person to exist without the same level of certainty, to navigate without the same clarity, to understand themselves without the same defined roles.

This is where identity begins to shift.

Not through resolution, but through exposure.

The person is exposed to the limits of the identity they have been holding. They begin to see that while it was coherent and meaningful, it was not exhaustive. It did not capture the full complexity of their experience or the reality they are now encountering.

This realization is not immediate.

It emerges gradually, often through continued engagement with the tension that grace introduces. The person may begin to notice that their identity, while still connected to the experience of harm, is not entirely defined by it. They may recognize that there are aspects of themselves that extend beyond the role they have occupied.

This recognition does not diminish the reality of what has happened.

The harm remains real. The experience continues to matter. But it introduces the possibility that identity is not fixed within a single narrative or role. It suggests that the self is not fully contained by the categories that have been used to interpret experience.

This suggestion is both unsettling and liberating.

It is unsettling because it removes the clarity that comes from fixed roles. The person can no longer rely on a single narrative to define who they are. They must navigate a more complex understanding of themselves, one that includes multiple dimensions that do not always align neatly.

It is liberating because it opens the possibility for growth.

The person is no longer confined to a single interpretation of their identity. They are able to engage with aspects of themselves that were not fully visible within the previous framework. They can begin to understand themselves in ways that are not limited to the role they have occupied.

This process is not linear.

The person may move back and forth between different understandings of themselves. At times, they may return to the clarity of the identity they once held, finding comfort in its stability. At other times, they may engage with the emerging complexity, exploring new ways of understanding who they are.

This movement reflects the ongoing nature of identity formation.

Identity is not a fixed state. It is a process that evolves over time, shaped by experience, interpretation, and engagement with the world. The disruption introduced by grace accelerates this process, bringing into view aspects of identity that were previously stable but are now in flux.

Within this process, the person begins to encounter a different way of understanding themselves.

Not as a fixed role within a moral structure, but as a participant in a reality that includes both structure and disruption, both clarity and ambiguity, both justice and grace. They begin to see that their identity is not determined solely by what has been done to them or by the roles they have occupied.

This does not eliminate the importance of those roles.

The person does not cease to be someone who has been harmed. The experience remains part of their story. But it is no longer the only way of understanding themselves. It becomes one aspect of a more complex identity.

This complexity requires a different kind of engagement.

The person must learn to hold multiple dimensions of their identity without reducing them to a single category. They must allow for the coexistence of elements that do not fully align, that may even feel in tension with one another.

This holding is not easy.

It requires patience, reflection, and a willingness to remain within uncertainty. It challenges the desire for a clear and consistent narrative, replacing it with a more fluid and dynamic understanding.

At the same time, this fluidity does not mean that identity becomes unstable in a destructive sense.

It becomes adaptable.

The person is able to engage with new experiences without needing to fit them into a fixed framework. They can respond to the presence of grace without being limited by the roles that once defined their understanding.

This adaptability allows for a different kind of coherence.

Not the coherence that comes from fixed roles and stable narratives, but the coherence that comes from integrating complexity over time. The person's identity becomes less about maintaining a single interpretation and more about engaging with the full range of their experience.

This engagement is ongoing.

It does not reach a final point of resolution. The person continues to encounter situations that challenge their understanding, to navigate tensions that do not fully resolve, to adapt their sense of self in response to what they experience.

But something has changed.

The threat that grace posed to identity is no longer experienced solely as a loss.

It is recognized as part of a process of becoming.

A becoming that does not rely on fixed roles or stable narratives, but on the capacity to remain engaged with a reality that is more complex than any single framework can contain.

This does not answer all the questions.

It does not eliminate the tension.

But it provides a way of moving forward.

Not by restoring what has been lost.

But by allowing something new to take shape.

CHAPTER 12

Grace Reopens What Was Closed

PART 1: WHEN CLOSURE IS INTERRUPTED

IF MORAL CLARITY ALLOWED the person to survive disruption by bringing events into a form that could be carried forward, then closure was the moment at which that process reached its limit. Closure did not necessarily mean that everything had been resolved or repaired. It meant that the person had reached a point at which the experience could be contained. The event had been named, categorized, and located within a narrative that allowed it to exist without overwhelming the present.

Closure, in this sense, is not superficial.

It is a form of stabilization.

It allows the person to move forward without needing to revisit the full weight of what has occurred. It creates a boundary between past and present, between what has been experienced and what is currently being lived. It establishes a sense of distance that makes continued engagement possible.

This distance is often hard-won.

The person may have labored to reach closure, working through the confusion and disruption that followed the initial event. They may have relied on moral clarity, on the affirmation of justice, on the support of others, to bring the experience into a form that could be held. Closure represents the outcome of that process.

It is not easily relinquished.

When closure is achieved, it becomes something to be protected. It provides a sense of stability that is necessary for ongoing life. It allows the person to engage with the present without being constantly drawn back into the past. It offers a way of living that does not require continuous reengagement with what has already been processed.

Grace interrupts this closure.

It does not simply add something new to the existing narrative. It reopens the narrative itself. It introduces a response that cannot be fully integrated into the structure that closure has established. It brings the past back into the present in ways that are not easily contained.

This reopening is not always recognized immediately.

At first, the person may experience grace as a new element, something that can be incorporated into the existing framework. They may attempt to understand it as an extension of the process that led to closure, as a continuation rather than a disruption.

But over time, the effect becomes clear.

Grace does not leave the closed structure intact.

It destabilizes it.

The boundaries that were established to contain the past begin to shift. The narrative that once provided a clear distinction between what was and what is becomes less stable. The person finds themselves drawn back into the event, not because they have failed to achieve closure, but because the conditions that made closure possible have changed.

This can be deeply unsettling.

The person may feel as though something they worked hard to establish is being undone. The stability they relied upon is no longer secure. The distance that allowed them to move forward is reduced, and the past becomes more present than it was before.

This experience is not simply a return.

It is a reopening.

The past does not reappear in the same form. It is encountered within a different context, shaped by the introduction of grace. The person is not revisiting the event as it was originally experienced, but as it is now being reinterpreted.

This reinterpretation can be disorienting.

The person may find that the categories they used to understand the event are no longer sufficient. The clarity that once defined the narrative is complicated by new possibilities. The roles that were fixed within the closed structure are now less certain.

This does not mean that the original understanding was wrong.

It means that it was not complete.

Closure allowed the person to stabilize their experience within a particular framework. Grace introduces the possibility that there are dimensions of the event that extend beyond that framework. It suggests that the narrative is not finished, that there are aspects of the situation that have not yet been fully engaged.

This suggestion is difficult to accept.

The person may resist the reopening.

They may seek to preserve the closure they have achieved, to maintain the boundaries that allowed them to move forward. They may interpret the reopening as a threat, as something that will undo the progress they have made.

This resistance is not irrational.

It reflects the cost of reopening.

To revisit what has been closed is to reengage with material that was difficult to process the first time. It is to expose oneself to the possibility of renewed disruption, of encountering again the weight of what has occurred. The person may fear that reopening will lead to instability, that it will undo the coherence they have worked to establish.

These fears are not unfounded.

Reopening does introduce risk.

It disrupts the stability of closure, reintroducing elements of uncertainty and ambiguity. It requires the person to engage with aspects of their experience that were previously contained. It challenges the boundaries that allowed for distance and control.

At the same time, the reopening introduced by grace is not identical to the original disruption.

The person is not the same as they were when the event first occurred. They have developed ways of understanding, coping, and engaging with their experience. They bring this development with them into the reopening.

This does not eliminate the difficulty.

But it changes the nature of the engagement.

The person is not starting from the beginning.

They are returning from a place of having already lived through the event, having already constructed a narrative that provided stability. The reopening occurs within this context, introducing new possibilities without entirely erasing what has been established.

This creates a complex dynamic.

The person must hold together the closure they have achieved and the reopening that grace introduces. They must navigate a space in which the past is both contained and active, both settled and unsettled.

This navigation is not straightforward.

The person may move between different positions, at times leaning into closure, at times engaging with the reopening. They may feel the pull of stability and the pressure of disruption simultaneously. They may struggle to determine how much of the past to revisit and how much to leave as it is.

This struggle reflects the tension between two necessary movements.

Closure allows for stability.

Reopening allows for transformation.

Grace introduces the second movement into a space that has already been shaped by the first.

This introduction is not optional.

It does not ask permission.

It occurs.

And when it does, the person must decide how to respond.

They can resist the reopening, seeking to preserve the closure they have achieved. They can attempt to contain the disruption, to limit its impact on their present experience. Or they can begin to engage with what has been reopened, allowing the narrative to expand beyond its previous boundaries.

This engagement is not immediate.

It requires a willingness to reenter a space that has already been navigated, to reconsider what has been understood, to allow for the possibility that the past is not fully settled.

At this stage, the person is not yet ready to fully embrace this movement.

They are still within the experience of interruption.

They are aware that something has been reopened, that the closure they relied upon is no longer complete. They are navigating the tension between preserving stability and engaging with disruption.

This is where the chapter begins.

Within the recognition that grace does not only offer something new.

It reopens what we believed was finished.

PART 2: WHY WE RESIST REOPENING

If closure provides stability and grace disrupts that stability by reopening what has been settled, then resistance is not only expected—it is necessary to understand. The person does not resist reopening because they are unwilling to grow or because they are opposed to grace in principle. They resist because reopening carries cost. It demands reengagement with what was difficult, destabilizes what has been secured, and introduces uncertainty into a space that had been made manageable.

This resistance is not superficial.

It is rooted in the work that closure required.

To reach closure, the person had to interpret what happened, locate it within a narrative, and establish boundaries that allowed for distance. They had to decide what the event meant, who was responsible, and how it would be carried forward. This process involved effort, reflection, and often pain. It was not simply a cognitive exercise. It was a restructuring of experience.

Closure represents the outcome of that restructuring.

It is the form that allows the person to live without being constantly overwhelmed by the past. It creates a sense of finality—not necessarily in the sense that everything is resolved, but in the sense that the event has been brought to a point where it no longer demands continuous engagement.

When grace reopens what has been closed, it threatens this finality.

It suggests that the work of closure is not complete, that the narrative is not finished, that the boundaries that were established are not as fixed as they appeared to be. This suggestion can feel like a reversal, as though the progress that was made is being undone.

The person resists because they recognize what reopening entails.

It requires reengagement.

Reengagement is not a neutral act. It involves returning to material that was difficult to process, revisiting emotions that may have been painful, and reconsidering interpretations that provided stability. The person must confront the possibility that what they have already worked through may need to be worked through again, but in a different way.

This prospect can be exhausting.

The person may feel that they have already done the necessary work, that they have already reached a point of understanding that allowed them to move forward. The idea of reopening can feel like an additional burden, a demand that exceeds what they are able or willing to carry.

This sense of exhaustion is not a sign of avoidance.

It reflects the reality that engaging with disruption requires energy. It requires attention, emotional capacity, and a willingness to confront uncertainty. The person may not have the resources to reenter that process, or they may feel that doing so would compromise their ability to function in the present.

In addition to the psychological cost, there is a moral dimension to the resistance.

Closure often involves a determination of responsibility.

The person identifies what has happened, who is accountable, and what that means for how the event is understood. This determination provides a sense of moral clarity. It allows the person to interpret the event in terms that align with their understanding of justice.

Reopening can challenge this clarity.

If grace introduces a response that does not align with the established sequence, then the moral interpretation that supported closure may no longer be sufficient. The person may be asked, implicitly or explicitly, to reconsider how they understand responsibility, accountability, and response.

This reconsideration can feel like a threat to justice.

The person may fear that reopening will lead to a weakening of the moral distinctions that were necessary to make sense of the event. They may worry that the clarity they achieved will be replaced by ambiguity, that the determination of responsibility will be diluted, that the significance of what happened will be diminished.

This fear is not unfounded.

Reopening does introduce ambiguity.

It complicates the narrative, introduces new possibilities, and challenges the simplicity of the categories that were used to achieve closure. The person must navigate a space in which the clarity they relied upon is no longer fully available.

This moral cost contributes to resistance.

The person is not only protecting their psychological stability. They are protecting their understanding of what is right. They are defending a framework that affirms the significance of the event and the necessity of a response that aligns with that significance.

There is also a relational dimension to the resistance.

Closure often involves adjustments in relationships.

The person may have established boundaries, redefined connections, or altered their engagement with others in response to what has happened. These adjustments are part of the process of stabilizing experience. They allow the person to move forward in ways that are consistent with their understanding of the event.

Reopening can unsettle these adjustments.

If the narrative shifts, if grace introduces the possibility of new forms of engagement, if relationships that were redefined are reconsidered, then the structures that supported the person's relational life may need to be revisited.

This can be destabilizing.

The person may fear that reopening will require changes that they are not prepared to make, that it will disrupt relationships that have been carefully managed, that it will introduce complexity into areas that have been simplified in order to maintain stability.

This fear can lead to resistance.

The person may seek to maintain the boundaries they have established, to preserve the relational structures that have allowed them to function. They may resist any movement that would require them to reconsider these structures, viewing it as a threat to their well-being.

At this stage, resistance is not only understandable.

It is necessary.

It reflects the person's attempt to preserve stability, to protect meaning, and to maintain a sense of coherence in the face of disruption. It is a response to real costs—psychological, moral, and relational—that reopening introduces.

To dismiss this resistance is to overlook these costs.

It is to treat reopening as if it were a simple extension of growth, rather than a process that requires the person to reengage with what has already been difficult. It is to ignore the work that closure represented and the significance of what is being threatened.

At the same time, resistance does not eliminate the reopening.

Grace continues to introduce the possibility that the narrative is not complete. It continues to unsettle the boundaries that closure established. The person may resist, but the tension remains.

This creates a difficult position.

The person is caught between the desire to preserve what has been achieved and the reality that something new is pressing against it. They are aware of the cost of reopening, but they are also aware that the closure they have relied upon is no longer fully stable.

This awareness can lead to a form of negotiation.

The person may attempt to control the reopening, to engage with it in limited ways that do not fully disrupt the stability they have achieved. They may revisit certain aspects of the past while maintaining boundaries around others. They may allow for partial reconsideration while resisting deeper changes.

This negotiation reflects the difficulty of the situation.

The person is trying to balance the need for stability with the reality of disruption. They are attempting to engage with grace without relinquishing the structures that have allowed them to move forward.

This balance is not easily maintained.

The tension between closure and reopening continues to shape the person's experience. They may move between resistance and engagement, at times holding tightly to what has been established, at times allowing for the possibility of something more.

At this stage, the person is not yet ready to fully embrace reopening.

They are still within resistance.

They are still protecting what closure provided, still aware of the cost of reengagement, still navigating the uncertainty that grace introduces.

But the presence of resistance itself reveals something important.

It shows that what is being reopened matters.

It indicates that the disruption is not superficial, that it touches something significant within the person's experience.

And it prepares the way for what comes next.

PART 3: REOPENING WITHOUT COLLAPSE

If closure provided stability and reopening introduces disruption, the question that follows is how to engage what has been reopened without losing what closure made possible. The person cannot simply return to the state they were in before closure, because that state was defined by instability, confusion, and the absence of a coherent narrative. At the same time, they cannot fully preserve the closure they achieved, because grace has already unsettled it. They must find a way to move forward that holds together both the need for stability and the reality of reopening.

This movement is not intuitive.

The instinct is often to choose between two options: to close again or to reopen completely. To close again is to attempt to restore the boundaries that were disrupted, to reassert the narrative that provided coherence, and to resist the implications of grace. To reopen completely is to relinquish those boundaries, to reengage the past without restraint, and to allow the disruption to unfold without limitation.

Both options carry risk.

Closing again may preserve stability, but it does so by ignoring what has been introduced. It requires the person to set aside the presence of grace, to return to a framework that no longer fully accounts for their experience. This can create a form of rigidity, where the person maintains coherence at the expense of engagement with reality.

Reopening completely may allow for full engagement with the disruption, but it risks overwhelming the person. Without the boundaries that closure provided, the past can reassert itself in ways that are difficult to manage. The person may find themselves drawn back into the intensity of the original experience, without the structures that allowed them to contain it.

The path forward lies between these extremes.

It involves engaging what has been reopened while maintaining enough structure to remain stable. It requires the person to hold boundaries differently—not as fixed barriers that prevent reengagement, but as flexible structures that allow for movement without collapse.

This distinction is critical.

Boundaries, in the context of closure, were often established to contain the past, to create distance, and to prevent the experience from overwhelming the present. They functioned as protective measures, ensuring that the person could continue to live without being constantly drawn back into what had occurred.

In the context of reopening, boundaries take on a different role.

They are no longer primarily about exclusion. They are about regulation. They allow the person to engage with what has been reopened in ways that are sustainable, that do not exceed their capacity, and that do not undo the stability they have achieved.

This regulation requires attentiveness.

The person must become aware of their own limits, of how much they can engage at a given time, of what aspects of the reopening are most pressing and which can remain at the periphery. They must learn to pace their engagement, to move in and out of the reopened space without becoming trapped within it.

This pacing is not passive.

It involves active discernment.

The person must decide when to engage and when to step back, when to revisit aspects of the past and when to allow them to remain as they are. These decisions are not guided by a fixed set of rules. They are shaped by the person's experience, their capacity, and the context in which they are engaging.

This discernment can be challenging.

There is no clear formula for how much reopening is appropriate or how it should be managed. The person must navigate this process without the certainty that comes from established structures. They must rely on their developing awareness of themselves and their situation.

At the same time, the person must also reconsider how they understand the past.

Closure often involved fixing the meaning of the event within a particular narrative. The person decided what had happened, what it meant, and how it would be carried forward. This narrative provided stability, but it also limited the range of possible interpretations.

Reopening introduces the possibility that this narrative is not final.

The person may begin to see aspects of the event that were not previously visible, to recognize complexities that were not fully accounted for, to consider interpretations that extend beyond the original framework. This does not negate the narrative that was established, but it expands it.

This expansion requires flexibility.

The person must be willing to hold multiple interpretations, to allow for the coexistence of different perspectives, to resist the urge to reduce the event to a single, fixed meaning. They must engage with the past as something that can be revisited and reinterpreted, rather than something that has been fully settled.

This engagement does not eliminate the need for stability.

The person does not abandon the structures that allowed them to move forward. They continue to rely on aspects of the narrative that provided coherence, even as they allow for its expansion. They hold the past in a way that is both stable and open.

This dual posture is difficult to maintain.

It requires the person to live within tension, to balance competing needs, to navigate a space that is neither fully closed nor fully open. It challenges the desire for simplicity, replacing it with a more complex and dynamic form of engagement.

At the same time, this posture allows for transformation.

By engaging what has been reopened without collapsing into it, the person creates the possibility for new understanding to emerge. They are able to integrate aspects of their experience that were not previously accessible, to develop a more nuanced understanding of what has happened, and to relate to the past in ways that are not limited by the original narrative.

This transformation is not immediate.

It unfolds over time, often in small shifts rather than dramatic changes. The person may notice subtle differences in how they interpret certain aspects of the event, in how they respond to reminders of the past, in how they understand their own role within the narrative.

These shifts indicate that something is changing.

The person is no longer relating to the past in the same way. They are engaging with it from a different position, one that allows for both stability and openness. They are not returning to the original disruption, but they are also not remaining entirely within the closure that followed it.

This new position is not fully defined.

It does not have the clarity of the original narrative or the stability of closure. It is characterized by movement, by the ongoing negotiation between engagement and distance, between openness and boundary.

This movement is the beginning of a different kind of relationship to the past.

The past is no longer something that must be contained in order to preserve stability. It becomes something that can be engaged without overwhelming the present, something that can be revisited without undoing the self.

This does not eliminate the difficulty.

Reopening remains challenging. It continues to require effort, discernment, and the willingness to engage with uncertainty. The person may still experience moments of resistance, of discomfort, of questioning whether the process is worth the cost.

But they are no longer without structure.

They have developed a way of engaging that allows them to remain stable while being open. They have learned to navigate the tension without collapsing into it. They have found a way to move forward that does not depend on either complete closure or complete reopening.

This way forward is not final.

It will continue to evolve as the person encounters new situations, new challenges, and new experiences of grace. But it provides a foundation for engaging with what has been reopened in a way that is both sustainable and transformative.

And it is from within this foundation that the next movement begins.

CHAPTER 13

The Community Fracture

PART 1: WHEN THE SAME EVENT MEANS DIFFERENT THINGS

If grace disrupts individual moral frameworks, destabilizes identity, and reopens what had been closed, it does not do so in isolation. These disruptions occur within communities—groups of people who share relationships, narratives, and structures of meaning. When grace enters a situation involving harm, its effects ripple outward, affecting not only the individuals directly involved, but the collective understanding of what has happened and what should follow.

It is here that fracture begins.

Communities, like individuals, rely on shared interpretations to maintain coherence. They develop collective narratives that explain events, assign meaning, and guide response. These narratives do not eliminate difference, but they provide enough alignment to allow the group to function as a unit. Members may disagree on details, but they share a basic framework within which those disagreements can be negotiated.

In situations of harm, this framework often centers on justice.

The community identifies what has occurred, recognizes those who have been affected, and establishes expectations for how the situation should be addressed. This process creates a shared understanding that stabilizes the group. It allows members to orient themselves in relation to the event and to one another.

Grace disrupts this shared understanding.

When grace is introduced—whether through forgiveness, restoration, or the reintroduction of someone who has caused harm—it does not affect all members of the community in the same way. Individuals bring different experiences, different commitments, and different interpretations to the situation. As a result, the same event begins to mean different things to different people.

This divergence is the beginning of fracture.

The community no longer operates within a single, coherent narrative. Instead, multiple interpretations emerge, each grounded in a different understanding of what is happening and why it matters. These interpretations do not simply coexist. They compete, each seeking to define the meaning of the event and to shape the response of the group.

At one level, this divergence may appear to be about facts.

Members may disagree about what has happened, about the details of the event, or about the actions of those involved. These disagreements can be significant, but they are often not the primary source of fracture. Even when the facts are broadly agreed upon, the interpretation of those facts can vary in ways that are far more consequential.

The fracture is not primarily about what happened.

It is about what it means.

Meaning is what connects events to response.

It determines how the community understands the significance of what has occurred, what it believes should follow, and how it evaluates the actions of its members. When meaning is shared, the community can move forward together. When meaning diverges, the community begins to separate.

Grace accelerates this divergence.

For some members, grace is understood as a necessary extension of the community's values. It is seen as an expression of compassion, a movement toward restoration, a way of engaging with complexity that goes beyond simple categorization. These members may view grace as consistent with the community's identity, even as it disrupts established patterns.

For others, grace is understood differently.

It may be seen as premature, as a bypassing of necessary processes, as a threat to the clarity that has been established. These members may interpret the introduction of grace as a departure from the principles that have guided the community's response. They may view it as undermining justice, as weakening accountability, or as introducing ambiguity where clarity is needed.

These differing interpretations create tension.

The same action—extending forgiveness, initiating restoration, altering the narrative—becomes a point of division rather than unity. Members of the community are no longer aligned in how they understand what is happening. They are interpreting the same event through different frameworks.

This tension is not easily resolved.

It is not simply a matter of providing more information or clarifying the facts. The divergence lies at the level of interpretation, where different values, priorities, and understandings of the community's purpose are brought to bear on the situation.

At this level, disagreement becomes more than a difference of opinion.

It becomes a difference in orientation.

Members of the community are not only seeing the situation differently. They are approaching it from different starting points, guided by different assumptions about what matters most and how the community should respond.

These orientations can be described, broadly, as justice-oriented and mercy-oriented.

The justice-oriented members emphasize the importance of maintaining moral clarity. They focus on accountability, on ensuring that actions have appropriate consequences, on preserving the integrity of the structures that allow the community to function. They are concerned that the introduction of grace may compromise these structures, leading to confusion or inconsistency.

The mercy-oriented members emphasize the importance of restoration. They focus on the possibility of change, on the value of extending compassion, on the potential for the community to move beyond the initial event. They are concerned that an exclusive focus on justice may limit the community's ability to engage with complexity and to respond in ways that reflect its deeper commitments.

These orientations are not mutually exclusive.

Most members of the community value both justice and mercy. They recognize the importance of accountability and the need for compassion. But when grace is introduced in a way that disrupts established patterns, these values can come into tension. Members may find themselves emphasizing one over the other, depending on how they interpret the situation.

This emphasis shapes how they respond.

Justice-oriented members may resist the introduction of grace, arguing that it is premature or inappropriate. They may call for a return to established processes, for a reaffirmation of the structures that have guided the community's response. They may view the movement toward grace as a deviation that needs to be corrected.

Mercy-oriented members may support the introduction of grace, seeing it as a necessary step toward healing and restoration. They may advocate for a reexamination of the narrative, for a willingness to move beyond the initial categories, for an openness to new possibilities. They may view resistance to grace as a limitation that needs to be overcome.

These responses can lead to conflict.

The community becomes divided not only in interpretation, but in action. Members align themselves with different approaches, forming groups that reflect their orientation. The shared narrative that once held the community together begins to fragment, replaced by competing narratives that pull the group in different directions.

This fragmentation can be painful.

Relationships are affected. Trust may be strained. Members may feel misunderstood or misrepresented by those who hold a different perspective. The sense of unity that once characterized the community is replaced by a sense of division.

At the same time, this fracture reveals something important.

It shows that the introduction of grace does not simply add to the community's understanding. It challenges the framework that has held that understanding together. It exposes the tensions that were present but not fully visible, bringing them into the open where they must be engaged.

This exposure is not comfortable.

It requires the community to confront differences that cannot be easily reconciled. It demands a level of engagement that goes beyond agreement on facts to a deeper consideration of meaning. It asks the community to navigate a space in which its shared narrative is no longer stable.

At this stage, the community is not yet resolving this fracture.

It is experiencing it.

Members are recognizing that they do not interpret the situation in the same way, that their responses are shaped by different orientations, that the introduction of grace has altered the ground on which they stand together.

This recognition is the beginning.

It marks the point at which the community must decide how to engage with the divergence that has emerged.

But that decision has not yet been made.

And it is within this unresolved tension that the chapter continues.

PART 2: WHEN WE MISREAD EACH OTHER

If the initial fracture emerges because members of the community interpret the same event differently, the next stage deepens the divide through misinterpretation. The tension is no longer only about differing meanings. It becomes about how those differences are understood. Each group begins to form a view of the other that simplifies, reduces, and, in doing so, distorts what the other is attempting to protect.

This shift is subtle.

At first, members recognize that there is disagreement. They may even acknowledge that others are acting from sincerely held convictions. But as the tension persists, as the interpretations remain unresolved, the effort to understand begins to give way to the need to explain. And explanation, under pressure, often becomes reduction.

The justice-oriented members begin to interpret the mercy-oriented response as a failure of seriousness.

They may perceive those who advocate for grace as minimizing the harm that has occurred, as moving too quickly toward restoration, as bypassing necessary processes. They may believe that the emphasis on mercy reflects a lack of commitment to accountability, a willingness to overlook what should not be overlooked.

From within this perspective, mercy appears irresponsible.

It seems to threaten the integrity of the community's moral structure. It appears to weaken the connection between action and consequence, to introduce ambiguity where clarity is needed, to prioritize compassion in ways that obscure responsibility.

These perceptions are not formed in abstraction.

They arise from genuine concern.

The justice-oriented members are attempting to protect something they believe is essential—the recognition of harm, the enforcement of accountability, the maintenance of structures that allow the community to function with integrity. When they see grace introduced in ways that seem to disrupt these elements, they interpret it as a threat.

At the same time, the mercy-oriented members begin to interpret the justice-oriented response differently.

They may perceive those who emphasize justice as rigid, as unwilling to engage with complexity, as prioritizing rules over people. They may believe that the insistence on process reflects a lack of compassion, a failure to recognize the possibility of change, a resistance to movement beyond the initial event.

From within this perspective, justice appears unyielding.

It seems to confine individuals within fixed categories, to limit the possibility of restoration, to maintain a focus on the past at the expense of the future. It appears to prioritize order in ways that restrict the community's ability to respond to what is emerging.

These perceptions, too, arise from genuine concern.

The mercy-oriented members are attempting to protect something they believe is essential—the possibility of transformation, the value of extending compassion, the need for the community to engage with complexity in ways that go beyond simple categorization. When they see resistance to grace, they interpret it as a limitation.

As these interpretations develop, each side begins to see the other not only as different, but as deficient.

The justice-oriented members may view the mercy-oriented as naïve or careless, unwilling to take seriously the implications of what has occurred. The mercy-oriented members may view the justice-oriented as harsh or inflexible, unable to move beyond established patterns.

This perception of deficiency intensifies the divide.

The disagreement is no longer only about how to interpret the situation. It becomes about the character of those who hold different interpretations. The focus shifts from the issue itself to the people involved.

This shift has consequences.

Once the other is understood as deficient, the possibility of genuine engagement decreases. The person is no longer seen as someone who is attempting to protect something important, but as someone who is failing to understand what matters. Their perspective is no longer approached with curiosity, but with skepticism or dismissal.

This change in posture alters the nature of the interaction.

Conversations become more defensive.

Members speak not only to express their understanding, but to defend it against what they perceive as misunderstanding or misrepresentation. They anticipate opposition, prepare counterarguments, and engage with one another in ways that reinforce the divide.

This defensiveness can lead to escalation.

Each side responds to the perceived deficiencies of the other by emphasizing their own position more strongly. The justice-oriented members may double down on the importance of accountability, reinforcing the need for clear consequences. The mercy-oriented members may intensify their emphasis on compassion, highlighting the importance of restoration.

As each side becomes more defined in its position, the space between them narrows.

There is less room for nuance, less capacity to hold complexity, less willingness to consider perspectives that do not align with the dominant orientation of the group. The conversation becomes polarized, with each side representing a more rigid version of its initial stance.

This polarization can obscure what is actually happening.

Both sides are responding to the same disruption—the introduction of grace into a situation that challenges established structures. Both are attempting to protect something they believe is essential. But in focusing on the perceived deficiencies of the other, they lose sight of what is shared.

They lose sight of the fact that both justice and mercy are valued.

They lose sight of the possibility that the tension between them may not be a problem to be solved, but a reality to be engaged. They become focused on defending their position rather than exploring the implications of the disruption.

This loss of shared perspective deepens the fracture.

The community becomes divided not only in interpretation, but in relationship. Members may begin to align themselves more strongly with those who share their orientation, forming subgroups that reinforce their understanding. These subgroups provide support and validation, but they also contribute to the separation.

As alignment increases, communication across the divide decreases.

Members may become less willing to engage with those who hold different perspectives, viewing such engagement as unproductive or even harmful. They may retreat into spaces where their views are affirmed, reducing exposure to alternative interpretations.

This retreat can create a feedback loop.

Within each subgroup, the dominant perspective is reinforced, and the perception of the other becomes more fixed. Without ongoing engagement, the opportunity to challenge assumptions or to recognize the complexity of the other's position diminishes.

This process is not unique to any particular type of community.

It can occur in religious settings, organizational contexts, families, or any group in which shared meaning is disrupted. The dynamics are consistent: divergence in interpretation, followed by misinterpretation, followed by polarization.

At this stage, the fracture is no longer only about grace.

It is about the community itself.

Members are not only asking how to respond to the situation. They are asking what kind of community they are part of, what values define it, and how those values should be expressed in practice. The disagreement becomes a question of identity at the collective level.

This question is not easily answered.

The community cannot simply return to its previous state, because the disruption has already occurred. The introduction of grace has exposed tensions that were not fully visible before. It has brought to the surface differences that cannot be easily reconciled.

At the same time, the community has not yet found a way to move forward.

The fracture remains.

Members are still interpreting, still reacting, still navigating the tension between justice and mercy. They are aware of the divide, but they do not yet know how to engage it in a way that allows for movement.

This is where the chapter deepens.

The misinterpretation that has taken place has not only revealed difference.

It has hardened it.

And it is from within this hardened division that the next movement must begin.

PART 3: STAYING TOGETHER WITHOUT AGREEMENT

If the fracture within a community emerges from divergent interpretations and is deepened by misinterpretation and polarization, the question that follows is not how to eliminate difference, but how to remain together in its presence. The instinct, at this stage, is often to seek resolution—to find a shared conclusion that restores unity by aligning interpretation and response. But when the divergence is rooted not in facts but in meaning, resolution may not be immediately possible.

The community is faced with a different task.

Not to agree.

But to remain.

This distinction is difficult.

Agreement provides clarity. It establishes a common narrative, aligns expectations, and allows for coordinated action. It restores a sense of coherence that makes collective life easier to navigate. Remaining without agreement, by contrast, introduces uncertainty. It requires the community to function without a unified interpretation, to act within a space of ongoing tension.

This tension is not easily sustained.

Members may feel the pull toward separation, toward aligning only with those who share their perspective. The discomfort of engaging with difference can lead to withdrawal, to the formation of subgroups, to the fragmentation of the community into smaller units that are more internally consistent.

To remain together requires resisting this pull.

It involves a commitment to relationship that is not dependent on agreement. It asks members to continue engaging with one another, even when their interpretations diverge, even when their responses to the situation are not aligned.

This commitment is not passive.

It requires intentional effort.

Members must choose to remain in conversation, to listen to perspectives that challenge their own, to engage with interpretations that they do not share. They must resist the tendency to reduce the other to a simplified version of their position, to hold open the possibility that there is more to the other's perspective than what is immediately apparent.

This effort is complicated by the fact that the disagreement is not trivial.

It involves deeply held convictions about justice, mercy, and the meaning of what has occurred. Members are not only expressing preferences. They are articulating values that they believe are essential to the integrity of the community.

To remain in relationship under these conditions requires a different kind of posture.

It involves recognizing that the other's perspective, while different, is not necessarily a threat to the community's existence. It requires acknowledging that the tension between justice and mercy is not a problem to be eliminated, but a reality that the community must learn to navigate.

This recognition shifts the focus.

Instead of seeking to resolve the tension, the community begins to explore how to hold it. Members ask not only what is right, but how to remain connected while holding different understandings of what is right.

This exploration is not straightforward.

It involves negotiating boundaries, determining how decisions will be made, and establishing practices that allow for continued engagement. The community must find ways to act, even in the absence of full agreement, to move forward without collapsing the tension into a single interpretation.

This may require new forms of communication.

Members may need to articulate their perspectives more clearly, to express not only what they believe, but why they believe it. They may need to listen more carefully, to attend not only to the content of what is being said, but to the concerns and commitments that underlie it.

This listening is not about agreement.

It is about understanding.

It involves recognizing that each perspective is attempting to protect something important—justice, accountability, compassion, restoration. It requires members to see that the divergence is not simply a conflict of opinions, but a reflection of different emphases within a shared moral landscape.

This recognition can create space.

When members understand what the other is trying to protect, they may be less inclined to dismiss or reduce the other's position. They may be more willing to engage with the complexity of the situation, to consider how different values can coexist without being fully reconciled.

At the same time, remaining together without agreement does not mean that all perspectives are treated as equivalent.

The community still makes decisions. It still acts. It still navigates the practical implications of the situation. But it does so with an awareness that its actions are not supported by a fully unified interpretation.

This awareness introduces humility.

The community recognizes that its decisions, while necessary, are not final. They are responses within a context of ongoing tension, shaped by competing values that have not been fully resolved. Members act with the understanding that their perspective is not the only one, that their interpretation does not exhaust the meaning of the situation.

This humility can be difficult to sustain.

It requires members to hold their convictions without absolutizing them, to act decisively without claiming complete certainty, to engage with others without requiring agreement. It challenges the desire for clarity, replacing it with a more complex and dynamic form of engagement.

But it also creates the possibility for a different kind of unity.

Not a unity based on agreement, but a unity based on commitment.

Members remain connected not because they share the same interpretation, but because they are committed to navigating the tension together. They recognize that the community is not defined by the absence of conflict, but by the way it engages with conflict.

This form of unity is more fragile.

It does not provide the same level of stability as agreement. It requires ongoing effort, continuous engagement, and a willingness to remain within tension. But it is also more resilient in a different way.

It allows the community to adapt.

By not requiring immediate resolution, the community remains open to new understanding. It can continue to engage with the implications of grace, to explore how justice and mercy can be held together, to respond to the situation in ways that are not limited by a single, fixed interpretation.

This adaptability is essential.

The introduction of grace has already altered the framework within which the community operates. It has exposed tensions that cannot be easily resolved. To insist on immediate agreement would be to force the community back into a structure that no longer fully accounts for its experience.

To remain together without agreement is to accept this change.

It is to recognize that the community is now operating within a more complex reality, one that requires a different approach to unity, to decision-making, and to engagement.

This acceptance is not the end of the process.

It is the beginning of a new way of being together.

The community continues to navigate the tension, to engage with differing perspectives, to make decisions within a context of uncertainty. It does not resolve the fracture, but it does not allow the fracture to define its future.

Instead, it holds the fracture as part of its ongoing life.

A reminder that the introduction of grace does not simply add to what was already there.

It changes how the community must live.

CHAPTER 14

Silence, Withdrawal, and Quiet Anger

PART 1: THE RELATIONAL RESPONSE

If grace disrupts moral logic, unsettles identity, reopens what has been closed, and fractures communities, it might be expected that the response would be equally visible. One might anticipate clear opposition, explicit disagreement, or open conflict. In some cases, this does occur. But more often, the response to grace is not loud. It is relational.

It shows up in distance.

In silence.

In subtle changes that are not immediately named but are deeply felt.

These responses are not always recognized as reactions to grace. They do not carry the same clarity as explicit disagreement. They are not articulated as arguments or framed as positions. They appear as shifts—small, often gradual, but significant in their cumulative effect.

The person begins to withdraw.

Not necessarily in a way that is obvious. They may still be present in the same spaces, participate in the same activities, engage in the same conversations. But something has changed in how they are present. There is less openness, less willingness to engage fully, less investment in the relational dynamics that once felt stable.

This withdrawal is not accidental.

It is a response.

It reflects the person's attempt to navigate a disruption that has not been resolved. When grace introduces tension that cannot be easily integrated, and when that tension affects identity, meaning, and community, the person may not know how to respond directly. Instead of confronting the disruption head-on, they adjust their level of engagement.

This adjustment creates distance.

Distance provides a form of protection. It allows the person to remain within the community without fully engaging with what has been disrupted. It reduces exposure to the tension, limiting the need to continually navigate the complexity that grace has introduced.

This protection is often necessary.

The person may not have the capacity to remain fully engaged with the disruption. They may need space to process, to stabilize, to regain a sense of coherence. Withdrawal offers a way of maintaining presence while reducing the intensity of engagement.

At the same time, this distance has consequences.

Relationships begin to shift.

Conversations become more guarded. Interactions lose some of their previous depth. The ease that once characterized engagement is replaced by a more cautious posture. The person is still there, but they are no longer participating in the same way.

These changes can be difficult to name.

They do not always present as clear conflicts or disagreements. They are experienced as a subtle alteration in relational dynamics, something that is felt more than articulated. Others may sense that something is different, but struggle to identify what has changed.

This ambiguity can create further tension.

Because the response is not explicit, it is not easily addressed. The person who is withdrawing may not feel able to articulate their experience, especially if they themselves are still trying to understand it. The community may not recognize the withdrawal as a response to grace, interpreting it instead as disengagement or disinterest.

This misrecognition can deepen the distance.

The person who is withdrawing may feel unseen, their response unacknowledged or misunderstood. The community may interpret the withdrawal as a lack of commitment, further straining the relationship. The subtle nature of the response makes it difficult to engage directly, allowing the shift to persist without resolution.

Silence often accompanies this withdrawal.

The person may choose not to voice their concerns, not because they do not have them, but because they do not see a way to express them that will be received or understood. They may feel that their perspective does not align with the direction the community is moving, or that raising their concerns would lead to further conflict without resolution.

Silence, in this context, is not absence.

It is a form of communication.

It indicates that something is present but not being expressed. It reflects the person's decision to withhold engagement, to step back from the conversation rather than enter into it under conditions that feel misaligned or unsafe.

This silence can be interpreted in multiple ways.

From within the community, it may be seen as agreement, as acquiescence, or as disengagement. From within the person, it may be experienced as restraint, as self-protection, or as an acknowledgment that the conversation cannot be held in a way that would be meaningful.

This divergence in interpretation contributes to the relational complexity.

The absence of explicit disagreement does not mean the absence of tension. It means that the tension is being carried differently, expressed through relational shifts rather than verbal articulation.

Alongside withdrawal and silence, there is often quiet anger.

This anger is not always visible.

It does not necessarily manifest in overt expressions of frustration or confrontation. It may be held internally, experienced as a persistent sense of unease, irritation, or resentment. It may surface in small ways—in tone, in timing, in the subtle choices the person makes about how and when to engage.

This quiet anger is rooted in the same dynamics that have been explored throughout this book.

It arises from the perception that something has been disrupted, that the structures that once provided stability are no longer intact, that the introduction of grace has altered the meaning of what has occurred. It reflects the person's ongoing engagement with a reality that does not align with their expectations.

Because this anger is not always expressed, it can be difficult to address.

The person may not feel that they have a place to voice it, or they may not be fully aware of its presence. The community may not recognize it, focusing instead on the visible aspects of participation and overlooking the underlying emotional dynamics.

This creates a situation in which the relational response to grace is present but not fully acknowledged.

The community may continue to function, but with an undercurrent of tension that is not explicitly named. The person may continue to participate, but with a sense of distance that affects how they engage.

These dynamics are not unusual.

They are common responses to situations in which disruption is introduced without clear resolution. They reflect the ways in which people navigate complexity when the available frameworks are insufficient to account for what is happening.

At this stage, the response to grace is not characterized by open conflict.

It is characterized by relational adjustment.

The person is not rejecting the community outright, nor are they fully embracing the changes that grace has introduced. They are navigating a middle space, maintaining connection while adjusting their level of engagement.

This middle space is not stable.

It can persist for a time, but it is often a transitional state. The person may eventually move toward greater engagement or greater withdrawal, depending on how the tension develops and how the community responds.

For now, the response remains quiet.

It is carried in relationships, expressed through presence and absence, through what is said and what is left unsaid. It reflects the person's attempt to live within a reality that has been altered by grace, without yet having a clear way to integrate that alteration into their understanding.

And it is within this quiet, often unspoken response that the chapter continues.

PART 2: DISENGAGEMENT AS MORAL PROTEST

If withdrawal and silence are relational responses to the disruption introduced by grace, they are not best understood as absence. They are forms of presence expressed differently. The person who disengages is not necessarily indifferent. They are often deeply engaged, but in a way that does not align with the structures or expectations of the community. Their withdrawal is not a lack of response. It is a response that takes the form of distance.

This distinction matters.

Disengagement is frequently interpreted as apathy, as a sign that the person no longer cares, no longer wishes to participate, or no longer sees value in the community. This interpretation can be convenient. It allows the community to categorize the response in ways that are easier to manage, to attribute the withdrawal to personal choice rather than to the complexity of the situation.

But disengagement, in the context of grace, is often something else.

It is a form of moral protest.

The person withdraws not because they have ceased to care, but because they care in a way that cannot be easily expressed within the current framework. They are responding to a disruption that they experience as significant, but for which they do not see a viable path of engagement. Their withdrawal is a way of maintaining integrity in a situation that feels misaligned.

This protest is quiet.

It does not announce itself.

It does not take the form of explicit opposition or public disagreement. Instead, it is expressed through absence—through reduced participation, limited engagement, and a reluctance to fully enter into the dynamics of the community. The person steps back, not as a rejection of relationship, but as a refusal to engage in ways that feel inconsistent with their understanding of what is right.

This refusal is not always fully articulated.

The person may struggle to put words to their response. They may sense that something is not right, that the introduction of grace has altered the meaning of what has occurred in ways they cannot accept, but they may not have the language to express this clearly. Disengagement becomes a way of responding without needing to resolve the complexity of articulation.

In this sense, disengagement functions as a boundary.

It marks a limit.

It indicates that the person cannot move forward within the current configuration, that there is a threshold beyond which they are not willing to go. This threshold is not arbitrary. It is shaped by the person's commitments, their understanding of justice, their need for coherence.

To disengage is to say, in effect, "I cannot participate in this as it is."

This statement may never be spoken directly.

But it is enacted.

It is present in the choices the person makes about where to be, how to engage, and how much of themselves to bring into the space. It is communicated through behavior rather than words.

This form of protest can be difficult for communities to recognize.

Because it is not explicit, it does not always register as disagreement. It can be overlooked, misinterpreted, or minimized. The absence of confrontation can be mistaken for the absence of concern. The quiet nature of the response can obscure its significance.

This misrecognition can lead to further misunderstanding.

The community may interpret disengagement as a personal issue rather than a relational one. They may attribute it to lack of commitment, to fatigue, or to other factors that do not fully account for what is happening. This interpretation can create distance, as the person feels that their response is not being understood.

At the same time, disengagement can serve a protective function.

It allows the person to maintain a connection to the community without fully participating in dynamics that feel misaligned. It provides space for processing, for reflection, for holding tension without being required to resolve it immediately. It creates a buffer that reduces the intensity of engagement.

This protection is often necessary.

The person may not have the capacity to engage fully with the disruption introduced by grace. They may need time to process, to understand their own response, to determine how they wish to move forward. Disengagement offers a way to remain present without being overwhelmed.

But this protection also has limits.

Over time, sustained disengagement can lead to further separation. The distance that was initially protective can become habitual, reducing the person's connection to the community. The lack of engagement can make it more difficult to reenter the relational space, as the gap between the person and the community widens.

This creates a tension within disengagement itself.

It both preserves and diminishes connection.

It allows the person to maintain integrity in the short term, but it can complicate the possibility of ongoing relationship in the long term.

The person must navigate this tension, deciding how much distance is necessary and how much connection they wish to preserve.

This navigation is not straightforward.

There is no clear guideline for how disengagement should be managed. The person must rely on their own sense of what is sustainable, what is necessary, and what is possible. They must balance their need for integrity with their desire for connection, their response to disruption with their commitment to relationship.

At the same time, disengagement is not the only possible response.

Some individuals may choose to remain fully engaged, to express their concerns directly, to participate actively in the tension. Others may move toward more complete withdrawal, stepping away from the community entirely. Disengagement occupies a space between these responses, allowing for partial engagement without full participation.

This in-between space is significant.

It reflects the complexity of the situation.

The person is not rejecting the community outright, nor are they fully embracing the changes that have occurred. They are holding themselves in a position that allows for both presence and distance, engagement and withdrawal.

This position is not static.

It may shift over time, depending on how the situation develops and how the person's understanding evolves. Disengagement may deepen, leading to further withdrawal, or it may lessen, allowing for greater engagement. The direction is not predetermined.

What remains constant is the underlying dynamic.

Disengagement is a response to disruption.

It is a way of navigating a reality that has been altered by grace, without yet having a clear path for integration. It reflects the person's attempt to remain true to their understanding while also remaining connected to a community that is changing.

This attempt is not always visible.

It does not always receive recognition or validation. But it is present, shaping the relational dynamics of the community in ways that are subtle but significant.

At this stage, disengagement has not yet been resolved.

It remains a form of protest, a boundary, a response that holds tension without eliminating it. The person is still within the process of navigating what grace has introduced, still determining how to engage with a reality that does not fully align with their expectations.

And it is within this quiet, often unspoken protest that the chapter continues.

PART 3: WHAT REMAINS UNSAID DOES NOT REMAIN INACTIVE

If silence, withdrawal, and quiet anger are the primary ways people respond to the disruption introduced by grace, then what is most significant is not only that these responses occur, but what happens when they persist. The absence of explicit conflict does not mean the absence of effect. What remains unspoken continues to shape the community, often in ways that are gradual, difficult to trace, and therefore harder to address.

Silence does not neutralize tension.

It relocates it.

When concerns are not voiced, they do not disappear. They move beneath the surface of interaction, becoming part of the unarticulated context within which relationships are lived. Conversations continue, decisions are made, the community functions—but all within an environment that is subtly altered by what is not being said.

This alteration is often first felt rather than recognized.

Members may sense that something is different, that interactions are less open, that engagement is more cautious. There may be a decrease in spontaneity, a hesitation in communication, a shift in tone that is difficult to define but noticeable over time. The community appears intact, but the quality of its life has changed.

This change is not immediate.

It develops gradually.

As disengagement persists, patterns begin to form. Certain conversations are avoided. Certain topics are left unaddressed. Members learn, often implicitly, where the boundaries of acceptable engagement lie. They adjust their behavior accordingly, navigating the relational space in ways that minimize conflict but also limit depth.

This adjustment creates a new form of stability.

Not the stability that comes from shared understanding, but the stability that comes from managed tension. The community finds ways to function without addressing the underlying divergence. It maintains coherence at the level of activity, even as coherence at the level of meaning remains unresolved.

This managed stability has advantages.

It allows the community to continue operating. It reduces the likelihood of open conflict. It provides a way of moving forward without requiring immediate resolution of complex issues. In contexts where the cost of conflict is high, this can be an effective strategy.

But it also has consequences.

Over time, the lack of engagement with what remains unspoken begins to affect trust.

Trust is not only built on agreement.

It is built on the expectation that what matters can be expressed and engaged. When members feel that certain aspects of their experience cannot be voiced, or that doing so would not be received in a meaningful way, this expectation is weakened. The community becomes a place where some things can be shared and others cannot.

This differentiation affects how members relate to one another.

They may become more selective in what they disclose, more cautious in how they engage, more guarded in their interactions. The openness that once characterized the community is replaced by a more measured form of participation, one that is attentive to what can and cannot be said.

This guardedness can extend beyond the initial issue.

It shapes how members approach other situations, how they interpret new events, how they engage with one another in general. The pattern of silence established in response to grace becomes part of the community's broader relational dynamic.

Quiet anger contributes to this pattern.

Because it is not expressed directly, it accumulates.

It does not dissipate through articulation or engagement. It remains present, influencing perception, shaping interpretation, and affecting response. The person may carry a sense of unresolved tension that informs how they experience the community, even if they do not explicitly connect it to the original disruption.

This accumulation can lead to subtle forms of distance.

Members may not withdraw completely, but they may invest less of themselves in the community. They may participate in ways that are functional but not fully engaged. The relational depth that once existed is reduced, replaced by a more limited form of connection.

This reduction is not always recognized as loss.

The community may continue to function effectively in many ways. Activities continue, roles are filled, goals are pursued. From an external perspective, little may appear to have changed. But internally, the quality of engagement has shifted.

This shift can be understood as a thinning of relational life.

The community remains connected, but the connections are less robust. They carry less weight, less openness, less capacity to hold complexity. The relational fabric is intact, but it is not as strong as it once was.

Over time, this thinning can affect the community's ability to respond to new challenges.

When future disruptions occur, the patterns established in response to earlier ones influence how the community engages. If silence and disengagement have become the default response, the community may be less equipped to address new tensions directly. The capacity for open engagement may be diminished.

This creates a cumulative effect.

Each unresolved tension contributes to the conditions under which future tensions will be addressed. The community's history of engagement—or lack of engagement—shapes its present capacity. What remains unspoken in one moment influences what can be spoken in the next.

At the same time, the persistence of unspoken tension does not eliminate the possibility of change.

It remains present as potential.

The silence that has been established can be broken. The disengagement that has occurred can be addressed. The quiet anger that has accumulated can be articulated. But this requires recognition.

The community must become aware of what has been happening beneath the surface.

It must recognize that the absence of conflict is not the same as the presence of health, that the continuation of activity does not necessarily indicate the resolution of tension. It must attend to the relational dynamics that have developed, even when they are not immediately visible.

This recognition is not always easy.

It requires a willingness to look beyond what is apparent, to engage with aspects of the community's life that are less defined, less structured, less easily measured. It asks members to consider not only what is happening, but how it is being experienced.

At this stage, the community has not yet reached this point of recognition.

It continues to function within the patterns that have developed, navigating the tension through silence, withdrawal, and quiet anger. These responses have allowed it to remain intact, but they have also reshaped its relational life in ways that are not fully acknowledged.

The effect of this reshaping is ongoing.

It influences how members relate to one another, how they engage with the community, how they interpret what is happening around them. It becomes part of the context within which future interactions occur.

And it sets the stage for what comes next.

Because what remains unspoken does not remain inactive.

It continues to work, shaping the community from within, until it is either engaged or allowed to define the limits of what the community can become.

PART IV

Scripture and the Scandal of Grace

(Biblical Witness to Disruptive Mercy)

CHAPTER 15

The Older Brother's Anger

PART 1: "THIS ISN'T FAIR"

If the offense of grace has been explored as disruption, as threat to identity, as fracture within community, and as the quiet withdrawal that follows unresolved tension, then it must also be recognized as something that is not new. It has been present within the tradition itself, embedded within one of the most familiar narratives of grace. The story commonly referred to as the Prodigal Son, found in Gospel of Luke 15:11–32, does not end with the return of the younger son. It culminates in the response of the older brother.

And it is in that response that the offense of grace is most clearly articulated.

The structure of the story is well known. A younger son demands his inheritance, leaves his father's house, and lives in ways that squander what he has been given. He returns, not out of transformation fully completed, but out of necessity, prepared to accept a reduced position. The father, instead of requiring repayment or imposing proportional consequence, receives him with celebration. A robe is placed on him, a ring is given, a feast is prepared. The narrative moves, unexpectedly, from loss to restoration without the intervening sequence that moral logic would anticipate.

It is here that the older brother enters.

He has remained.

He has not left, has not squandered, has not disrupted the order of the household. He has been faithful, consistent, aligned with the expectations that define his place within the family. His identity is rooted in this faithfulness. He understands himself in relation to what he has done and how he has remained.

When he learns of the celebration, his response is immediate.

He refuses to enter.

This refusal is not passive.

It is deliberate.

He stands outside the celebration, not because he is unaware of it, but because he cannot accept what it represents. The father comes out to him, inviting him to join, but the older brother's response reveals the depth of his offense.

"Look," he says, "these many years I have served you, and I never disobeyed your command, yet you never gave me a young goat, that I might celebrate with my friends. But when this son of yours came, who has devoured your property. . . you killed the fattened calf for him."

This is not merely complaint.

It is protest.

And at the center of that protest is a statement that echoes throughout the experience of grace:

This isn't fair.

The older brother articulates what has been present throughout the chapters that precede this one. He names the disruption. He identifies the break in sequence. He points to the absence of proportion. His response is not a misunderstanding of grace. It is an accurate perception of what grace has done.

From within his framework, the father's action violates moral logic.

The younger son has acted. The consequence has been lived. But the return is not followed by a measured response that reflects the gravity of what has occurred. Instead, it is followed by celebration. The sequence is interrupted. The expected connection between action and outcome is broken.

The older brother does not deny that the younger has returned.

He denies that the return should be received in this way.

This distinction is crucial.

His protest is not against restoration itself, but against the manner of restoration. He is not opposing the idea that the younger son might be reintegrated into the family. He is opposing the absence of proportion in how that reintegration is being enacted.

This is the classic offense of grace.

It is not that grace is misunderstood.

It is that grace is understood and rejected.

The older brother sees clearly what is happening. He recognizes that the father is acting outside the structures that have defined the household. He sees that faithfulness has not been rewarded in the way he expected, that transgression has not been met with the consequences he anticipated. His protest arises from a coherent moral framework.

"I have served you."

This statement reveals the structure he has been living within.

Service, obedience, consistency—these have been the basis of his identity. They have defined his place within the family. They have shaped his understanding of what should follow. His expectation is not arbitrary. It is grounded in a system in which action corresponds to response.

Within that system, his faithfulness should be recognized.

It should lead to reward, to acknowledgment, to celebration. The absence of such recognition is not neutral. It is perceived as a failure of the system to function as it should.

At the same time, the presence of celebration for the younger son intensifies the offense.

It is not only that the older brother has not received what he expected. It is that the younger has received what he does not deserve. The disparity between these outcomes highlights the break in moral logic.

The older brother's anger is not only about deprivation.

It is about inversion.

What should be has not been.

What should not be has occurred.

This inversion destabilizes his identity.

If faithfulness does not lead to the expected outcome, then what has his faithfulness meant? If obedience does not result in recognition, then what has it secured? The structure that has supported his identity is no longer stable. The connection between his actions and his place within the family is no longer clear.

This is where the offense deepens.

The older brother is not only protesting the father's action.

He is confronting the possibility that the framework through which he has understood himself is incomplete.

"This son of yours. . ."

In this phrase, the relational fracture becomes visible.

He distances himself from the younger brother, refusing to claim him as part of the same identity. The disruption introduced by grace does not only affect his understanding of fairness. It affects how he understands relationship.

The family, as he has known it, is no longer structured in the same way.

The categories that defined belonging are being altered. The distinctions that separated faithful from unfaithful, obedient from disobedient, are being reconfigured. The older brother finds himself unable to locate himself within this new structure.

His refusal to enter the celebration is, therefore, more than a personal reaction.

It is a boundary.

He remains outside because he cannot participate in a reality that does not align with his understanding of how things should be. To enter would be to accept a structure that contradicts the one he has relied upon. His refusal is a way of maintaining integrity within that framework.

This refusal echoes the responses explored in earlier chapters.

It is a form of disengagement, a withdrawal that is not rooted in indifference but in conviction. The older brother remains present—he does not leave the household—but he does not participate in the celebration. He occupies the space between belonging and separation, holding his position without resolving the tension.

The father's response does not resolve the tension either.

He does not correct the older brother's perception by appealing to fairness. He does not explain the decision in terms that would restore proportional logic. Instead, he speaks in relational terms: "Son, you are always with me, and all that is mine is yours. It was fitting to celebrate. . ."

The language shifts.

From fairness to relationship.

From proportion to presence.

From what has been done to what is.

This shift does not eliminate the offense.

It intensifies it.

Because it does not answer the older brother's protest on its own terms. It introduces a different framework, one that does not align with the structure he has been defending.

At this point, the narrative does not tell us what the older brother does.

It ends with the tension unresolved.

The question remains open.

Will he enter?

Will he remain outside?

Will he be able to inhabit a reality in which grace disrupts the structure he has relied upon?

This open ending is not accidental.

It reflects the ongoing nature of the offense.

The older brother's protest is not resolved within the story because it is not easily resolved within experience. It continues to shape how grace is encountered, how it is resisted, how it is understood.

And it is from within this unresolved tension that the chapter continues.

PART 2: WHEN THE PROTEST IS NOT WRONG

If the older brother's response in Gospel of Luke 15 is understood as the classic offense of grace, then it must be approached with care. It is tempting to resolve the tension quickly by identifying the older brother as the figure who "does not understand grace," whose anger reflects a limitation that must be corrected. But such a reading risks overlooking what is most significant about his response.

The older brother is not wrong in the way he sees the situation.

He perceives accurately the break in moral sequence. He recognizes that the expected relationship between action and outcome has been interrupted. He sees that faithfulness has not been rewarded in proportion to its consistency and that transgression has not been met with the consequences it would ordinarily carry. His protest is not based on error. It is grounded in a coherent moral framework.

This framework has been affirmed throughout the narrative of human experience.

Action leads to consequence.

Commitment leads to recognition.

Deviation leads to cost.

These connections are not arbitrary. They are essential for the maintenance of moral life. They provide structure, stability, and a sense of order that allows individuals and communities to function. Without them, the world becomes difficult to navigate.

The older brother's protest arises from this structure.

He is not inventing a new standard. He is appealing to one that has been operative throughout his life. His faithfulness has been lived within this framework. His understanding of his relationship to the father, to the household, and to his own identity has been shaped by it.

"I have served you. . . I never disobeyed. . ."

These are not empty claims.

They are statements of fact.

They reflect a pattern of life that has been consistent, reliable, and aligned with the expectations that define the household. The older brother's identity is rooted in this pattern. It is not performative. It is lived.

Within this context, his expectation is reasonable.

He expects that his faithfulness will be recognized in ways that correspond to its consistency. He expects that the structure he has operated within will hold. He expects that the return of the younger brother will be met with a response that reflects the gravity of what has occurred.

These expectations are not excessive.

They are proportionate.

They align with the logic that has governed his experience. They reflect a commitment to a system that has provided meaning and stability. The older brother is not asking for something extraordinary. He is asking for what makes sense within the framework he has been given.

This is why his protest carries moral weight.

"This isn't fair" is not a trivial complaint.

It is a theological statement.

It asserts that the distribution of response does not align with the principles that have been assumed to govern the household. It calls into question the coherence of the system itself. It challenges the integrity of the framework that connects action to outcome.

To dismiss this protest as misunderstanding is to avoid its force.

The older brother is not confused.

He is confronted.

He is encountering a reality that does not align with the structure he has relied upon. His protest is the articulation of that misalignment.

At the same time, the coherence of his protest does not resolve the tension.

It intensifies it.

Because if the protest is valid within its framework, and if the father's action stands, then the issue is not one of correction within the system. It is a question of whether the system itself is complete.

This is where the older brother's position becomes limited.

Not because it is incorrect, but because it is contained.

His framework is coherent, but it is not exhaustive.

It accounts for a significant dimension of reality—the dimension of justice, of proportion, of correspondence between action and response. But it does not account for everything that is present in the situation.

The father's action introduces something that exceeds this framework.

It does not negate the structure the older brother is defending, but it operates beyond it. It introduces a response that cannot be fully explained in terms of fairness or proportion. It reflects a different logic—one that is not opposed to justice, but not contained by it.

This is the point of tension.

The older brother is standing within a framework that is real and necessary.

The father is acting from a reality that is also real, but not reducible to that framework.

The conflict is not between right and wrong.

It is between partial understanding and expanded reality.

This distinction is difficult to hold.

It challenges the desire for clear resolution.

If one side were simply wrong, the tension could be resolved by correction. But when both sides are grounded in something real, the tension cannot be eliminated. It must be engaged.

The older brother's protest must be taken seriously.

It must be recognized as an articulation of a valid concern. It must be understood as a defense of something essential. It must be allowed to stand without being dismissed.

At the same time, it cannot be the final word.

Because it does not fully account for what is happening.

The father's response is not arbitrary.

It is not a rejection of justice, nor is it an indifference to the older brother's faithfulness. It is an expression of a different dimension of reality—one that operates alongside justice but is not governed by the same rules.

"It was fitting to celebrate. . ."

This statement does not answer the older brother's protest in terms of fairness.

It introduces a different criterion.

Fittingness.

Not what is deserved, but what corresponds to the reality of the moment.

The son was lost and is found.

This is the basis for celebration.

Not the completion of a sequence, but the recognition of a reality that cannot be reduced to that sequence. The father is responding to something that the older brother's framework does not fully capture.

This does not invalidate the older brother's perspective.

It reveals its limits.

His protest is correct within the system he is using.

But the system is not complete.

This incompleteness is not immediately evident.

From within the older brother's position, the framework appears sufficient. It has explained his experience, guided his actions, and provided coherence for his identity. There is no obvious reason to question it—until grace is introduced.

Grace exposes the limits of the framework.

It reveals that there are aspects of reality that cannot be accounted for within it. It shows that the connection between action and outcome, while real, is not the only principle at work.

This exposure is what creates offense.

Not because the older brother is wrong.

But because what he is right about is not enough.

This is the tension that must be held.

The older brother's protest must be affirmed as morally coherent.

And at the same time, it must be recognized as incomplete.

To hold both of these truths is difficult.

It resists simplification.

It requires a willingness to engage with a reality that cannot be reduced to a single framework. It asks the person to remain within tension, to acknowledge the validity of their protest while also remaining open to what exceeds it.

At this stage, the older brother has not yet moved.

He remains outside.

His protest stands.

The father's response stands.

The tension remains unresolved.

And it is from within this unresolved tension that the chapter continues.

PART 3: ENTERING WITHOUT AGREEMENT

If the older brother's protest is morally coherent and yet incomplete, then the question that remains is not whether his objection can be corrected, but whether he can move without fully resolving it. The narrative leaves him outside, standing at the threshold of a celebration he cannot yet accept. The father's invitation remains open, but it does not come with an explanation that would satisfy the framework the older brother has been using. There is no argument that restores proportional logic, no clarification that reestablishes the expected sequence. There is only invitation.

To enter would require something different.

Not agreement.

Movement.

This distinction is critical.

The older brother cannot enter the celebration by resolving the tension in his mind. He cannot first make the father's action conform to his understanding of fairness and then step inside. The narrative does not provide him with the conditions for that kind of resolution. If he is to enter, it must be without the satisfaction of having his protest answered on its own terms.

This is where the difficulty lies.

The older brother is not being asked to deny what he sees. He is not being told that his perception of unfairness is incorrect. He is not being instructed to abandon his commitment to justice or to reinterpret his faithfulness as insignificant. None of these are required.

What is required is something more subtle and more demanding.

He must be willing to act in a reality he does not fully agree with.

This willingness is not easily formed.

It challenges the expectation that action should follow understanding, that participation should be grounded in agreement, that movement should be secured by clarity. The older brother has lived within a structure in which these connections hold. To act without them is to step into uncertainty.

This uncertainty is not abstract.

It is relational.

To enter the celebration is to join in what the father is doing, to participate in a response that he does not yet accept. It is to stand within a reality that contradicts his framework, to engage with others in a way that does not align with his interpretation of what should be happening.

This engagement carries risk.

The older brother may fear that entering the celebration will compromise his integrity, that it will signal acceptance of something he believes is wrong, that it will undermine the framework that has guided his life. These fears are not trivial. They reflect the cost of moving without resolution.

At the same time, remaining outside carries its own cost.

The older brother preserves his framework, but at the expense of relationship. He maintains his protest, but he does so in isolation. The household continues without him, the celebration unfolds, and he stands apart, holding his position but separated from the life that is taking place.

This separation is not neutral.

It reshapes his relationship to the father, to the brother, and to the household itself. By remaining outside, he defines his identity in opposition to what is happening inside. His protest becomes not only a response to an event, but a position that structures his place within the family.

To enter, then, is not simply to join a celebration.

It is to risk a reconfiguration of identity.

The older brother must consider whether he can participate in a reality that does not fully align with his understanding without losing the integrity of who he is. He must ask whether his commitment to justice can remain intact even as he engages with something that exceeds it.

This question does not have an easy answer.

It cannot be resolved through argument alone. It requires a different kind of engagement, one that holds together conviction and openness, protest and participation, clarity and uncertainty.

The father's response offers a clue, though not a solution.

"Son, you are always with me, and all that is mine is yours."

This statement does not address the fairness of the situation.

It addresses relationship.

It shifts the focus from what has been distributed to what is shared, from the sequence of actions to the presence of connection. The father does not deny the older brother's faithfulness. He affirms it. He does not diminish what has been lived. He places it within a different context.

This context is not based on comparison.

It is based on belonging.

The older brother's identity has been structured around what he has done and what has followed. The father's response invites him to consider an identity rooted in relationship rather than in outcome. It suggests that his place within the household is not contingent on the distribution of rewards, but on his presence within the relationship.

This invitation does not eliminate the tension.

It reframes it.

The older brother is not asked to stop caring about fairness.

He is asked to consider whether fairness is the only lens through which he understands his place.

To enter the celebration, then, is not to abandon justice.

It is to allow justice to be held within a larger reality.

The older brother's concern for fairness does not disappear. His protest does not become invalid. But it is no longer the sole determinant of his response. He begins to act within a space where justice is real, but not exhaustive.

This movement is difficult.

It requires the older brother to hold his convictions without allowing them to close him off from participation. It asks him to remain honest about what he sees while also remaining open to what he does not yet understand. It calls for a posture that is both grounded and flexible.

This posture is not stable in the way his previous framework was.

It does not provide clear guidelines for action or predictable outcomes. It introduces a level of uncertainty that cannot be resolved in advance. The older brother must act without the assurance that his action is fully justified within his existing framework.

At the same time, this posture allows for something that was not previously possible.

It allows for participation without full agreement.

It creates space for relationship to continue even when interpretation diverges. It makes it possible for the older brother to remain connected to the household, to engage with what is happening, without requiring that everything align with his understanding.

This possibility does not resolve the tension.

It holds it.

The older brother may still feel the pull of his protest, the weight of his questions, the desire for fairness to be restored in the ways he expects. These do not disappear when he enters. They remain part of his experience.

But they no longer determine his position.

He is no longer defined by his refusal to participate. He becomes someone who engages despite unresolved tension, who remains within the relationship even when the framework is incomplete.

This is the movement that grace invites.

Not the elimination of offense.

Not the correction of perception.

But the possibility of participation without resolution.

The narrative does not tell us whether the older brother makes this movement.

It leaves him at the threshold.

This silence is intentional.

It places the question in the hands of the reader.

Will you enter?

Will you remain outside?

Will you require resolution before participation?

Or will you step into a reality that exceeds your framework, holding your protest even as you move?

These questions do not have immediate answers.

They cannot be resolved within a single moment or through a single decision. They reflect an ongoing process, one that continues to unfold as the person encounters grace in different contexts.

But the invitation remains.

Not to agree.

But to enter.

CHAPTER 16

Workers in the Vineyard

PART 1: WHEN EQUAL PAY FEELS UNEQUAL

IF THE OLDER BROTHER in Gospel of Luke 15 gives us the interior protest of offended grace, then the parable of the workers in the vineyard, found in Gospel of Matthew 20:1–16, widens that protest into a collective experience. Here, the offense of grace is not confined to a single relationship within a family. It unfolds within a system of labor, compensation, and expectation—a space where fairness is not only personal but structural.

The narrative is simple, but its implications are not.

A landowner hires laborers at different points throughout the day. Some begin early in the morning, committing themselves to a full day's work under agreed terms. Others are brought in later—midday, afternoon, even near the end of the workday. Each group enters under different conditions, with varying amounts of time and effort invested.

At the end of the day, the workers are paid.

And this is where the disruption occurs.

Those who worked only a short time receive the same wage as those who labored from the beginning. The distribution does not reflect the amount of labor performed. It does not correspond to the duration of effort or the degree of contribution. It is equal.

And it is precisely this equality that creates the offense.

The early workers do not protest their own payment.

They receive what was agreed upon.

Their complaint arises when they see what others have received. The problem is not that they have been treated unjustly in isolation. The problem is that, in comparison, the distribution does not align with their understanding of fairness.

"These last worked only one hour," they say, "and you have made them equal to us who have borne the burden of the day and the scorching heat."

This statement captures the essence of the disruption.

The issue is not only about compensation.

It is about equivalence.

To be made equal under conditions that are not equal is experienced as a violation of moral logic. The connection between effort and reward has been interrupted. The structure that allows labor to be measured, valued, and compensated has been altered.

The workers' protest is not irrational.

It is grounded in a widely shared understanding of justice.

Within most human systems, effort corresponds to reward. Time invested, energy expended, and conditions endured contribute to what is considered fair. These factors create a scale by which outcomes can be evaluated and compared.

The early workers have operated within this scale.

They have given more time, endured more conditions, and contributed more labor. Their expectation that this would result in a greater reward is not excessive. It is consistent with the framework that governs most economic and social interactions.

When this expectation is not met, the result is not confusion.

It is offense.

The equal payment does not simply surprise them.

It disrupts the system they rely on to interpret their experience.

The problem is not that they are underpaid.

It is that the relationship between input and output has been altered.

This alteration introduces instability.

If the amount of labor no longer determines the amount of reward, then the system that organizes work and compensation becomes less predictable. The workers can no longer rely on the same connections to understand how their effort will be valued. The coherence of the system is compromised.

This is where the parable moves beyond economics.

It exposes a deeper structure.

The workers' protest is not only about money.

It is about meaning.

Their labor has been interpreted through a framework that assigns value based on measurable contribution. The longer they worked, the more they expected their work to mean in terms of outcome. The equal payment disrupts that meaning, suggesting that value is being assigned according to a different logic.

This is the economic expression of grace.

Grace, in this context, is not abstract.

It is enacted through distribution.

It appears in the decision to give to each worker the same, regardless of their contribution. It manifests as generosity that is not governed by proportionality. It introduces a form of equality that is not derived from sameness of effort.

This form of equality is destabilizing.

It challenges the assumption that fairness must be tied to measurable difference. It suggests that there are circumstances in which distribution is determined by something other than input. It introduces a logic that does not negate effort, but does not use it as the sole basis for outcome.

The landowner's response makes this explicit.

"Friend, I am doing you no wrong. Did you not agree with me for a denarius? . . . Am I not allowed to do what I choose with what belongs to me? Or do you begrudge my generosity?"

The question shifts.

From fairness to freedom.

From proportion to generosity.

The landowner does not deny the structure that the workers are appealing to.

He affirms that the agreement has been honored. The early workers have received what was promised. Their expectation, within that agreement, has been met.

But he also introduces another dimension.

The freedom to give beyond proportion.

The generosity that is not constrained by the logic of equivalence.

This introduction does not resolve the workers' protest.

It intensifies it.

Because it reveals that the system they have relied upon is not the only system in operation. There is another logic at work—one that intersects with their own, but does not conform to it.

This intersection is where the offense of grace is most acute.

The workers are not operating within a system that has been entirely replaced.

They are operating within a system that has been expanded.

The logic of labor and reward still exists.

But it is no longer exclusive.

It is now accompanied by a logic of generosity that does not align with it.

This coexistence creates tension.

The workers must now interpret their experience within a framework that includes both proportion and gift, both effort and generosity. The categories that once provided clarity are no longer sufficient to account for what is happening.

This insufficiency leads to comparison.

The workers measure their outcome not only in relation to their own labor, but in relation to the labor and reward of others. The equal payment becomes a point of reference that highlights the disparity between effort and outcome.

This comparison amplifies the offense.

If each worker had received the same wage without knowledge of the others, thedisruption might have been less pronounced. But the visibility of the distribution creates a relational context in which fairness is evaluated comparatively.

The early workers see themselves in relation to the late workers.

And in that comparison, the system they rely on appears to fail.

This relational dimension is critical.

Grace does not only disrupt individual expectations.

It disrupts shared systems.

It alters how people understand their place in relation to others, how they evaluate outcomes, how they interpret what is just. It introduces a form of equality that cannot be fully reconciled with proportional logic.

This is why the parable does not end with resolution.

It ends with a statement that reinforces the inversion:

"So the last will be first, and the first last."

This inversion is not a correction within the existing system.

It is a reordering.

It suggests that the categories used to determine position—first and last, more and less, deserving and undeserving—are not fixed in the way they have been assumed to be.

This suggestion does not eliminate the logic of justice.

It reveals that it is not complete.

The workers' protest remains.

Their perception of unfairness is not dismissed.

But it is placed within a reality that includes more than what their framework can contain.

And it is within this unresolved tension that the chapter continues.

PART 2: THE WEIGHT OF COMPARISON

If the early workers' protest in Gospel of Matthew 20 arises from the disruption of proportional logic, it is sharpened and intensified through comparison. The equal payment becomes offensive not only because it breaks the connection between labor and reward, but because it is seen in relation to others. What might have been experienced as acceptable in isolation becomes intolerable when placed within a comparative framework.

This is where the offense deepens.

The workers do not begin by questioning their own wage.

They question the equivalence.

"They have been made equal to us."

This statement reveals the shift from individual assessment to relational evaluation. The workers are no longer interpreting their outcome based solely on their agreement with the landowner. They are interpreting it in light of what others have received. The meaning of their compensation is altered by comparison.

Comparison introduces a new dimension of judgment.

It allows individuals to evaluate not only whether they have been treated fairly in absolute terms, but whether they have been treated fairly relative to others. This relational evaluation is not incidental. It is central to how people understand justice within shared systems.

In most contexts, fairness is not only about what is received.

It is about how what is received compares.

People assess outcomes by measuring them against the outcomes of others, using these comparisons to determine whether the distribution aligns with their expectations of equity. When differences in input are visible, differences in output are expected. When those differences are not reflected, the result is perceived as imbalance.

The workers in the vineyard operate within this framework.

They see their extended labor, the conditions they endured, the time they invested. They also see the limited contribution of those who arrived later. The equal payment, viewed through this lens, appears to erase the distinction between these experiences.

This erasure is what generates the sense of injustice.

It is not that the workers have been deprived.

It is that their additional effort has not been recognized in a way that differentiates them from others. The distinction that should matter does not matter in the way they expect.

This is where comparison becomes morally charged.

The workers' response is not simply emotional.

It is interpretive.

They are making a judgment about what the situation means. They are asserting that the lack of differentiation in outcome fails to reflect the reality of differentiation in effort. Their protest is not based on envy alone. It is grounded in a claim about fairness.

And yet, envy is present.

Not as a primary motive, but as a consequence.

The workers see what others have received, and in that seeing, their own outcome is reinterpreted. What was sufficient in isolation becomes insufficient in comparison. The equal wage becomes a source of dissatisfaction not because it fails to meet their needs, but because it fails to distinguish them.

This distinction is important.

Envy, in this context, is not simply a desire for more.

It is a response to perceived equivalence.

The workers do not necessarily want more than they were promised. They want their greater effort to result in greater recognition. They want the distribution to reflect difference.

When that reflection is absent, the result is a form of envy that feels justified.

"They got what we got."

This statement carries weight.

It expresses a sense that something meaningful has been overlooked, that the system has failed to account for what should matter. The workers are not only reacting to what others have received. They are reacting to what that reception implies about their own contribution.

If all receive the same regardless of effort, then what does effort mean?

This question lies beneath the protest.

It is not always articulated, but it shapes the response. The workers are not only concerned with the immediate outcome. They are concerned with the implications for how value is assigned. The equal payment suggests that effort is not the determining factor, and this suggestion destabilizes the framework they rely on.

This destabilization affects identity.

The workers have understood themselves as those who labored more, who endured more, who contributed more. Their identity is tied to this distinction. It provides a sense of worth, a way of understanding their place within the system.

When the outcome does not reflect this distinction, their identity is affected.

They are no longer differentiated in the way they expected. The narrative that connected their effort to their value is disrupted. The meaning of their labor is called into question.

This is why the offense is not easily resolved.

It is not only about compensation.

It is about recognition.

The workers are seeking a confirmation that their effort matters in a way that is visible and measurable. The equal payment obscures this confirmation, introducing ambiguity into the relationship between effort and value.

The landowner's response addresses this ambiguity, but not in the terms the workers expect.

"Am I not allowed to do what I choose with what belongs to me? Or do you begrudge my generosity?"

The question shifts the focus from the workers' comparison to the landowner's intention.

It reframes the distribution as an act of generosity rather than a calculation of proportion. It suggests that the equal payment is not meant to reflect equivalence of effort, but to express a different kind of value—one that is not derived from comparison.

This reframing does not eliminate the workers' concern.

It challenges the basis on which that concern is formed.

If the distribution is not intended to reflect proportional fairness, then the comparison that generates the offense is no longer the appropriate measure. The workers are evaluating the outcome according to a framework that the landowner is not using.

This misalignment is the source of tension.

The workers are operating within a system of justice that relies on comparison and proportion. The landowner is operating within a system of generosity that does not use comparison as its primary metric. These systems intersect in the distribution of wages, but they do not align.

The result is a situation in which the same action is interpreted differently.

For the workers, it is unfair.

For the landowner, it is generous.

These interpretations are not easily reconciled.

They arise from different understandings of what the distribution is meant to accomplish. The workers see it as a reflection of labor. The landowner presents it as an expression of freedom.

This divergence leaves the workers in a difficult position.

They must decide how to interpret what has happened. They can continue to evaluate it within the framework of comparison, maintaining their sense of injustice. Or they can attempt to engage with the possibility that the distribution reflects a different logic, one that does not negate their effort but does not center it.

This engagement is not simple.

It requires a shift in perspective.

The workers must consider whether their comparison, while valid within one framework, is sufficient to account for the reality they are encountering. They must ask whether there is a way of understanding the situation that does not rely on differentiation as the primary measure of value.

At this stage, they are not yet able to make this shift.

Their protest remains.

The comparison continues to shape their interpretation.

The weight of what others have received presses against their understanding of fairness, and the tension remains unresolved.

And it is from within this unresolved tension that the chapter continues.

PART 3: LIVING BEYOND COMPARISON

If the offense in Gospel of Matthew 20 arises from the disruption of proportional fairness and is intensified through comparison, then the question that follows is not whether comparison can be eliminated, but whether it can be held differently. The workers do not invent comparison. They inherit it. It is the framework through which they have learned to interpret labor, value, and reward. It is how they have understood themselves in relation to others. To ask them to abandon comparison entirely would be to ask them to step outside the very structure that has given their experience coherence.

And yet, the parable does not allow that structure to remain unchanged.

The equal payment introduces a reality that cannot be fully contained within comparative logic. It does not deny the difference in labor. It does not erase the fact that some have worked longer, endured more, contributed differently. But it refuses to allow those differences to determine the outcome in the way the workers expect.

This refusal creates a tension that cannot be resolved by returning to the previous framework.

The workers cannot simply reassert proportional fairness and move on, because the landowner's action stands. The distribution has already occurred. The system has already been disrupted. The reality they must now interpret includes both their experience of labor and the landowner's act of generosity.

To live within this reality requires a different posture.

Not the abandonment of justice.

But the relinquishment of its exclusivity.

Justice, as the workers understand it, remains real. Their perception of difference is accurate. Their sense that effort matters is not negated. But it is no longer sufficient to account for what has happened. It must now be held alongside something that exceeds it.

This "alongside" is where the difficulty lies.

The instinct is to resolve the tension by choosing one framework over the other—to insist that fairness must prevail, or to accept generosity at the expense of proportion. But the parable does not allow for this kind of resolution. It holds both realities in place, refusing to collapse one into the other.

The workers are left with a choice.

Not about what has happened.

But about how they will inhabit it.

They can continue to interpret the situation through comparison, allowing the equal payment to diminish their own experience. They can remain within the logic that measures value by difference, and in doing so, maintain their sense of injustice. This path preserves the coherence of their framework, but it does so by resisting the reality that has been introduced.

Or they can begin to engage with a different possibility.

They can consider that the landowner's generosity does not negate their labor, but reframes its meaning. That their work, while real and significant, is not the sole determinant of what they receive. That value may be assigned in ways that are not reducible to measurable input.

This consideration does not come easily.

It challenges deeply held assumptions about how the world works. It requires the workers to loosen their reliance on comparison as the primary means of interpretation. It asks them to see their experience not only in relation to others, but in relation to the one who gives.

This shift is subtle but profound.

Comparison focuses attention horizontally—on the relationship between workers, on the differences in their labor, on the disparities in their outcomes. Generosity redirects attention vertically—toward the source of the gift, toward the intention behind the distribution, toward a reality that is not governed by equivalence.

To live beyond comparison is not to ignore difference.

It is to refuse to let difference determine meaning.

The workers' labor remains what it was. The conditions they endured are not erased. Their contribution is not diminished. But the significance of that contribution is no longer derived solely from how it compares to others.

This does not eliminate the sense of tension.

The workers may still feel the pull of comparison, the instinct to measure, to evaluate, to differentiate. These impulses do not disappear. They remain part of how the world is navigated. But they are no longer the only lens through which the situation is understood.

This multiplicity of lenses introduces a different kind of coherence.

Not the coherence that comes from a single, unified framework, but the coherence that emerges from holding multiple realities together. The workers begin to understand that their experience can be interpreted in more than one way, that their labor can have meaning beyond its measurable output.

This understanding is not immediate.

It develops over time, through continued engagement with the tension that the parable introduces. The workers must learn to live within a reality that does not resolve neatly, that does not provide a single, definitive explanation for what has occurred.

This learning involves risk.

To move beyond comparison is to relinquish a form of control.

Comparison allows for predictability. It provides a way of anticipating outcomes, of understanding how effort will be rewarded, of navigating systems with a sense of assurance. To loosen this reliance is to enter a space where outcomes are less certain, where generosity can disrupt expectation.

This uncertainty can be unsettling.

The workers may fear that without comparison, their labor will lose its significance, that their effort will no longer be recognized, that the system will become arbitrary. These fears are not unfounded. The introduction of generosity does change the terms of evaluation.

But it also introduces a different kind of security.

If value is not solely determined by comparison, then it is not solely threatened by it either. The workers' worth is no longer dependent on being more than others, on having done more, endured more, contributed more. It is grounded in a reality that is not contingent on relative difference.

This grounding does not eliminate the importance of effort.

It recontextualizes it.

The workers continue to labor. Their work continues to matter. But its meaning is no longer confined to the scale of comparison. It is situated within a broader reality in which generosity plays a role.

To inhabit this reality is to accept a form of tension that does not resolve.

The workers must hold together the knowledge that their labor is real and that their reward is not determined solely by that labor. They must live with the awareness that fairness and generosity operate alongside one another, without collapsing into a single system.

This awareness changes how they engage with others.

Comparison, when it is no longer the primary lens, loses some of its power to generate resentment. The presence of others' gain does not necessarily diminish their own. The equal payment no longer functions as a measure of their worth, but as an expression of something that extends beyond it.

This does not mean that the workers become indifferent.

They remain aware of difference, of effort, of contribution. But they are less compelled to interpret these differences as determining their value. They are able to engage with the presence of generosity without immediately translating it into a loss.

This shift is the beginning of a different way of living.

A way that does not deny justice, but does not confine reality to it.

A way that recognizes the validity of comparison, but does not allow it to define meaning.

A way that holds tension without requiring resolution.

The parable does not tell us whether the workers make this shift.

It leaves them within the tension.

Their protest stands.

The landowner's generosity stands.

The question remains open.

How will they live in a world where both are true?

And it is from within this open question that the chapter ends.

CHAPTER 17

The Woman Who Was Not Condemned

PART 1: WHEN PUNISHMENT DOES NOT ARRIVE

IF THE PARABLE OF the workers in the vineyard exposes the offense of grace within systems of distribution, then the account of the woman brought before Jesus in Gospel of John 8:1–11 brings that offense into a more immediate and volatile setting. Here, the tension is not mediated through economic structures or narrative distance. It is present in real time, in a public confrontation, with clear wrongdoing, visible accusation, and an expected outcome that does not occur.

The scene is direct.

A woman is brought forward, placed at the center of a gathering, identified as having been caught in adultery. The accusation is not ambiguous. It is not inferred or debated. It is stated plainly, presented as fact, and anchored in a framework that provides a clear response. The law is cited. The expectation is articulated. The question is posed.

"What do you say?"

This question is not neutral.

It is designed to force alignment.

The accusers are not seeking clarification. They are establishing a context in which the appropriate response is already known. The woman's guilt has been named. The law has been invoked. The sequence that connects wrongdoing to punishment has been activated. What remains is the enactment of that sequence.

This is the structure of moral clarity at its most exposed.

There is an act.

There is a violation.

There is a prescribed consequence.

The alignment between these elements is not in question. The system is functioning as it is designed to function. The situation is not ambiguous. It is defined.

And within that definition, the expectation is clear.

Punishment should follow.

This expectation is not rooted in cruelty.

It is rooted in coherence.

The presence of wrongdoing calls for a response that acknowledges it. The law provides a structure through which that acknowledgment is enacted. The community, in bringing the woman forward, is participating in a process that affirms the seriousness of what has occurred.

This is justice as sequence.

Wrong → judgment → consequence.

The sequence is not arbitrary.

It is what allows the community to maintain order, to assign meaning, to ensure that actions are not without response. It is what makes the moral world intelligible.

Jesus is placed within this sequence.

The question directed toward him is not simply about his opinion. It is about his alignment with the structure that is already in motion. To answer is to position himself either within or against the established framework.

His response does not follow the expected path.

He does not immediately engage the accusation. He does not dispute the facts. He does not reinterpret the law. Instead, he bends down and writes on the ground. The narrative pauses.

This pause is not incidental.

It interrupts the sequence.

The momentum of accusation, which is moving toward consequence, is slowed. The clarity of the situation isnot denied, but it is not immediately acted upon. The expected progression is suspended.

The accusers press.

They repeat the question, seeking to restore the sequence, to move the situation forward toward resolution. The interruption is not allowed to stand without challenge. The pressure to act remains.

Jesus responds with a statement that reframes the situation without denying its elements.

"Let the one among you who is without sin be the first to throw a stone."

This statement does not negate the law.

It does not deny the wrongdoing.

It does not remove the possibility of punishment.

What it does is introduce a condition that shifts the focus from the accused to the accusers. It redirects attention from the act that has been committed to the position of those who are prepared to respond.

This redirection alters the dynamic.

The sequence is no longer straightforward.

The act of judgment now requires self-examination. The clarity that once defined the situation becomes complicated by the presence of the accusers' own condition. The focus is broadened, and in that broadening, the immediacy of punishment is disrupted.

The narrative moves in silence.

One by one, the accusers leave.

The sequence dissolves.

The structure that was in place—the alignment of accusation, law, and consequence—remains conceptually intact, but it is no longer enacted. The process that would have led to punishment is not completed.

The woman remains.

Jesus remains.

And in that space, the expected outcome has not occurred.

This absence is the point of disruption.

The woman is not declared innocent.

Her wrongdoing is not reinterpreted.

The law is not overturned.

And yet, punishment does not arrive.

This is the offense of grace in its most direct form.

The sequence has been interrupted.

Not by denial.

But by non-completion.

The expected connection between wrongdoing and consequence is not carried through. The act remains. The violation stands. But the response does not follow the established path.

This creates discomfort.

Not only for the accusers, who have already departed, but for any who remain within the framework that expects coherence. The situation no longer aligns with the structure that has been relied upon to interpret it.

The absence of punishment raises questions.

What does this mean for the law?

What does it mean for justice?

What does it mean for the seriousness of the act?

These questions are not answered within the moment.

They remain.

Jesus turns to the woman.

"Woman, where are they? Has no one condemned you?"

She responds, "No one, Lord."

And he says, "Neither do I condemn you. Go, and from now on do not sin again."

This statement holds tension.

It does not dismiss wrongdoing.

"Do not sin again" affirms that what has occurred matters, that the act is not neutral, that change is expected. But this acknowledgment is not paired with punishment. The consequence that should have followed does not.

This pairing—recognition without condemnation—is what destabilizes the framework.

The woman is neither justified in her action nor punished for it. She is addressed as someone who has acted and who is now released. The sequence is neither completed nor denied. It is altered.

This alteration is difficult to interpret.

It does not fit within the categories that have been used to understand such situations. It introduces a form of response that acknowledges wrongdoing without enacting the expected consequence. It creates a space in which the act is real, but the punishment is absent.

This absence is not neutral.

It carries meaning.

It suggests that the response to wrongdoing is not limited to the execution of consequence. It introduces the possibility that there are ways of engaging with violation that do not follow the established sequence, without denying the reality of the violation itself.

This possibility is what creates collective discomfort.

The community, represented by the accusers, has been operating within a framework that provides clarity and order. The interruption of that framework introduces uncertainty. It raises questions about how such situations are to be understood and addressed.

The discomfort is not only about the specific event.

It is about the implications.

If punishment does not follow wrongdoing in this instance, what does that mean for other instances? If the sequence can be interrupted here, where else might it be interrupted? The stability of the framework is called into question.

This questioning does not lead to immediate resolution.

The narrative does not provide a systematic explanation. It does not reconcile the tension in a way that restores clarity. It presents the disruption and leaves it in place.

The woman walks away.

Not condemned.

Not declared innocent.

But released.

The sequence remains incomplete.

And it is from within this incompleteness that the chapter continues.

PART 2: WHEN MERCY FEELS LIKE MORAL COLLAPSE

If the interruption of punishment in Gospel of John 8 disrupts the expected sequence of wrongdoing and consequence, the full weight of that disruption is most clearly felt not only by the one who is released, but by those who witness it. The woman's experience is one of unexpected reprieve. The bystanders' experience, however, is more complex. What appears as mercy to one can register as instability to another.

This instability is not abstract.

It is immediate.

The situation begins with clarity. There is a defined act, a known law, a prescribed response. The alignment between these elements provides a sense of coherence. Those present understand what is happening and what should follow. They are not navigating ambiguity. They are operating within a structure that is familiar and intelligible.

When that structure is interrupted, the clarity does not simply disappear.

It fractures.

The bystanders are left with a situation that contains all the elements of moral judgment—wrongdoing, law, accusation—but lacks the expected conclusion. The sequence has been initiated but not completed. The result is not neutrality, but dissonance.

This dissonance is experienced as a form of moral disruption.

The bystanders must now interpret a reality in which the usual connections do not hold. The presence of wrongdoing without corresponding punishment creates a gap in the framework they rely on. The system has not been denied, but it has not been enacted.

This gap raises questions.

If wrongdoing does not lead to punishment in this instance, what determines when it does? If the law is not applied here, under what conditions is it applied? If the sequence can be interrupted, what governs that interruption?

These questions are not theoretical.

They affect how the bystanders understand the world.

The moral framework they have relied upon is not only a set of rules. It is a way of organizing experience. It provides predictability, allowing individuals to anticipate outcomes and navigate situations with a sense of order. When that framework is disrupted, the predictability it offers is weakened.

This weakening can be experienced as a loss of control.

The bystanders are no longer able to rely on the same connections to interpret what is happening. The structure that once guided their understanding is no longer fully reliable. They must now engage with a reality that is less predictable, less contained, less aligned with their expectations.

This experience can lead to discomfort.

Not because mercy itself is rejected, but because the manner in which it appears does not align with the established framework. The bystanders may recognize the value of compassion, the importance of forgiveness, the possibility of release. But when these are introduced in a way that bypasses the expected sequence, they can feel destabilizing.

This is where mercy begins to feel like moral collapse.

The bystanders are not only observing an act of grace.

They are witnessing a disruption of the system that has made moral life intelligible. The absence of punishment does not register simply as kindness. It registers as a failure to carry through the process that affirms the seriousness of wrongdoing.

This perception is not necessarily articulated.

It may remain implicit, shaping how the situation is experienced without being fully expressed. The bystanders may not say, "This is a collapse of moral order," but they may feel that something essential has been unsettled.

This feeling can take different forms.

Some may experience confusion, unsure of how to interpret what has occurred. Others may feel frustration, sensing that the situation has not been resolved in a way that aligns with their understanding of justice. Still others may feel concern, wondering what this means for future situations and for the application of the law.

These responses are not uniform.

They reflect the diversity of perspectives within the group. But they share a common element: the recognition that the expected sequence has been interrupted, and that this interruption has implications.

One of the most significant implications is the redefinition of authority.

The bystanders have brought the situation to Jesus, expecting him to affirm the established framework. His response does not reject that framework, but it does not simply apply it either. He introduces a different mode of engagement, one that complicates the straightforward application of the law.

This complication shifts how authority is understood.

The bystanders must now consider that the application of justice is not as direct as they assumed. The presence of authority does not guarantee the enactment of the expected sequence. Instead, authority may involve discernment, interruption, and responses that do not align with established patterns.

This shift can be unsettling.

It introduces uncertainty into the role of leadership, into the interpretation of law, into the process of judgment. The bystanders can no longer assume that situations will be handled in predictable ways. They must engage with a form of authority that operates differently.

This engagement requires adjustment.

The bystanders must reconsider how they understand the relationship between law and response, between wrongdoing and consequence. They must account for the possibility that the framework they have relied upon is not exhaustive, that there are dimensions of judgment that do not fit within its structure.

This reconsideration is not easy.

It challenges deeply held assumptions.

The bystanders have been formed within a system that provides clarity and stability. To question that system is to question the basis of their understanding. It requires a willingness to engage with uncertainty, to hold together elements that do not fully align.

At the same time, the disruption does not eliminate the need for coherence.

The bystanders still seek to understand what has happened, to interpret it in ways that make sense. They do not abandon their desire for order. They attempt to integrate the new reality into their existing framework, even as that framework is being stretched.

This integration may take different forms.

Some may attempt to reinterpret the situation in ways that preserve the framework, emphasizing aspects of the narrative that align with their understanding. Others may begin to adjust their framework, allowing for the possibility that it needs to be expanded. Still others may resist the disruption, holding tightly to the structure that has provided stability.

These responses reflect different ways of navigating the tension.

There is no immediate resolution.

The bystanders remain within the experience of disruption, attempting to make sense of a situation that does not fully align with their expectations. The absence of punishment continues to shape their interpretation, even as they seek to understand it.

This is where the weight of the moment becomes apparent.

The woman walks away.

The crowd disperses.

The event concludes.

But the implications remain.

The bystanders carry with them a memory of what has occurred, a recognition that the moral sequence can be interrupted, that the expected response may not always follow. This recognition becomes part of their ongoing experience, influencing how they interpret future situations.

The disruption introduced by grace does not end with the moment.

It extends beyond it.

It becomes part of the context within which moral life is lived, shaping expectations, informing responses, and contributing to the ongoing negotiation between justice and mercy.

At this stage, the bystanders have not resolved this tension.

They are still within it.

They are aware that something has shifted, that the framework they rely on is no longer fully stable, that the presence of grace introduces complexity that cannot be easily integrated.

And it is from within this unresolved awareness that the chapter continues.

PART 3: HOLDING TRUTH WITHOUT CONDEMNATION

If the account in Gospel of John 8 leaves us with a disruption that neither denies wrongdoing nor completes the expected sequence of punishment, then the question that follows is not how to resolve the tension, but how to remain within it without collapsing into one side or the other. The woman has not been condemned, and yet she has not been declared innocent. The act remains named. The consequence has not been enacted. The structure has been interrupted but not abolished.

This creates a space that is difficult to inhabit.

The instinct, when faced with such tension, is to move toward resolution. One might attempt to restore the sequence by reasserting the necessity of punishment, or to eliminate the tension by reframing the wrongdoing in ways that reduce its significance. Both responses seek to restore coherence by simplifying the situation.

But the narrative resists this simplification.

It holds together elements that do not easily align. It presents a form of engagement that acknowledges wrongdoing without enacting condemnation, that maintains truth without completing the sequence that would ordinarily follow from it.

To remain within this space requires a different kind of posture.

Not the posture of judgment that moves directly from recognition to consequence, and not the posture of denial that minimizes the act in order to preserve comfort. It requires a way of holding truth that does not immediately translate into punishment.

This distinction is subtle.

Truth, as it appears in the narrative, is not avoided. The woman is not told that nothing has happened. She is not reassured that her actions are inconsequential. The statement "do not sin again" affirms that what has occurred matters, that it carries weight, that it calls for change.

At the same time, this truth is not accompanied by condemnation.

"Neither do I condemn you."

This pairing is what defines the space.

Truth is spoken.

Condemnation is withheld.

To hold these together is not intuitive.

In many frameworks, the acknowledgment of wrongdoing leads directly to the enactment of consequence. The connection between truth and punishment is assumed. To break that connection is to disrupt the sequence that provides moral clarity.

And yet, the narrative insists on this disruption.

It suggests that truth does not require condemnation in order to be real. It introduces the possibility that wrongdoing can be named without immediately assigning the full weight of consequence that would ordinarily follow.

This possibility is difficult to accept.

It can feel as though the seriousness of the act is being diminished, as though the absence of punishment signals a lack of concern, as though the structure that affirms the importance of truth is being weakened. These concerns reflect the depth of the connection between truth and consequence in the frameworks we rely on.

To hold truth without condemnation, then, is not to weaken truth.

It is to alter how it is engaged.

The woman stands within the reality of what has occurred.

She is not shielded from it.

She is addressed within it.

The absence of condemnation does not remove the weight of the act. It changes the manner in which that weight is carried.

This change is not easily understood within existing categories.

It does not fit within a system that requires immediate correspondence between action and response. It introduces a delay, a suspension, a refusal to complete the sequence in the expected way.

This suspension creates space.

Not empty space.

But relational space.

The woman is not left alone with her act.

She is engaged.

She is addressed.

She is released.

The response she receives is not one of abandonment or indifference. It is a form of engagement that does not take the shape of punishment.

This engagement allows for a different kind of movement.

Instead of being defined solely by what she has done and what must follow, the woman is given the possibility of acting differently. "Do not sin again" is not a condition for avoiding punishment that has already been withheld. It is an invitation into a different way of being.

This invitation is grounded in truth.

It does not ignore the act.

It calls for change.

But it does so without anchoring that call in condemnation. The motivation for change is not the avoidance of consequence, but the recognition of what is.

This shift has implications for how wrongdoing is understood.

If truth can be held without immediate condemnation, then the response to wrongdoing is not limited to punishment. It includes the possibility of engagement that seeks transformation without relying on the completion of the sequence.

This does not eliminate the role of consequence.

The narrative does not establish a general rule that wrongdoing is never followed by punishment. It presents a specific instance in which the sequence is interrupted. The broader framework remains, but it is no longer exclusive.

To live within this expanded framework is to accept that the relationship between truth and response is not singular.

There are multiple ways of engaging with wrongdoing.

Some involve consequence.

Some involve interruption.

Some involve a combination of both.

The challenge is not to determine a single, consistent rule that applies in all cases.

It is to discern how to hold truth in ways that do not collapse into condemnation by default.

This discernment requires attentiveness.

It cannot be reduced to a formula.

It involves recognizing the complexity of each situation, the dynamics at play, the potential for different forms of response. It asks for a level of engagement that goes beyond the application of established sequences.

At the same time, this approach introduces risk.

To hold truth without condemnation can be misinterpreted as permissiveness. It can be seen as a failure to take wrongdoing seriously, as a reluctance to enforce necessary boundaries, as a weakening of the structures that maintain order.

These risks are real.

They reflect the difficulty of operating outside a framework that provides clear guidelines. Without the certainty of sequence, the response must be shaped in more complex ways, and the potential for misjudgment increases.

But the narrative does not avoid this risk.

It embodies it.

The interruption of the sequence in this moment doesnot come with guarantees. It does not ensure that the woman will act differently. It does not provide a mechanism for enforcing the invitation that is given. It leaves open the possibility that the outcome is not controlled.

This openness is part of what makes the response an expression of grace.

It is not secured by consequence.

It is not enforced by structure.

It is extended within uncertainty.

To hold truth without condemnation, then, is to accept this uncertainty.

It is to engage with wrongdoing in a way that does not rely solely on the mechanisms of control. It is to remain within a space where the outcome is not guaranteed, where the response is not determined by a fixed sequence.

This does not resolve the tension.

It deepens it.

The person must now navigate a reality in which truth and mercy coexist without collapsing into one another. They must learn to engage with wrongdoing in ways that are both honest and open, both grounded and flexible.

This engagement is ongoing.

It does not arrive at a final position.

It continues to unfold as new situations arise, as different contexts present themselves, as the tension between justice and mercy remains active.

The narrative of the woman who was not condemned does not provide a conclusion.

It provides a pattern.

A pattern of holding truth without condemnation.

A pattern of engaging wrongdoing without completing the expected sequence.

A pattern of remaining within tension without resolving it.

And it is from within this pattern that the next movement begins.

CHAPTER 18

The Thief on the Cross

PART 1: WHEN GRACE ARRIVES TOO LATE TO MAKE SENSE

If grace in previous chapters has disrupted sequence, destabilized identity, fractured communities, and interrupted expected outcomes, then the account of the thief on the cross in Gospel of Luke 23 brings that disruption to its most compressed and irreversible form. Here, there is no time for process, no opportunity for restitution, no possibility of extended transformation. The narrative unfolds at the edge of death, where the usual structures that govern moral life—time, effort, change—are no longer available.

The scene is stark.

Three figures are present.

One at the center, two on either side.

All are under sentence.

All are nearing the end.

The context is not one of ambiguity or potential.

It is final.

Within this setting, the categories that have been used to interpret moral life are compressed into a moment that cannot be extended. There is no future in which actions can be corrected, no space in which consequences can be worked through, no process by which restoration can unfold over time.

The structure that connects wrongdoing to response is present, but it is nearing its conclusion.

The thieves have been judged.

Their punishment is in progress.

The sequence has been enacted.

And yet, within this finality, something occurs that disrupts even this compressed form of moral logic.

One of the criminals speaks.

He recognizes something.

He names his own condition, acknowledging the justice of what he is experiencing: "We are receiving what we deserve for our deeds." This statement affirms the structure that has governed the narrative up to this point. It acknowledges wrongdoing. It accepts consequence. It aligns with the framework of justice.

Within this acknowledgment, there is coherence.

The sequence holds.

Wrongdoing → judgment → consequence.

The man does not resist this sequence.

He affirms it.

And then, within that affirmation, he turns.

"Jesus, remember me when you come into your kingdom."

This request does not interrupt the sequence in the way earlier narratives have.

It does not challenge the judgment.

It does not seek to avoid the consequence.

It occurs within the acceptance of both.

The man is not asking to be removed from the cross.

He is not asking for the sequence to be undone.

He is asking for recognition beyond it.

This request introduces a different dimension.

It does not negate justice.

It moves alongside it.

The response comes immediately.

"Truly I tell you, today you will be with me in paradise."

There is no delay.

No process.

No condition.

No requirement that must be fulfilled before the promise is given.

The response is not deferred to a future in which the man has demonstrated change, made restitution, or engaged in transformation. It is given in the present, within the final moment, without the structures that would ordinarily support it.

This is grace at its most immediate.

And it is precisely this immediacy that creates offense.

In earlier chapters, grace has disrupted sequence by interrupting expected processes. Here, there is no process to interrupt. There is no time for sequence to unfold. The usual progression from wrongdoing to transformation to restoration is not bypassed—it is absent.

The man has not had time to change his life.

He has not repaired what he has done.

He has not demonstrated a sustained commitment to a different way of being.

There is no evidence, within the narrative, of anything beyond this moment.

And yet, the promise is given.

This creates a form of dissonance that is distinct from previous instances.

The offense is not only that grace is unearned.

It is that it is immediate.

There is no space between request and response.

No interval in which the logic of justice might be reasserted or the conditions of grace clarified.

The response arrives fully formed, without the intermediary steps that would make it intelligible within existing frameworks.

This immediacy challenges the role of time in moral life.

Time, in most systems, is essential.

It allows for development, for change, for the working out of consequences. It provides the space in which transformation can occur, in which actions can be evaluated over duration, in which the relationship between past and future can be negotiated.

In this narrative, time is removed.

There is no duration.

Only a moment.

And within that moment, the full weight of grace is extended.

This removal of time disrupts the expectation that transformation must precede restoration.

The man is not restored because he has become something different over time.

He is restored within the moment in which he recognizes and requests.

This recognition is significant.

It is not dismissed.

The man's acknowledgment of his condition, his awareness of justice, his turning toward Jesus—these are not irrelevant. They are part of the moment.

But they are not part of a process.

They do not unfold over time.

They do not demonstrate sustained change.

They occur within the immediacy of the situation.

This immediacy raises questions.

What does this mean for the role of effort?

For the importance of time?

For the necessity of process?

If grace can be given in this way, without the structures that have been assumed to support it, then the framework that connects transformation to restoration is called into question.

This questioning is not easily resolved.

It does not negate the value of time, of effort, of process.

These remain essential in most contexts.

But it reveals that they are not the only conditions under which grace operates.

There is a dimension of grace that is not governed by duration.

A dimension that does not require the unfolding of transformation over time.

A dimension that can be expressed in a moment.

This dimension is difficult to integrate.

It challenges the coherence of systems that rely on sequence.

It introduces a form of response that cannot be predicted or managed.

It suggests that there are circumstances in which the usual connections do not apply.

For those who observe this narrative, the offense is clear.

How can this be?

How can someone who has lived in wrongdoing, who has not had the opportunity to change, who cannot make restitution, receive such a promise?

The question is not about the man's request.

It is about the response.

The immediacy of the response appears to bypass the structures that have been used to understand how such things should occur.

This bypass is not explained within the narrative.

It is presented.

The man dies.

The promise stands.

The sequence is not completed in the expected way.

And the reader is left with a tension that cannot be resolved within the framework that has been used to interpret moral life.

Grace has arrived.

Too late for process.

Too late for restitution.

Too late for transformation as it is usually understood.

And yet, not too late to be given.

This is the offense.

And it is from within this offense that the chapter continues.

PART 2: THE WEIGHT OF A LIFETIME

If the immediacy of grace in Gospel of Luke 23 disrupts the expectation that time, effort, and process are necessary for restoration, then its full weight is most clearly felt in contrast to those who have lived within those very structures. The man on the cross receives in a moment what others have pursued over a lifetime. It is this contrast that intensifies the offense.

The narrative itself does not include these others explicitly.

There are no lifelong disciples standing beside the cross asking why this man should receive what they have labored toward. There is no direct comparison within the text. But the structure of the story invites that comparison. It calls forth an imagined audience—those who have followed, struggled, repented, endured, and sought to align their lives over time with what they believe to be right.

For such individuals, the immediacy of grace raises a question that is difficult to ignore.

What was the point of the time?

If restoration can be granted at the final moment, without the intervening process that has shaped their lives, then what meaning does that process hold? If the endpoint can be reached without the path, then how is the path to be understood?

This question is not rooted in resentment alone.

It is rooted in coherence.

Those who have lived within a framework that connects time, effort, and transformation to outcome have relied on that framework to make sense of their experience. Their choices, their sacrifices, their endurance—all have been interpreted through a system that assigns meaning based on duration and commitment.

Within that system, time matters.

It allows for growth, for correction, for the gradual alignment of one's life with what is considered right. It provides the space in which transformation is not only possible but expected. It gives weight to the journey, not only to the destination.

The man on the cross appears to bypass this.

He arrives at the end.

Without the journey.

Without the extended process.

Without the accumulation of effort that has defined the lives of others.

This creates a tension that is not easily resolved.

It is not that the value of the journey is denied.

It is that the necessity of the journey is called into question.

If the endpoint can be granted in a moment, then the relationship between journey and destination becomes less clear. The connection that has provided meaning is loosened.

This loosening can be experienced as loss.

Those who have lived within the framework of time and effort may feel that what they have done is diminished. Not because it is undone, but because it is no longer required in the way they believed. The significance of their endurance, their discipline, their persistence is not negated, but it is no longer the sole path to what they have received.

This shift affects identity.

The person who has understood themselves as someone who has walked a long road, who has remained committed over time, who has engaged in the process of transformation, now encounters a reality in which that process is not the only way. The narrative that has shaped their identity is no longer exclusive.

This does not mean that their journey is without value.

It means that its value is not tied exclusively to its necessity.

The journey matters.

But it is not the condition upon which the endpoint depends.

This distinction is difficult to hold.

It challenges the assumption that effort must be required in order for something to be meaningful. It introduces the possibility that something can be given without the accumulation of time and labor that would ordinarily justify it.

This possibility is what creates the sense of injustice.

It is not only that the man on the cross receives something without having done what others have done.

It is that the system that connects effort to outcome appears to have been bypassed.

For those who have lived within that system, this can feel like a devaluation.

Not of their effort itself, but of its role.

If what they have pursued can be granted without the path they have taken, then what distinguishes their journey? What sets their experience apart? What affirms the significance of the time they have invested?

These questions are not easily answered.

They cannot be resolved by simply affirming the value of the journey, because the tension remains. The presence of last-minute grace continues to stand as a counterpoint to the narrative of lifelong pursuit.

At the same time, the comparison itself must be examined.

The imagined contrast between the man on the cross and those who have lived faithfully over time is not identical to the comparison in the parable of the workers in the vineyard, but it carries similar dynamics. It places two different experiences side by side and evaluates them according to a shared outcome.

This evaluation assumes that the outcome should reflect the difference in experience.

It assumes that time and effort should result in a different form of reception than what is given in a moment. It applies a logic of proportionality to a situation in which that logic is not the primary framework.

This is where the tension must be held.

The lives of those who have engaged in long-term transformation are not equivalent to the moment of the man on the cross.

They are different.

Their experiences are not the same.

Their journeys are not interchangeable.

But the outcome—being with Christ, being received—is not determined by that difference in the way one might expect.

This does not erase the distinction.

It reframes its significance.

The journey is no longer understood as the condition for the outcome.

It is understood as a different form of participation.

Those who have lived within the process of transformation have experienced something that the man on the cross has not.

They have known the gradual shaping of their lives, the ongoing engagement with change, the extended experience of relationship. Their journey has formed them in ways that a final moment cannot replicate.

This formation is real.

It carries its own value.

It is not diminished by the presence of last-minute grace.

But it is different.

It is not the same as the endpoint.

And it is not required for the endpoint to be given.

This distinction allows for a different understanding.

The value of a lifetime is not in securing what can be given at the end.

It is in the life itself.

In the process.

In the relationship that unfolds over time.

This understanding does not eliminate the tension.

It does not fully resolve the sense of injustice that may arise when the man on the cross is considered in relation to those who have lived differently. The comparison continues to press against the framework, raising questions that do not have simple answers.

But it begins to shift the focus.

From what is received to what is lived.

From the endpoint to the journey.

From the equivalence of outcome to the difference of experience.

This shift does not negate the offense.

It reframes it.

The presence of last-minute grace remains disruptive.

It continues to challenge the assumption that time and effort must determine outcome. It continues to introduce a reality that cannot be fully integrated into the framework of proportionality.

And those who have lived within that framework must decide how to engage with this reality.

They can hold to the comparison, allowing it to generate a sense of injustice.

Or they can begin to explore the possibility that the value of their lives is not dependent on the exclusivity of the path they have taken.

This exploration is not complete.

It remains open.

The tension persists.

And it is from within this persistent tension that the chapter continues.

PART 3: HOLDING THE LIFETIME AND THE MOMENT TOGETHER

If the immediacy of grace in Gospel of Luke 23 challenges the necessity of time, and if the comparison between the thief on the cross and those who have lived faithfully over a lifetime introduces a sense of imbalance, then the question that follows is not how to resolve this tension by privileging one over the other, but how to hold both realities together without diminishing either.

The lifetime and the moment are not the same.

They cannot be made equivalent.

The person who has lived within a long process of transformation has experienced something that unfolds through time—through repeated choices, sustained engagement, gradual change. This experience carries weight. It shapes identity, forms character, and establishes patterns of living that extend beyond isolated moments.

The thief on the cross does not have this experience.

His life, as it is presented in the narrative, has not been defined by sustained alignment with what is right. His recognition occurs at the end, within the final moments, without the extended process that characterizes the lives of others.

These differences are real.

They matter.

They must not be erased in the effort to reconcile the tension.

At the same time, the outcome—being received, being with Christ—is not distributed according to these differences. The promise given to the thief is not reduced or delayed because of the absence of process. It is immediate and complete.

This creates a situation in which two distinct realities coexist.

A lifetime of formation.

A moment of recognition.

Both are real.

Both are meaningful.

But they do not function in the same way.

The difficulty arises when one is used to measure the other.

If the lifetime is evaluated primarily in terms of the outcome it secures, then the presence of last-minute grace appears to diminish it. If the moment is evaluated in terms of the process it lacks, then it appears insufficient or incomplete.

In both cases, the comparison collapses the distinction.

It attempts to place two different kinds of experience within a single framework of evaluation.

But the narrative resists this collapse.

It does not suggest that the lifetime is unnecessary.

Nor does it suggest that the moment is inadequate.

It presents both without resolving the tension between them.

To hold them together requires a shift in how they are understood.

The lifetime is not primarily about securing the endpoint.

It is about participation.

It is about living within a relationship over time, engaging with transformation as an ongoing process, experiencing the unfolding of change in ways that cannot be compressed into a single moment.

This participation has its own value.

It is not a means to an end.

It is an end in itself.

The life lived in alignment, however imperfectly, is not only a path toward something else. It is a form of being that carries significance in its own right.

The moment, by contrast, is not about participation over time.

It is about recognition within immediacy.

The thief's request is not the culmination of a long process.

It is an acknowledgment that occurs at the edge of his life. It is a turning that does not unfold gradually, but happens within a single exchange.

This recognition has its own significance.

It is not less real because it is brief.

It is not less meaningful because it lacks duration.

It is different.

And it is received.

To hold these together is to allow for multiple forms of engagement with grace.

It is to recognize that grace does not operate exclusively through process, nor exclusively through moment, but can be present in both. It does not require that all experiences conform to a single pattern.

This recognition challenges the assumption that there must be one way.

One path.

One sequence.

Instead, it introduces plurality.

Different ways of encountering, engaging, and receiving.

This plurality does not eliminate tension.

It increases it.

Because it removes the simplicity of a single framework and replaces it with a more complex reality in which different forms coexist without being reduced to one another.

The person who has lived faithfully must now consider that their life is not validated by the absence of last-minute grace.

Their journey does not derive its meaning from being the only path.

It stands on its own.

Its value is intrinsic.

Not comparative.

This shift is significant.

It frees the lifetime from the need to be exclusive in order to be meaningful. It allows the person to see their experience not as something that must be justified by contrast with others, but as something that carries its own weight.

At the same time, the presence of last-minute grace must be held without minimizing its disruption.

It does not fit within the structures that assign value based on time and effort. It continues to challenge the coherence of those structures.

It remains an expression of grace that cannot be fully explained within existing frameworks.

To accept it is not to resolve it.

It is to allow it to stand.

This acceptance requires a willingness to live without full alignment.

The person must hold together realities that do not neatly fit, to acknowledge both the importance of process and the reality of immediacy, to engage with a system that is not singular.

This engagement is not passive.

It involves ongoing interpretation, continual adjustment, and the ability to remain within tension without forcing resolution. It asks the person to relinquish the need for a single, comprehensive explanation and to live within a reality that is more complex than that.

This complexity does not eliminate meaning.

It reshapes it.

Meaning is no longer derived from a single structure that explains all experiences in the same way. It emerges from the interaction of different elements, from the coexistence of multiple forms of engagement, from the recognition that reality cannot be reduced to one pattern.

Within this reshaped meaning, both the lifetime and the moment are held.

Neither is diminished.

Neither is made to serve as the measure of the other.

Each is allowed to stand within its own context.

This does not remove the emotional weight of the comparison.

The sense of imbalance may still arise.

The questions may remain.

But they are held differently.

They are no longer required to be resolved in order for the person to continue.

This holding is the beginning of integration.

Not the merging of justice and grace into a single, unified system, but the capacity to live within their tension, to allow both to be present without collapsing one into the other.

The thief on the cross and the person who has lived faithfully over time do not cancel each other out.

They reveal the range.

The breadth of how grace can appear.

The limits of the frameworks used to contain it.

And the necessity of learning to live within a reality that exceeds those frameworks.

The narrative does not conclude with a resolution.

The thief dies.

The promise stands.

The lifetime continues elsewhere.

And the tension remains.

But it is no longer only a source of offense.

It becomes a space in which a different kind of understanding can begin.

CHAPTER 19

Jesus and the Collapse of Moral Categories

PART 1: WHEN THE LINES DO NOT HOLD

IF THE PREVIOUS CHAPTERS have traced the offense of grace through specific encounters—the older brother, the workers in the vineyard, the woman not condemned, the thief on the cross—then what begins to emerge is not a series of isolated disruptions, but a pattern. These moments are not exceptions within the ministry of Jesus. They are expressions of a consistent way of engaging with people, situations, and structures. Taken together, they reveal something more unsettling than any single event.

They reveal that the categories themselves do not hold.

Within the narratives of the Gospels, the distinction between sinner and righteous, outsider and insider, deserving and undeserving, is repeatedly brought into question. These distinctions are not erased in the sense that behavior becomes irrelevant or actions lose significance. They remain present. But they are no longer stable in the way they were assumed to be.

This instability is not accidental.

It is introduced.

It emerges from the way Jesus engages with those who are identified within these categories. He does not avoid them. He does not deny their existence. But he does not treat them as fixed boundaries that determine how people are to be approached or what they are to receive.

This becomes visible in the repeated pattern.

Sinners are welcomed.

Insiders are unsettled.

Those who are expected to be at a distance are brought near. Those who are assumed to be secure find themselves questioned. The alignment between category and response is disrupted. The moral map that organizes who belongs where begins to shift.

This shift is not primarily about inclusion in the way it is often understood.

It is not simply that those who were excluded are now included.

It is that the basis upon which inclusion and exclusion have been determined is no longer sufficient.

The categories remain, but their function changes.

They no longer serve as reliable indicators of how grace will be extended.

This is where the destabilization becomes theological.

The categories are not merely social.

They are moral.

They carry weight in determining how people understand themselves, how they interpret others, and how they believe God relates to both. To disrupt these categories is not only to alter social dynamics. It is to challenge the framework through which moral reality is understood.

For those who have lived within this framework, the disruption is disorienting.

The categories have provided clarity.

They have allowed individuals to locate themselves within a moral landscape, to understand their position in relation to others, to interpret their experiences with a sense of coherence. The distinction between sinner and righteous, insider and outsider, has functioned as a guide.

When these distinctions no longer operate in the same way, the guidance they provide is weakened.

The person is no longer able to rely on the same markers to determine where they stand. The categories that once provided stability now introduce uncertainty. The moral landscape becomes less defined, more complex, more difficult to navigate.

This complexity is not easily embraced.

It challenges the desire for clarity.

The person may seek to reestablish the categories, to reinforce the boundaries, to restore the distinctions that have been disrupted. They may attempt to reinterpret the actions of Jesus in ways that preserve the existing framework, to integrate the disruption without allowing it to alter the structure.

But the pattern resists this integration.

It persists.

Again and again, those who are identified as sinners are engaged in ways that do not align with the expectations attached to that category. They are not simply tolerated. They are not merely acknowledged. They are welcomed, addressed, and, in many cases, affirmed in ways that exceed what the category would suggest.

At the same time, those who are identified as insiders are not left undisturbed.

They are questioned.

They are challenged.

They are placed in situations where their assumptions are exposed, where their understanding of their own position is unsettled. The security that comes from being within the category is disrupted.

This dual movement is essential.

If only sinners were welcomed, the pattern might be understood as a simple extension of inclusion. If only insiders were challenged, it might be interpreted as a correction within the existing framework. But the combination of both creates a more profound disruption.

The categories are not only expanded.

They are destabilized.

They no longer function as fixed points.

They become fluid.

This fluidity introduces a different kind of engagement.

People are no longer approached primarily on the basis of the category they occupy. They are engaged within the complexity of their situation, their actions, their responses. The interaction is not determined in advance by the category. It unfolds in a way that resists simple classification.

This does not eliminate moral evaluation.

It complicates it.

Actions still matter.

Responses still carry weight.

But they are not interpreted solely through the lens of fixed categories. The relationship between behavior and identity becomes more dynamic, less confined to predefined structures.

For those observing this pattern, the effect is unsettling.

The expectation that moral categories will provide a reliable framework for understanding and response is challenged. The predictability that comes from knowing who is inside and who is outside, who is right and who is wrong, is diminished.

This diminution creates a sense of instability.

The person may feel that the ground beneath them is shifting, that the markers they have relied upon are no longer sufficient. They may experience confusion, uncertainty, even resistance, as they attempt to navigate a reality that does not align with their expectations.

This resistance is not irrational.

It reflects the depth of reliance on these categories.

To question them is to question the basis of moral understanding. It is to engage with the possibility that the framework that has provided coherence is incomplete.

This engagement is not optional.

The pattern presented in the narratives does not allow for a simple return to the previous structure. The disruption has already occurred. The categories have already been shown to be unstable.

The question is how to respond.

The person may attempt to reinforce the categories, to draw the lines more sharply, to reassert the distinctions that have been blurred. This response seeks to restore stability by narrowing the framework, by limiting the impact of the disruption.

Or they may begin to explore what it means to live within a reality where the categories are no longer fixed.

This exploration is not about abandoning moral distinctions.

It is about recognizing that those distinctions do not function in the same way.

It is about learning to engage with people and situations without relying solely on predefined classifications.

This learning requires a different kind of attention.

The person must attend to what is actually happening, rather than what the category suggests should be happening. They must engage with the particular, rather than relying on the general. They must be open to responses that do not fit within established patterns.

This openness is not comfortable.

It introduces uncertainty.

It requires the person to navigate without the same level of guidance, to make judgments without the assurance that comes from fixed categories. It calls for a form of engagement that is more responsive, more attentive, more complex.

At the same time, it creates the possibility for a different kind of understanding.

One that is not limited by the constraints of rigid classification, that can account for the nuances of human experience, that can engage with the ways in which people do not fit neatly into predefined roles.

This understanding does not resolve the tension.

It holds it.

The categories remain, but they no longer function as they once did.

They are present.

But they are not final.

And it is within this ongoing destabilization that the chapter continues.

PART 2: WHEN STABILITY FEELS LIKE IT IS BEING TAKEN AWAY

If the repeated pattern within the Gospels destabilizes moral categories by welcoming those identified as sinners and unsettling those understood as insiders, then the impact of this destabilization is not evenly distributed. Those who have existed on the margins may experience this disruption as unexpected access, as the opening of space that was previously closed. But those who have lived within the center of the framework—those who have understood themselves as aligned, as faithful, as inside—experience something different.

They experience loss.

Not necessarily the loss of position in a visible sense, not an immediate removal from the community or a denial of their identity, but a more subtle and profound loss: the loss of stability. The categories that have supported their understanding of themselves begin to shift, and with that shift, the clarity that has defined their place is altered.

This loss is not always recognized at first.

It does not announce itself as deprivation. It emerges through disorientation. The insider finds that the markers they have relied upon to understand their position are no longer functioning in the same way. The distinction between themselves and others becomes less clear. The boundaries that once defined their identity become permeable.

This permeability introduces uncertainty.

The insider has lived within a structure that provides orientation. They have known where they stand, how they are to be understood, what their actions signify. Their identity has been shaped not only by what they have done, but by how those actions are interpreted within a stable framework.

When that framework is destabilized, the interpretation becomes less certain.

The insider may begin to question what their faithfulness means, what their consistency signifies, how their actions are to be understood if the categories that once defined them are no longer fixed. The connection between identity and category is loosened.

This loosening can feel like diminishment.

Not because the actions themselves are undone, but because the structure that affirmed their significance is no longer as clear. The insider may feel that what they have relied upon to define themselves is being taken away, even if nothing external has changed.

This perception of loss is often accompanied by a sense of threat.

The insider is not only losing stability. They are confronting the possibility that the system they have trusted is not as reliable as they believed. The framework that has provided coherence is being questioned, and with that questioning comes the fear that the foundation itself may not hold.

This fear is not irrational.

It reflects the depth of dependence on the framework.

The categories have not only organized experience. They have provided meaning. They have allowed the insider to interpret their life, to understand their relationship to others, to locate themselves within a moral landscape.

To destabilize these categories is to introduce the possibility that this meaning is not secure.

This possibility can lead to resistance.

The insider may seek to reassert the categories, to reinforce the boundaries, to restore the clarity that has been disrupted. They may emphasize the distinctions more strongly, drawing sharper lines between themselves and others, attempting to preserve the structure that has provided stability.

This response is not simply defensive.

It is protective.

The insider is attempting to maintain coherence, to preserve the system that has allowed them to navigate their experience. The reassertion of categories is a way of holding onto what has been reliable.

At the same time, the destabilization introduced by Jesus resists this reassertion.

The pattern persists.

Those identified as sinners continue to be engaged in ways that do not align with their categorization. Those understood as insiders continue to be unsettled, their assumptions exposed, their positions questioned. The effort to restore the categories is met with further disruption.

This ongoing disruption intensifies the sense of threat.

The insider may begin to experience the pattern not only as confusing, but as undermining. The stability they have relied upon is not only shifting—it is being actively challenged. The system is not simply evolving. It is being reconfigured in ways that are difficult to control.

This loss of control is significant.

The insider has not only relied on the categories for identity, but for predictability. The framework has allowed them to anticipate how situations will be interpreted, how responses will be enacted, how their actions will be understood. It has provided a sense of order.

When the categories are destabilized, this predictability is weakened.

The insider can no longer assume that the same actions will lead to the same interpretations, that the same categories will produce the same responses. The system becomes less controllable, less manageable, less aligned with expectation.

This shift affects how the insider engages with others.

They may become more cautious, more guarded, more attentive to the ways in which the framework is being altered. They may seek to protect their position by aligning more strongly with those who share their perspective, forming subgroups that reinforce the stability they are losing.

These subgroups provide temporary reassurance.

They allow the insider to maintain a sense of coherence within a smaller context, to preserve the categories within a more controlled environment. But they also contribute to the broader fracture, reinforcing the divide between those who are willing to engage with the destabilization and those who are resisting it.

At a deeper level, the insider's experience is not only about loss and threat.

It is about identity.

The categories have shaped not only how they understand themselves, but who they believe themselves to be. They have provided a narrative that connects their actions, their values, and their place within the community.

When these categories are destabilized, the narrative is disrupted.

The insider may find that the story they have been telling about themselves no longer holds in the same way. The connection between their identity and the categories that have defined it is loosened.

This creates a sense of uncertainty that extends beyond the immediate situation.

It raises questions about the nature of their identity, about what defines them if the categories are not fixed, about how they are to understand themselves within a shifting framework.

These questions are not easily answered.

They cannot be resolved by simply reasserting the categories or by dismissing the disruption. They require a deeper engagement with the reality that is emerging, a willingness to consider that identity may not be as tightly bound to category as it has been assumed to be.

At this stage, the insider is not yet able to make this shift.

They remain within the experience of loss and threat, attempting to navigate a reality that is less stable, less predictable, less aligned with their expectations. The destabilization introduced by Jesus continues to challenge the framework, and the insider continues to feel its impact.

This is where the tension deepens.

The insider is not only confronted with a different way of engaging with others.

They are confronted with a different way of understanding themselves.

And it is from within this confrontation that the chapter continues.

PART 3: LIVING WITHOUT FIXED LINES

If the repeated pattern in the Gospels reveals that moral categories do not hold in the way they were assumed to, and if this destabilization produces confusion for some and threat for others, then the question that follows is not whether the categories can be restored, but how life is to be lived when they no longer function as fixed lines. The collapse of categories does not eliminate the need for moral orientation. It intensifies it.

Without fixed lines, the person cannot rely on predefined distinctions to determine how to interpret situations, how to respond to others, or how to understand themselves. The absence of stable categories does not create neutrality. It creates a different kind of demand—one that requires attentiveness rather than classification.

This shift is significant.

Categories allow for efficiency.

They provide immediate frameworks for understanding, enabling quick judgments and predictable responses. They reduce complexity by assigning people and situations to established types. This reduction is not inherently negative. It allows for navigation within a complex world.

But it also limits perception.

When categories are treated as fixed, they can obscure the particularities of individual situations. They can lead to responses that are determined more by classification than by attention. They can create distance between what is perceived and what is present.

The collapse of categories removes this distance.

It forces the person into direct engagement.

Without the ability to rely on fixed classifications, the person must attend more closely to what is actually happening. They must engage with the specifics of each situation, the nuances of each interaction, the complexity of each person.

This engagement is more demanding.

It requires time, attention, and discernment.

The person can no longer default to established patterns. They must actively interpret, rather than passively apply. They must respond in ways that are shaped by the particular, rather than determined by the general.

This does not mean that moral clarity is lost.

It means that it is located differently.

Clarity is no longer derived from the application of categories.

It emerges from the interaction between the person and the situation.

It is not given in advance.

It is formed in the moment.

This form of clarity is less stable, but not less real.

It does not provide the same level of predictability, but it allows for a more responsive engagement. It makes it possible to hold together elements that do not fit within fixed categories, to respond in ways that are attentive to complexity rather than constrained by classification.

This responsiveness is evident in the way Jesus engages with people throughout the narratives.

He does not apply a uniform response based on category.

He responds to individuals in ways that reflect their particular situation, their actions, their openness, their resistance. The same category—sinner, insider, outsider—does not determine the same response. The interaction is shaped by what is present, not by what is assumed.

To live in this way requires a reorientation.

The person must shift from a reliance on categories to a practice of attention.

This attention is not passive observation.

It is active engagement.

It involves listening, perceiving, discerning.

It requires the person to be present to what is happening, rather than relying on what has already been determined.

This presence is not easy to maintain.

It requires a willingness to remain within uncertainty.

Without fixed lines, the person cannot be sure in advance that their response will align with a stable framework. They must act without the assurance that comes from predefined categories, trusting that clarity will emerge through engagement.

This trust is not automatic.

It develops over time.

It is formed through repeated encounters in which the person learns to navigate complexity without collapsing into simplicity. It is sustained by the recognition that the absence of fixed categories does not mean the absence of meaning, but the presence of a different kind of meaning.

At the same time, living without fixed lines does not eliminate the need for boundaries.

The collapse of categories is not the collapse of all distinction.

It does not mean that all actions are equivalent, that all responses are interchangeable, that all situations are to be treated the same. It means that the basis for distinction is no longer located in fixed classifications.

Boundaries are still present.

But they are not predetermined.

They are discerned.

They emerge from engagement rather than being imposed by category.

This distinction is critical.

Without it, the collapse of categories could be mistaken for a collapse of moral structure.

But the narrative does not support this.

It presents a form of engagement that is both attentive and discerning, responsive and grounded. The absence of fixed lines does not lead to indifference. It leads to a different kind of responsibility.

The person must now participate in the formation of their response.

They cannot rely on the system to determine it for them.

This participation carries weight.

It requires the person to be accountable for how they engage, how they interpret, how they respond. It removes the possibility of deferring responsibility to the category, of saying "this is what is done in this situation" without attending to the particular.

This responsibility can be experienced as burden.

It demands more of the person.

It requires a level of engagement that is more complex, more nuanced, more involved. It asks the person to remain present in ways that are not always comfortable.

But it also creates possibility.

Without fixed categories, the person is not constrained by the limitations those categories impose. They are able to respond in ways that are more closely aligned with what is needed in the moment, to engage with others in ways that reflect their actual condition rather than their assigned classification.

This possibility is not easily realized.

It requires practice.

It involves learning to hold tension without resolving it prematurely, to remain within uncertainty without retreating to simplicity, to engage with complexity without being overwhelmed by it.

This learning is ongoing.

It does not arrive at a final state.

It continues to develop as the person encounters new situations, new challenges, new forms of disruption. The collapse of categories is not a one-time event. It is an ongoing condition that shapes how the person lives.

Within this condition, identity is also reshaped.

The person can no longer define themselves primarily by their position within fixed categories. They must find a different basis for understanding who they are, one that is not dependent on stable classifications.

This basis is not given explicitly.

It emerges through engagement.

Through relationship.

Through the ongoing process of living within a reality that does not conform to simple structures.

This emergence is not without tension.

The person may still feel the pull of categories, the desire for clarity, the need for stability. These impulses do not disappear. They remain part of the experience, creating an ongoing negotiation between the desire for fixed lines and the reality of their collapse.

To live without fixed lines, then, is not to eliminate this negotiation.

It is to remain within it.

To hold the tension between clarity and complexity, between structure and responsiveness, between category and attention.

This holding is not resolution.

It is participation.

It is the way in which the person engages with a reality that exceeds the frameworks that once defined it.

The collapse of moral categories does not leave the person without orientation.

It invites them into a different form of orientation.

One that is less defined by fixed lines and more shaped by the ongoing work of attention, discernment, and engagement.

And it is from within this reorientation that the next movement begins.

PART V

Living With Unresolved Grace

(Pastoral and Practical Theology)

CHAPTER 20

Do Not Rush Grace

PART 1: WHEN MERCY COMES TOO SOON

If the preceding chapters have traced the disruption of grace—how it unsettles moral logic, destabilizes identity, fractures communities, and resists categorization—then a new danger emerges at this stage of the work. It is not the rejection of grace, but its premature application. Having recognized the power of grace to interrupt expected sequences, there can be a tendency to move toward it too quickly, to invoke it before the situation can bear its weight, to deploy it as a resolution rather than to receive it as a reality.

This movement, though often well-intentioned, introduces a different form of harm.

Grace, when rushed, does not heal.

It silences.

It bypasses.

It closes what has not yet been fully opened.

This is not immediately obvious.

The language of grace carries positive associations. It is linked to forgiveness, reconciliation, restoration. To speak of grace is to speak of something that is desired, something that is understood as good. As a result, the introduction of grace into a situation is often assumed to be inherently beneficial.

But timing matters.

The presence of grace does not negate the conditions under which it is introduced. When grace arrives before truth has been fully engaged, before harm has been named, before the reality of what has occurred has been allowed to surface, it does not function as restoration. It functions as interruption.

This interruption is different from the interruptions described in earlier chapters.

There, grace disrupted the expected sequence of punishment. Here, it disrupts the necessary process of recognition. It prevents the full articulation of what has happened. It moves the situation forward before it has been adequately understood.

This movement can be subtle.

It may appear in the form of language that encourages immediate forgiveness, that emphasizes the need to "move on," that frames lingering pain as a failure to embrace grace. It may be expressed through the expectation that reconciliation should occur quickly, that conflict should be resolved without extended engagement, that the presence of grace should eliminate the need for continued attention to the situation.

These expressions are not always imposed externally.

They can arise internally.

The person who has been harmed may feel pressure—whether from others or from themselves—to move toward forgiveness, to release the tension, to align with what is perceived as the appropriate response. The discomfort of unresolved conflict can create a desire for closure, and grace can be invoked as the means by which that closure is achieved.

In these moments, grace becomes a tool.

It is used to manage tension, to reduce discomfort, to restore a sense of order. It is applied as a solution, rather than received as something that may or may not emerge within the situation.

This instrumentalization of grace alters its function.

It shifts grace from being a response that arises within reality to a mechanism that is imposed upon it. Instead of engaging with what is present, it seeks to override it. Instead of allowing the situation to unfold, it attempts to bring it to resolution prematurely.

This premature resolution can have significant consequences.

When harm has not been fully named, forgiveness can feel like erasure. The person who has been affected may experience the movement toward grace as a dismissal of their experience, as an indication that what has happened is not being taken seriously. The call to forgive can be heard not as an invitation, but as a demand to relinquish something that has not yet been processed.

This creates tension.

The language of grace, which is intended to restore, becomes associated with pressure. It is no longer experienced as a gift, but as an expectation. The person may feel that they are being asked to conform to a response that does not align with their current reality.

This misalignment can lead to resistance.

The person may withdraw, not because they reject grace itself, but because they cannot receive it in the form in which it is being presented. The premature introduction of grace creates a barrier rather than an opening, complicating the possibility of genuine engagement.

At the same time, premature forgiveness can obscure the nature of the harm.

When the focus shifts too quickly to reconciliation, the specifics of what has occurred may be left unexamined. The details are not fully articulated, the impact is not fully acknowledged, the reality is not fully engaged. The movement toward grace bypasses the process of recognition.

This bypass has implications for justice.

Justice requires attention.

It involves naming what has happened, understanding its effects, and engaging with the reality of the situation. When grace is introduced too quickly, this attention can be shortened or skipped, leaving the work of justice incomplete.

This does not mean that grace and justice are opposed.

It means that their relationship is not sequential in a simple way.

Grace does not eliminate the need for attention to harm. It does not replace the process of recognition. When it is used to do so, it becomes something other than grace.

This distinction is important.

To say "do not rush grace" is not to say "do not extend grace."

It is to recognize that grace cannot be forced into a situation before the conditions are present for it to be received. It must emerge within the context of what is real, not be imposed as a solution to what is unresolved.

This emergence requires time.

Not time in the abstract, but time for engagement.

Time for truth to be spoken.

Time for harm to be acknowledged.

Time for the complexity of the situation to surface.

Without this time, the introduction of grace risks becoming a form of avoidance.

It allows the community or the individuals involved to move past the discomfort without fully engaging it. It provides a way of restoring order without addressing what has disrupted it.

This restoration is fragile.

It is built on an incomplete foundation.

The unresolved elements remain beneath the surface, shaping future interactions, influencing how trust is experienced, affecting the capacity for genuine relationship. The appearance of resolution masks the presence of ongoing tension.

This tension does not disappear.

It persists.

It may be expressed in subtle ways—in guarded interactions, in reduced openness, in the quiet distance that develops over time. The premature application of grace does not eliminate the effects of harm. It relocates them.

This relocation can make them more difficult to address.

Because the situation has been labeled as resolved, there may be less space for revisiting it. The expectation of forgiveness may create resistance to further engagement, making it harder to return to what was not fully addressed.

At this stage, the call is not to abandon grace.

It is to allow it to take its place.

To resist the urge to deploy it as a solution.

To recognize that grace, if it is to function as grace, must be received within the reality of the situation, not imposed upon it.

This requires patience.

A willingness to remain within tension.

A commitment to engage with what is present without rushing toward resolution.

It asks the person to trust that grace does not need to be forced in order to be real.

That it can emerge in its own time.

That its presence is not dependent on our ability to produce it, but on our willingness to remain open to it.

This openness is not passive.

It is active engagement with what is.

It involves holding space for truth, for pain, for complexity, without prematurely closing it.

It is within this space that grace, when it comes, can be received.

Not as a requirement.

But as a gift.

And it is from within this refusal to rush that the chapter continues.

PART 2: WHEN GRACE IS USED TO AVOID THE WORK

If premature grace at the personal level can function as a form of interruption, then at the communal and institutional level it can become something more structured, more embedded, and more difficult to challenge. The language of grace, when adopted by communities, carries authority. It is not only an individual response. It becomes part of the shared vocabulary through which situations are interpreted and addressed. This shared vocabulary shapes expectations, defines what is considered appropriate, and influences how members engage with one another.

Within this context, grace can begin to function in ways that are not immediately apparent.

It can be used not only to restore, but to regulate.

Not only to heal, but to contain.

The community may speak of forgiveness, of reconciliation, of moving forward, and in doing so create an environment in which these responses are expected rather than offered. The language of grace becomes normative, establishing a pattern that members are encouraged—implicitly or explicitly—to follow.

This normativity can introduce pressure.

The individual who has experienced harm may find that the expected response is already defined. Forgiveness is not presented as a possibility among others. It is framed as the appropriate next step, the response that aligns with the values of the community, the expression of maturity or faithfulness.

This framing can be subtle.

It may not take the form of direct instruction.

It may appear in the way situations are discussed, in the emphasis placed on reconciliation, in the absence of space for alternative responses. The community may not say, "You must forgive now," but it may communicate that lingering in tension is undesirable, that expressing ongoing pain is a sign of resistance, that moving toward resolution is the mark of belonging.

In this way, grace becomes prescriptive.

It is no longer something that emerges within the complexity of the situation. It is something that is expected to be enacted, often on a timeline that does not account for the realities of those involved.

This expectation can silence.

The person who is not ready to extend forgiveness may feel that their response is out of alignment with the community. They may hesitate to speak, to express their experience, to name the ongoing impact of what has occurred. The presence of a prescribed response creates a boundary around what can be said.

This silence is not always enforced.

It is often internalized.

The individual may adopt the language of grace even when it does not reflect their reality, using it to describe a response they have not yet fully experienced. They may speak of forgiveness while still carrying unresolved tension, aligning their words with the expectations of the community even as their internal experience remains unchanged.

This misalignment can create fragmentation.

The external expression does not match the internal state.

The person appears to have moved forward, but the underlying experience has not been engaged. The use of grace language masks the presence of unresolved tension, creating a disconnect between what is said and what is lived.

At the institutional level, this dynamic can serve to protect the system.

When situations of harm arise, the movement toward forgiveness can function as a way of restoring stability without fully addressing the underlying issues. The focus shifts from examining the conditions that allowed the harm to occur to facilitating reconciliation between individuals.

This shift can be efficient.

It allows the community to move past disruption, to reestablish a sense of order, to maintain continuity. But it can also obscure the need for deeper engagement with the structures and dynamics that contributed to the situation.

Grace, in this context, becomes a means of containment.

It limits the extent to which the situation is examined, reducing the need for systemic reflection. It allows the community to address the immediate relational tension without engaging with the broader context.

This containment is not always intentional.

It often arises from a genuine desire to restore harmony, to prevent division, to maintain unity. The community may believe that emphasizing forgiveness is the best way to move forward, to avoid prolonged conflict, to preserve relationships.

But when this emphasis is not accompanied by space for truth, it can have unintended consequences.

The harm that has occurred may not be fully named.

The impact may not be fully acknowledged.

The conditions that allowed it may remain unexamined.

The movement toward grace bypasses the work that justice requires.

This bypass can undermine trust.

Members of the community may begin to sense that certain aspects of their experience are not fully recognized, that the emphasis on reconciliation comes at the expense of acknowledgment, that the language of grace is being used to movepast issues rather than engage with them.

This perception can lead to disengagement.

The individual may withdraw, not because they reject the community, but because they do not see a way to participate honestly within its current framework. The expectation of grace, when it is not aligned with their experience, becomes a barrier rather than an invitation.

At the same time, those who promote the language of grace may not recognize its impact.

They may understand themselves as advocating for what is good, for what is consistent with their values, for what will ultimately lead to healing. The possibility that their approach may be contributing to harm is not always visible.

This lack of visibility complicates the situation.

The dynamic is not one of clear opposition, but of misalignment.

The intention to restore meets the need to be heard.

The desire for unity encounters the reality of unresolved tension.

The language of grace, instead of bridging this gap, can widen it when it is used without attentiveness to timing and context.

This is where the concept of spiritual bypassing becomes relevant.

Grace is used to move around the difficult work rather than through it.

The language of forgiveness is employed to avoid engagement with pain, conflict, and complexity. The emphasis on reconciliation becomes a way of sidestepping the processes that would allow for deeper understanding.

This bypassing does not eliminate the need for that work.

It delays it.

The unresolved elements remain present, influencing how individuals relate to one another, how trust is experienced, how the community functions over time. The appearance of resolution conceals the persistence of underlying tension.

To recognize this dynamic is not to reject the language of grace.

It is to examine how it is being used.

It is to ask whether grace is emerging within the situation or being imposed upon it, whether it is creating space for engagement or limiting it, whether it is aligned with the reality of those involved or functioning as a substitute for that reality.

This examination requires honesty.

It involves acknowledging that good intentions do not guarantee good outcomes, that the desire to restore can coexist with the effect of silencing, that the language of grace can be used in ways that do not reflect its deeper meaning.

At this stage, the task is not to eliminate grace from the communal vocabulary.

It is to allow it to be situated properly.

To resist the urge to use it as a tool for managing tension.

To create space in which it can emerge as a response that is received, rather than required.

This space is not easily maintained.

It requires a willingness to remain within discomfort, to allow tension to persist, to engage with situations that do not resolve quickly. It asks the community to prioritize truth alongside grace, to hold both without allowing one to displace the other.

This holding is not simple.

It challenges established patterns.

It requires a shift in how situations are approached, how language is used, how responses are framed. It calls for a form of engagement that is more attentive, more patient, more aligned with the complexity of what is present.

And it is within this shift that the chapter continues.

PART 3: WHEN GRACE IS ALLOWED TO ARRIVE

If grace, when rushed, silences and distorts, and when institutionalized can be used to avoid the necessary work of truth, then the question that follows is not how to produce grace more effectively, but how to create the conditions in which it can arrive without being forced. The movement here is subtle but decisive. Grace is not something that can be generated on demand. It is not a response that can be required, scheduled, or prescribed. It emerges, or it does not.

To allow grace to arrive is to relinquish control over its timing.

This relinquishment is difficult.

It runs counter to the desire for resolution, for closure, for the restoration of order. When harm has occurred, the impulse is to move toward healing as quickly as possible, to bring the situation to a point where it can be considered complete. Grace, when understood as forgiveness or reconciliation, can appear to offer that completion.

But when grace is allowed to emerge rather than imposed, it does not follow this timeline.

It does not arrive according to expectation.

It does not conform to the needs of the system.

It is shaped by the reality of those involved, by the depth of what has occurred, by the extent to which truth has been engaged.

This engagement with truth is foundational.

Grace that is allowed to arrive does not bypass truth.

It grows out of it.

The naming of harm, the acknowledgment of impact, the articulation of what has been experienced—these are not obstacles to grace. They are the ground within which grace can take form.

Without this ground, grace lacks substance.

It becomes abstract, disconnected from the reality it is meant to address. It may be spoken, but it is not held. It may be expressed, but it is not embodied. It floats above the situation, rather than emerging from within it.

To remain with truth, then, is not to delay grace unnecessarily.

It is to prepare the space in which grace can be real.

This preparation is not a technique.

It is a posture.

It involves staying present to what is, without moving too quickly toward what should be. It requires the willingness to hear what is difficult, to sit with what is unresolved, to allow the full weight of the situation to be felt.

This posture resists urgency.

Not the urgency of care, but the urgency of resolution.

It recognizes that the desire to fix, to restore, to move on can lead to actions that are out of alignment with the reality of the situation. It holds back from applying solutions prematurely, allowing the process to unfold at a pace that is responsive rather than imposed.

Within this unfolding, grace begins to take a different shape.

It is no longer something that is demanded.

It is something that becomes possible.

The person who has been harmed may begin to experience shifts—not as a result of pressure, but as a response to the way the situation has been engaged. As truth is named and held, as their experience is recognized and validated, the conditions for a different kind of response begin to form.

This formation is not predictable.

It does not follow a set path.

It may involve movement toward forgiveness.

It may not.

It may include reconciliation.

It may not.

Grace, in this sense, is not defined by a specific outcome.

It is defined by the way in which the response emerges from within the reality of the situation.

This emergence is relational.

It involves the interaction between those who have been affected, the acknowledgment of what has occurred, the engagement with the present. It is not something that one person produces independently. It is shaped within the space that is created through attention, honesty, and presence.

This relational dimension is important.

Grace is not isolated.

It is connected to the dynamics of the situation, to the way individuals engage with one another, to the environment that allows or constrains expression. When grace is allowed to arrive, it reflects the quality of this engagement.

This means that the role of the community shifts.

Instead of promoting grace as a goal to be achieved, the community becomes responsible for maintaining the conditions in which grace can emerge. It creates space for truth, supports the articulation of experience, resists the urge to impose resolution, and remains present within the tension.

This presence is not passive.

It is active.

It involves listening, attending, holding space without filling it prematurely. It requires the community to tolerate discomfort, to remain engaged even when there is no clear path forward, to trust that something can emerge without being forced.

This trust is not easy to sustain.

It challenges the impulse to control.

It asks the community to relinquish the need to manage outcomes, to accept that grace cannot be engineered. It requires a different kind of confidence—not in the ability to produce results, but in the capacity to remain present.

At the same time, allowing grace to arrive does not mean that nothing is done.

It does not imply passivity or neglect.

The work of truth, of acknowledgment, of engagement is active and demanding. It requires attention and effort. It involves confronting difficult realities, navigating complex dynamics, and remaining committed to the process even when it is challenging.

Grace, when it emerges within this context, carries a different weight.

It is not a response that has been imposed.

It is one that has been formed.

It reflects the depth of engagement that has preceded it, the reality that has been honored, the space that has been maintained. It is received not as an obligation, but as something that becomes possible.

This possibility is not uniform.

It does not manifest in the same way in every situation.

In some cases, it may take the form of forgiveness.

In others, it may be a release from the need to resolve.

In still others, it may be the ability to remain in relationship without full reconciliation.

Grace is not a single outcome.

It is a way of being that emerges within the complexity of what is.

This understanding resists simplification.

It does not allow for easy formulas or predictable results. It requires ongoing discernment, continual engagement, and a willingness to remain within tension without forcing resolution.

This is not a comfortable place.

It does not provide the clarity that comes from fixed sequences or predetermined outcomes. It introduces uncertainty, requiring the person and the community to navigate without the assurance of immediate resolution.

But it is within this space that grace, when it arrives, is real.

Not as a concept.

Not as a requirement.

But as a response that has grown out of truth, that has been shaped by engagement, that has been received rather than imposed.

This is the difference.

Between grace that is used and grace that is lived.

Between grace that silences and grace that speaks.

Between grace that closes and grace that opens.

To not rush grace is to remain open to this difference.

To allow for the possibility that grace, when it comes, will not look like a solution, but like a presence.

And it is from within this presence that the next movement begins.

CHAPTER 21

Let Offense Speak

PART 1: WHEN ANGER CARRIES MEANING

IF GRACE DISRUPTS MORAL expectation, destabilizes identity, fractures communities, and resists resolution when rushed, then the responses it generates cannot be treated as secondary or incidental. They are part of the reality grace creates. Among these responses, anger is often the most immediate and the most misunderstood. It is frequently interpreted as resistance, as immaturity, or as a failure to align with what is good. It is corrected, redirected, or dismissed in the effort to restore order.

But anger, within the context of moral disruption, is not simply a problem to be solved.

It is data.

It carries information about how the situation is being experienced, about what has been perceived as violated, about the expectations that have been disrupted. To treat anger as failure is to overlook the meaning it contains.

This meaning is not always clear.

Anger can be expressed in ways that are sharp, reactive, or difficult to receive. It may be directed toward individuals, toward decisions, toward the system itself. It can take forms that make it tempting to focus on the expression rather than the content, to respond to how it is said rather than to what is being communicated.

This focus on expression can obscure the underlying reality.

The person who is angry is responding to something.

They are engaging with a situation that has disrupted their understanding, their expectations, their sense of what is right. The anger is not arising in isolation. It is connected to a perception, to an interpretation, to a judgment about what has occurred.

To understand anger as data is to shift the point of attention.

From the expression to the source.

From the reaction to the meaning.

This shift does not justify all forms of anger.

It does not suggest that every expression is appropriate or that all responses should be affirmed without question. But it does require that anger be taken seriously as an indicator of something that needs to be understood.

This requirement is often resisted.

There is a strong impulse to move quickly toward correction, to address the anger by explaining why it is misplaced, by offering a different interpretation, by guiding the person toward what is considered a more appropriate response. This impulse is rooted in a desire to restore alignment, to bring the person back into coherence with the framework that is being presented.

But when correction precedes understanding, it can reinforce the disruption.

The person who is angry may feel that their experience is not being recognized, that their response is being evaluated before it is being heard. The attempt to correct can be experienced as dismissal, as an indication that what they are perceiving does not matter.

This experience can deepen the anger.

Not because the original issue has intensified, but because the response to it has added another layer of misalignment. The person is now not only responding to the initial disruption, but to the way their response is being handled.

To let offense speak is to resist this movement toward premature correction.

It is to create space for the expression of anger to be heard without immediately being evaluated. It involves listening to what is being said, attending to the content of the response, and allowing the meaning to surface.

This listening is not passive.

It requires attention.

It involves asking what the anger is pointing to, what expectations have been disrupted, what values are being defended, what interpretations are being made. It seeks to understand the internal logic of the response, even if that logic is not ultimately adopted.

This process can be uncomfortable.

Listening to anger requires a willingness to remain present in the face of strong emotion, to engage with perspectives that may challenge one's own, to hold space for responses that are not easily resolved. It asks for patience, for restraint, for the ability to tolerate tension without immediately moving to reduce it.

This tolerance is not indifference.

It is engagement.

It reflects a commitment to understanding the reality of the situation as it is being experienced, rather than imposing a different interpretation prematurely. It acknowledges that the person's response, even if it is not fully aligned with the broader framework, contains elements that are important to recognize.

At the same time, letting offense speak does not mean that all interpretations are accepted without question.

It means that they are engaged.

The distinction is important.

Engagement involves entering into the perspective of the other, seeking to understand how they are making sense of the situation, identifying the connections they are drawing between events and meanings. It does not require agreement. It requires attentiveness.

This attentiveness creates the possibility for a different kind of response.

When anger is heard, when its meaning is recognized, the person may begin to feel that their experience is being taken seriously. This recognition can reduce the need to intensify the expression, to defend the response more strongly, to escalate in order to be understood.

The conversation can then move.

Not away from the anger, but through it.

From expression to exploration.

From reaction to reflection.

This movement does not eliminate the tension.

It deepens the engagement with it.

The person is still grappling with the disruption that has occurred, still navigating the misalignment between expectation and reality. But they are doing so within a context that allows for their experience to be articulated and considered.

This has significant pastoral implications.

In many settings, the response to anger is to contain it.

To redirect it.

To move it toward resolution as quickly as possible.

This approach is often motivated by a desire to maintain order, to prevent conflict from escalating, to preserve the stability of the community.

But when anger is treated primarily as something to be managed, its meaning is often lost.

The underlying issues remain unaddressed.

The responses are shaped by surface-level engagement rather than by a deeper understanding of what is occurring.

To approach anger as data is to adopt a different posture.

It is to see the expression of offense not as a disruption to be minimized, but as a source of information that can inform how the situation is understood and engaged. It is to recognize that the presence of anger indicates that something significant is at stake.

This recognition changes the role of the pastoral response.

Instead of moving immediately to correct or to resolve, the pastoral role becomes one of facilitation.

Creating space for expression.

Encouraging articulation.

Helping to clarify the meaning of what is being communicated.

This facilitation is not neutral.

It is guided by a commitment to truth, to the recognition of harm, to the integrity of the community. It involves holding together the expression of anger with the broader context in which it occurs, ensuring that the engagement remains grounded.

But it does not begin with correction.

It begins with listening.

This order matters.

When listening precedes correction, the response that follows is more likely to be aligned with the reality of the situation. It is informed by an understanding of how the person is experiencing the disruption, rather than by an assumption about how they should experience it.

This alignment does not guarantee agreement.

But it creates the conditions for meaningful engagement.

The person is more likely to remain in the conversation, to consider alternative perspectives, to engage with the complexity of the situation, when they feel that their own perspective has been heard.

At this stage, the focus is not on resolving the anger.

It is on understanding it.

To let offense speak is to recognize that anger is not the end of the conversation.

It is the beginning.

And it is from within this beginning that the chapter continues.

PART 2: WHAT SILENCE DOES TO THE SOUL

If anger carries meaning and must be heard in order to be understood, then the suppression of anger is not a neutral act. It is not simply the absence of expression. It is the interruption of a process through which individuals and communities make sense of disruption. When offense is silenced—whether externally through pressure or internally through self-regulation—the data it carries is not removed. It is displaced.

This displacement has consequences.

At the individual level, the silencing of anger alters the relationship a person has with their own experience. The initial disruption—whether it is caused by perceived injustice, moral confusion, or the destabilizing presence of grace—produces a response that seeks expression. When that expression is constrained, the person is required to hold the response internally without the opportunity to articulate it.

This internal holding changes the quality of the experience.

Anger that cannot be spoken does not simply remain intact.

It transforms.

It may become diffuse, less clearly connected to its source. It may shift into other forms—resentment, withdrawal, fatigue, or a generalized sense of disorientation. The clarity that anger can provide, pointing directly to what has been perceived as wrong, begins to fade, replaced by a more ambiguous internal state.

This ambiguity complicates self-understanding.

The person may no longer be able to clearly identify what they are responding to, why they feel as they do, or how to engage with the situation. The initial data that anger carried has been obscured, making it more difficult to interpret the experience.

At the same time, the act of suppression introduces a second layer.

The person is not only managing the original disruption.

They are managing their response to it.

They may feel the need to monitor their own expression, to ensure that what they say aligns with what is expected, to avoid revealing responses that might be judged as inappropriate. This monitoring requires energy, attention, and effort.

Over time, it can lead to exhaustion.

The continual management of internal responses, without the opportunity for external articulation, creates strain. The person is engaged in an ongoing process of containment, holding back what arises, redirecting it, attempting to align it with acceptable forms.

This strain can affect how the person relates to themselves.

They may begin to question the validity of their own experience, to doubt whether what they are feeling is appropriate, to internalize the idea that their response is a problem rather than a signal. The suppression of anger can lead to a suppression of trust in one's own perception.

This loss of trust is significant.

If the person no longer feels confident in their ability to interpret their own experience, they become more dependent on external frameworks to define what is real and what is not. Their internal sense of orientation is weakened, replaced by a reliance on what is communicated by others.

This dynamic can lead to disconnection.

The person may feel increasingly distant from their own experience, less able to engage with what is happening within them, more inclined to adopt responses that do not fully align with their internal reality. This disconnection can manifest as numbness, as a reduction in emotional engagement, or as a sense of being out of alignment with oneself.

At the communal level, the silencing of offense has parallel effects.

When expressions of anger are constrained, the community loses access to important information about its own functioning. The responses that would indicate where tension exists, where misalignment is present, where harm has occurred, are not fully available.

This lack of information affects how the community understands itself.

Without the articulation of offense, the community may assume that alignment has been achieved, that situations have been resolved, that members are in agreement. The absence of visible conflict can be interpreted as the presence of harmony.

But this harmony may be superficial.

The underlying tensions have not been eliminated.

They have been relocated.

They exist beneath the surface, influencing interactions in ways that are not immediately visible. The community continues to function, but the quality of that functioning is affected by what has not been expressed.

This can lead to fragmentation.

Not in the form of open division, but in the development of parallel realities. Individuals or groups within the community may hold different experiences, different interpretations, different responses, but without the opportunity to bring these into shared space, they remain separate.

These parallel realities can create distance.

Members may begin to relate to one another based on assumptions rather than understanding, to navigate interactions cautiously, to avoid areas where tension might surface. The sense of connection that comes from shared engagement is weakened.

At the same time, the suppression of offense can affect how the community responds to future situations.

Without access to the data that anger provides, the community may lack the awareness needed to address underlying issues. Patterns that contribute to disruption may go unrecognized, repeated without being examined.

This repetition can reinforce the conditions that lead to harm.

The absence of expressed offense allows the community to continue operating within the same framework, without the interruption that would prompt reflection or change. The system remains stable on the surface, but the underlying dynamics persist.

This persistence can erode trust.

Members may begin to sense that certain aspects of their experience are not fully acknowledged, that the community does not have the capacity to engage with difficult realities, that there are limits to what can be said. This perception can lead to withdrawal, as individuals seek spaces where their experience can be expressed more fully.

The loss of trust is not always immediate.

It develops over time, through repeated instances in which expression is constrained and meaning is not fully engaged. The cumulative effect of these instances shapes how members understand their relationship to the community.

In some cases, the silencing of offense can lead to a form of compliance.

Members may learn to align their expressions with what is expected, to present responses that fit within the accepted framework, even when these responses do not reflect their internal experience. This alignment can create the appearance of unity, but it is not rooted in shared understanding.

In other cases, it can lead to disengagement.

Members may choose to reduce their participation, to limit their involvement, to withdraw from spaces where they do not feel able to express themselves fully. This disengagement can be quiet, not marked by overt conflict, but by a gradual reduction in connection.

Both compliance and disengagement represent adaptations to an environment in which offense is not fully heard.

They allow individuals to navigate the community, but they do not resolve the underlying tension. The absence of expression does not eliminate the need for engagement. It delays it.

To recognize the cost of silence is to acknowledge that the suppression of anger is not a solution.

It is a deferral.

It postpones the work that needs to be done, allowing the community to maintain a sense of stability in the short term, but at the expense of deeper coherence over time.

This recognition does not imply that all expressions of anger should be unfiltered or unexamined.

It does not suggest that the community should abandon discernment in how responses are engaged. But it does require that space be created for offense to be articulated, that the meaning it carries be accessed, that the data it provides be considered.

Without this space, the community operates with incomplete information.

With it, the possibility for deeper understanding emerges.

The movement from silence to expression is not easy.

It involves risk.

It requires the community to tolerate tension, to engage with perspectives that may challenge its assumptions, to remain present in the face of discomfort. It asks individuals to speak, even when doing so may feel uncertain or vulnerable.

But it is within this movement that the possibility for genuine engagement begins.

And it is from within this possibility that the chapter continues.

PART 3: CREATING SPACE WHERE TRUTH CAN BE HEARD

If anger carries meaning and its suppression fragments both individuals and communities, then the task before us is not merely to permit its expression, but to cultivate environments in which that expression can occur without distortion. To "let offense speak" is not simply to allow people to say whatever they feel. It is to create a space in which what is spoken can be heard, engaged, and held without immediate collapse into correction, defensiveness, or resolution.

This space does not emerge automatically.

It must be formed.

And its formation depends less on rules than on posture.

The first element of this posture is restraint.

Not silence, but the deliberate withholding of immediate response. When offense is expressed, especially in its early form, it often carries intensity. It may be sharp, unrefined, or directed in ways that feel uncomfortable. The instinct in such moments is to respond quickly—to clarify, to correct, to redirect the conversation toward what is more manageable.

But quick response can close what has just begun to open.

Restraint creates time.

Time for the expression to unfold.

Time for the speaker to articulate more fully what they are experiencing.

Time for the listener to move beyond initial reaction and into deeper attention.

This restraint is not passive.

It is active listening.

It involves focusing on what is being communicated, attending to both the content and the underlying meaning, resisting the urge to filter the expression through immediate evaluation. It asks the listener to remain present, even when the expression is difficult to receive.

Presence is the second element.

To create space where offense can be heard, the listener must be fully engaged. This engagement is not only cognitive, but relational. It involves recognizing the person who is speaking, acknowledging their experience, and communicating that what is being expressed matters.

This recognition does not require agreement.

It requires attention.

The distinction is critical.

Agreement aligns with the content.

Attention aligns with the person.

To attend is to say, in effect, "I am here with you in what you are expressing, even if I do not yet share your interpretation." This presence allows the speaker to continue, to move beyond surface-level expression into deeper articulation.

Without presence, expression can stall.

The speaker may sense that their words are not being received, that the listener is disengaged or preoccupied, that the space is not safe for continued articulation. In such cases, the expression may become more forceful in an attempt to be heard, or it may withdraw entirely.

Presence stabilizes the space.

It provides a foundation upon which the expression can rest.

The third element is curiosity.

To listen well requires more than hearing what is said. It involves seeking to understand how the speaker is making sense of the situation, what connections they are drawing, what meanings they are assigning. Curiosity moves the listener from reaction to inquiry.

This inquiry is not interrogative.

It is exploratory.

It asks questions not to challenge, but to clarify. It seeks to uncover the internal logic of the speaker's response, to understand the perspective from which the anger arises. It recognizes that even when the conclusion is not shared, the reasoning that leads to it can be engaged.

Curiosity opens space.

It invites the speaker to expand, to elaborate, to reflect more deeply on what they are expressing. It signals that the listener is not merely waiting to respond, but is actively engaged in understanding.

This engagement can transform the nature of the conversation.

The focus shifts from defending positions to exploring meanings, from asserting correctness to seeking clarity. The interaction becomes less about winning or resolving and more about understanding.

The fourth element is patience.

The articulation of offense is rarely immediate or complete. It unfolds over time, often in stages, as the speaker moves from initial expression into deeper reflection. This process cannot be rushed without distorting what is being communicated.

Patience allows the process to continue.

It resists the urge to move quickly toward resolution, to bring the conversation to a point of closure before it has fully developed. It recognizes that understanding is not instantaneous, that meaning emerges through sustained engagement.

This patience can be challenging.

It requires the listener to remain within uncertainty, to tolerate the lack of immediate clarity, to engage with a process that does not follow a predetermined path. It asks for a willingness to stay present even when the outcome is not yet visible.

The fifth element is containment.

Not suppression, but holding.

As offense is expressed, especially in communal settings, there is a need to ensure that the space remains stable, that the conversation does not escalate into forms that are destructive or unsafe. Containment provides the boundaries within which expression can occur.

This involves guiding the conversation when necessary, helping to maintain focus, ensuring that all participants are able to engage without being overwhelmed. It does not restrict expression, but it shapes the environment in which expression takes place.

Containment is a form of care.

It recognizes that the articulation of offense can be intense, that it can evoke strong reactions, and that the space must be able to hold these without collapsing. It provides a structure that supports engagement without limiting it.

Within a space formed by restraint, presence, curiosity, patience, and containment, offense can be spoken in ways that are both honest and engaged.

The speaker is able to articulate their experience without immediate correction.

The listener is able to receive that articulation without defensive reaction.

The community is able to hold the interaction without moving prematurely to resolution.

This does not eliminate tension.

It sustains it.

But it sustains it in a way that allows for meaning to emerge.

Over time, this kind of space can reshape how individuals and communities relate to offense.

Anger is no longer seen as a problem to be eliminated, but as a signal to be understood. The expression of offense becomes part of the process of engagement, rather than a disruption to be managed.

This shift has implications for how truth is held.

When offense can be spoken and heard, the community gains access to a fuller understanding of its own dynamics, its own tensions, its own areas of misalignment. The data that anger carries becomes available, informing how the community interprets itself and how it responds to situations.

This access does not guarantee agreement.

But it creates the possibility for deeper engagement.

The conversation can move beyond surface-level resolution into more substantive exploration, allowing for a more nuanced understanding of what is occurring.

At the same time, the creation of such spaces requires ongoing commitment.

It is not a one-time achievement.

It must be maintained through repeated practice, through continual attention to posture, through a willingness to adjust as situations evolve. The elements that support this space must be actively sustained.

This sustainability depends on leadership.

Not only formal leadership, but the distributed leadership that emerges within a community. Individuals must be willing to model restraint, to practice presence, to engage with curiosity, to exercise patience, to contribute to containment. The culture of the community is shaped by these practices.

When this culture is established, the expression of offense becomes less threatening.

It is no longer something that signals breakdown.

It becomes part of the ongoing life of the community, a way of engaging with the complexities that arise, a means of maintaining connection through honest articulation.

This does not remove the difficulty of these moments.

They remain challenging.

But they are no longer avoided or suppressed.

They are engaged.

To let offense speak, then, is not simply to permit expression.

It is to create the conditions in which that expression can be heard, understood, and held within a space that does not collapse under its weight.

It is to recognize that within offense there is meaning, and that within the articulation of that meaning there is the possibility for deeper engagement.

And it is from within this engagement that the next movement begins.

CHAPTER 22

Holding Justice Without Collapsing Mercy

PART 1: WHEN RESOLUTION IS REFUSED

If the previous chapters have insisted that grace cannot be rushed, that offense must be heard, and that moral categories do not hold in the way we once assumed, then we arrive at a point where the question is no longer how to choose between justice and mercy, but how to live when both remain present and neither can be reduced to the other. The instinct, at this stage, is to seek resolution—to find a way of integrating these realities into a coherent system that removes tension and restores clarity.

But the work resists this instinct.

It does not move toward balance.

It moves toward tension.

This distinction is essential.

Balance suggests that justice and mercy can be measured, adjusted, and brought into proportion. It implies that there is a point at which the two are harmonized, where the demands of one are satisfied without compromising the other. It offers the promise of resolution, of a stable position from which the person can operate with confidence.

Tension offers no such promise.

It does not resolve the relationship between justice and mercy.

It holds them together without collapsing either into the other.

This holding is not comfortable.

It requires the person to remain within a space where clarity is partial, where the connection between action and response is not fully defined, where the outcome is not predetermined by a single framework. It introduces a form of living that is shaped by paradox.

Paradox is not contradiction.

It is the coexistence of realities that do not fully align but are both true.

Justice insists on acknowledgment, on the naming of harm, on the recognition that actions have consequences. Mercy interrupts, extends, offers what is not earned, refuses to be constrained by proportionality. Both are real. Both carry weight. Both make claims on how situations are to be understood and engaged.

To collapse one into the other is to simplify.

To reduce mercy to justice is to make grace conditional, to tie it to the fulfillment of requirements, to ensure that it follows the sequence that justice demands. To reduce justice to mercy is to minimize harm, to bypass acknowledgment, to move too quickly toward release.

Both collapses offer relief.

They remove tension.

They provide clarity.

But they do so at a cost.

They diminish the complexity of what is real.

The refusal of resolution, then, is not a failure to integrate.

It is a recognition that integration does not take the form of synthesis.

It takes the form of coexistence.

Justice and mercy remain distinct, each retaining its integrity, each resisting absorption into the other. The person is not given a framework that explains how they fit together in a single, unified system. They are asked to live within the space that their coexistence creates.

This space is not empty.

It is charged.

It is where decisions are made, where responses are formed, where engagement takes place. It is not a theoretical construct, but a lived reality that shapes how individuals and communities navigate situations.

Within this space, the absence of resolution creates pressure.

The person may feel the need to resolve the tension, to choose a side, to move toward a position that provides stability. This pressure is not accidental. It arises from the discomfort of holding realities that do not align.

The temptation to resolve is strong.

It offers the possibility of relief.

It allows the person to act with certainty, to apply a consistent framework, to avoid the complexity that tension introduces.

But the work calls for a different response.

Not the elimination of tension.

But the endurance of it.

This endurance is not passive.

It is active engagement with the realities that are present, without reducing them to a single framework. It involves holding justice and mercy in view simultaneously, allowing each to inform the response without allowing either to dominate.

This is not a neutral position.

It requires discernment.

The person must attend to the specifics of each situation, to the nature of the harm, to the context in which it has occurred, to the possibilities for response. They must navigate without the assurance that comes from a fixed sequence, relying instead on attentiveness and engagement.

This navigation is shaped by paradox.

The person must be willing to affirm that harm is real and that it matters, while also remaining open to responses that are not determined solely by that harm. They must be able to hold the weight of justice without allowing it to close off the possibility of mercy, and to receive mercy without allowing it to obscure the reality of justice.

This dual holding creates a different kind of coherence.

Not the coherence of a system that resolves tension, but the coherence of a posture that can sustain it. The person develops the capacity to remain within complexity, to engage with situations that do not fit neatly into categories, to respond in ways that reflect the full reality of what is present.

This capacity is not immediate.

It is formed over time.

Through repeated engagement with situations that resist resolution, through the practice of holding tension without collapsing it, through the willingness to remain present even when clarity is incomplete.

At the communal level, this posture has significant implications.

Communities often seek resolution.

They aim to establish shared frameworks, to define responses, to create structures that provide consistency. These aims are not inherently problematic. They support coordination, clarity, and shared understanding.

But when it comes to the relationship between justice and mercy, the pursuit of resolution can lead to simplification.

The community may adopt a stance that prioritizes one over the other, creating a dominant framework that shapes how situations are addressed. This dominance can provide stability, but it can also limit the community's ability to engage with the full complexity of what arises.

To hold justice without collapsing mercy is to resist this movement.

It is to create a communal posture that allows both to remain present, that does not force alignment into a single system, that recognizes the necessity of tension.

This recognition changes how situations are approached.

The community does not move immediately to resolution.

It allows space for both justice and mercy to be considered, for their implications to be explored, for responses to emerge that are informed by both without being determined solely by either.

This approach is slower.

It requires more engagement.

It introduces uncertainty.

But it also allows for responses that are more aligned with the complexity of what is present.

The refusal of false resolution is not an avoidance of responsibility.

It is an acceptance of it.

It acknowledges that the work of holding justice and mercy together cannot be reduced to a formula, that it requires ongoing discernment, that it involves living within paradox.

This paradox is not something to be solved.

It is something to be inhabited.

To live in this way is to accept that clarity will be partial, that tension will remain, that the desire for resolution will not always be satisfied. It is to trust that meaning can emerge within this space, that engagement can occur without complete alignment, that responses can be formed without collapsing complexity.

This trust is not automatic.

It is cultivated.

Through practice.

Through experience.

Through the recognition that attempts to force resolution often lead to distortion, while the willingness to remain within tension allows for a deeper engagement with reality.

At this stage, the work is not to resolve the paradox.

It is to remain within it.

And it is from within this remaining that the chapter continues.

PART 2: WHEN ONE SIDE TAKES OVER

If the work of this chapter is to hold justice and mercy in tension without collapsing one into the other, then it becomes necessary to examine what happens when that tension is not sustained. The pressure to resolve is real, and in the absence of a posture that can endure paradox, individuals and communities often move toward simplification. This simplification does not always appear as an explicit choice. It emerges gradually, through patterns of response, through the accumulation of decisions, through the shaping of assumptions.

Over time, one side begins to take precedence.

Justice becomes dominant.

Or mercy does.

In either case, the tension is reduced.

And with that reduction comes distortion.

The collapse toward justice is often easier to recognize.

It aligns with a strong sense of order, with the desire for accountability, with the need to affirm that actions have consequences. Within this frame, the primary task is to ensure that wrongdoing is named, that responsibility is assigned, that appropriate responses are enacted. The coherence of the system depends on the consistency of these connections.

In this context, mercy begins to feel like a threat.

It appears as a disruption to the order that justice seeks to maintain. It introduces uncertainty into a system that relies on predictability. It raises the possibility that the sequence may not be completed, that the expected outcome may not occur.

As a result, mercy is often constrained.

It is allowed only after justice has been satisfied, only within limits that do not threaten the structure, only in ways that can be controlled. It becomes conditional, tied to the fulfillment of requirements, dependent on the completion of processes that affirm the primacy of justice.

This conditioning alters mercy.

It is no longer free.

It becomes an extension of justice rather than a distinct reality. It is permitted within the system, but it does not challenge it. The possibility that mercy might interrupt or exceed the sequence is minimized.

This minimization has consequences.

The system becomes rigid.

It prioritizes consistency over responsiveness, structure over discernment. The focus remains on maintaining order, on ensuring that the connections between action and consequence are preserved. Situations are interpreted through a framework that emphasizes alignment with established patterns.

Within this rigidity, the complexity of human experience can be reduced.

Individuals may be understood primarily in terms of their actions, categorized according to their behavior, engaged with in ways that reflect their position within the system. The particularities of each situation, the nuances of each person's experience, may be overshadowed by the need to maintain consistency.

This reduction can lead to a form of moral clarity that is stable but limited.

It provides a clear framework for response, but it may not fully account for the realities it seeks to address. The emphasis on justice ensures that wrongdoing is taken seriously, but it may constrain the possibility of responses that do not fit within the established sequence.

At the same time, the collapse toward mercy produces a different kind of distortion.

It often arises as a reaction to the rigidity of justice, as an attempt to create space for compassion, for understanding, for release. Within this frame, the emphasis shifts from accountability to restoration, from consequence to relationship, from structure to openness.

This shift can be necessary.

It can correct imbalances.

It can introduce flexibility into systems that have become too rigid.

But when mercy becomes dominant, it can also obscure.

The focus on restoration may lead to a minimization of harm, to a reluctance to name wrongdoing clearly, to an avoidance of the discomfort that comes with acknowledging the full weight of what has occurred.

The desire to maintain connection can take precedence over the need to engage with truth.

In this context, justice begins to feel excessive.

It appears as harsh, as unnecessary, as a barrier to the relationships that mercy seeks to preserve. The naming of harm may be softened, the assignment of responsibility blurred, the consequences deferred or avoided.

This softening alters justice.

It is no longer fully engaged.

The seriousness of actions may be diminished, the impact of harm underrecognized, the need for accountability weakened. The system becomes more flexible, but it may lose the capacity to address certain realities with the depth they require.

This loss has implications.

Without a clear engagement with justice, the community may struggle to maintain boundaries, to address patterns of harm, to create environments in which individuals can trust that their experiences will be taken seriously. The emphasis on mercy, when it is not held in tension with justice, can lead to a form of instability that is different from rigidity, but no less significant.

In both collapses, something is lost.

When justice dominates, mercy is constrained.

When mercy dominates, justice is diminished.

In each case, the complexity of reality is reduced to a single framework.

This reduction provides clarity.

But it is a partial clarity.

It does not fully account for the range of what is present.

The distortion becomes apparent over time.

In systems where justice dominates, there may be an accumulation of responses that feel overly rigid, that fail to account for the nuances of individual situations, that prioritize consistency at the expense of responsiveness. Individuals may feel categorized, defined by their actions, engaged with in ways that do not reflect the full scope of their experience.

In systems where mercy dominates, there may be an accumulation of unresolved tensions, of harms that have not been fully addressed, of patterns that persist without being examined. Individuals may feel that their experiences are minimized, that the emphasis on reconciliation comes at the expense of acknowledgment, that the space for truth is limited.

These outcomes are not always immediate.

They develop gradually, as the dominant framework shapes how situations are interpreted and addressed. The effects accumulate, influencing the culture of the community, the nature of relationships, the way individuals understand their place within the system.

To recognize these distortions is not to reject either justice or mercy.

It is to see the necessity of both.

The collapse occurs not because one is wrong, but because one is isolated.

Removed from the tension that holds it in relation to the other.

This isolation simplifies.

But it also narrows.

The person or community operating within a single dominant frame may experience a sense of clarity, but it is a clarity that does not fully engage with the realities it encounters. It provides a way of navigating, but it limits the capacity to respond to complexity.

The work, then, is not to choose between justice and mercy.

It is to resist the collapse.

To remain within the tension, even when it is uncomfortable.

To allow both realities to inform response, without allowing either to define it completely.

This resistance is not easy.

It requires awareness of the tendencies toward simplification, attentiveness to the ways in which one side may be taking precedence, a willingness to adjust and recalibrate.

It involves recognizing that the desire for clarity can lead to reduction, and that the maintenance of tension, though more demanding, allows for a fuller engagement with reality.

At this stage, the person or community is not yet fully inhabiting this tension.

They are learning to see where it is lost.

To identify the points at which collapse occurs.

To understand the patterns that lead to distortion.

And it is from within this understanding that the chapter continues.

PART 3: PRACTICING THE TENSION

If the work of this chapter has moved from the refusal of false resolution to the recognition of how easily we collapse toward one side, then the remaining question is not theoretical. It is practical. How does a person live within this tension in actual situations, where decisions must be made, responses must be formed, and the absence of resolution cannot be sustained indefinitely without direction?

To "practice the tension" is not to maintain a state of indecision.

It is not hesitation.

It is not the avoidance of action.

It is a way of engaging that refuses to allow action to be determined by a single frame.

This requires the development of habits.

Not rigid procedures, but practices that shape how attention is given, how interpretation is formed, and how response emerges.

The first of these practices is double attention.

To hold justice and mercy together, one must learn to see both simultaneously. This sounds simple, but it is not. The natural tendency is to focus on one dimension of a situation—the harm that has occurred or the possibility of release, the need for accountability or the opportunity for restoration. Attention narrows, and with that narrowing, the other dimension recedes.

Double attention resists this narrowing.

It requires the person to remain aware of the harm—its reality, its impact, its significance—while also remaining open to the presence of mercy, to the possibility that the response may not be determined solely by the harm. It asks the person to hold both in view, even when they pull in different directions.

This holding is not static.

It shifts.

At times, justice may demand more attention.

At other times, mercy may come forward.

But neither is allowed to disappear.

Both remain part of the field of awareness, informing how the situation is engaged.

The second practice is delayed closure.

The impulse to resolve is strong.

It offers relief.

It provides a sense of completion.

But when justice and mercy are held in tension, immediate closure often comes at the cost of reduction. One side is privileged in order to bring the situation to an end.

Delayed closure does not avoid resolution indefinitely.

It resists premature resolution.

It allows time for the complexity of the situation to be more fully understood, for the implications of different responses to be considered, for the tension to be engaged rather than escaped.

This delay is not inactivity.

It is active waiting.

It involves continued attention, continued engagement, continued reflection. It recognizes that some responses require time to form, that clarity may emerge through sustained interaction rather than immediate decision.

The third practice is relational anchoring.

The tension between justice and mercy is not held in abstraction.

It is held in relationship.

The person who has been harmed, the one who has caused harm, the community that surrounds them—these relationships shape how the tension is experienced and engaged.

Relational anchoring means that decisions are not made solely on the basis of principle, but in the context of people.

It requires attention to how responses will affect those involved, to how they will be experienced, to how they will shape the ongoing relationship. It resists the application of abstract rules without regard for the relational dynamics at play.

This does not mean that principles are abandoned.

It means that they are engaged within the context of relationship.

Justice is not only about what is right in the abstract, but about what it means for those who have been affected.

Mercy is not only about what can be given, but about how that giving is received.

The fourth practice is truthful naming.

To hold mercy without collapsing justice requires that harm be named clearly.

Without this naming, mercy becomes untethered.

It risks minimizing what has occurred, softening its impact, obscuring its significance. Truthful naming grounds the engagement, ensuring that the reality of the situation is not lost.

This naming is not accusatory.

It is descriptive.

It seeks to articulate what has happened, to acknowledge its effects, to bring into shared awareness the elements that must be considered. It provides a foundation upon which response can be built.

At the same time, truthful naming is not the end of the process.

It is part of it.

It must be held alongside openness to what may follow, to the possibility that the response will not be determined solely by what is named.

The fifth practice is non-final judgment.

In many frameworks, judgment is understood as a final determination.

A conclusion that defines the situation and dictates the response.

Within the tension of justice and mercy, judgment takes on a different form.

It becomes provisional.

Responsive.

Open to revision.

This does not mean that nothing is decided.

It means that decisions are made with an awareness of their partiality, of the fact that they do not fully resolve the tension, that they remain open to further engagement.

Non-final judgment allows for action without closure.

It enables the person to respond while recognizing that the response is not the final word, that it may need to be revisited, that the situation may continue to evolve.

This openness is not indecisiveness.

It is humility.

It acknowledges the limits of any single response, the complexity of the situation, the possibility that further understanding may emerge.

The sixth practice is communal discernment.

Holding tension is not solely an individual task.

It is a communal one.

The complexity of justice and mercy exceeds the capacity of any single perspective. It requires the input of others, the engagement of different experiences, the interaction of multiple viewpoints.

Communal discernment creates space for this engagement.

It allows for the tension to be held collectively, for different aspects of the situation to be brought forward, for the response to be shaped through interaction rather than imposed by a single perspective.

This discernment is not always harmonious.

It involves disagreement.

It requires the community to engage with differing interpretations, to hold space for multiple voices, to resist the urge to unify prematurely.

But it also provides depth.

The response that emerges from communal discernment is more likely to reflect the complexity of the situation, to account for different dimensions, to be shaped by a broader understanding.

These practices do not eliminate tension.

They sustain it.

They provide ways of living within it, of engaging with it, of allowing it to inform response without forcing resolution.

To practice the tension is to accept that there will be no final position from which all situations can be addressed.

It is to live within a reality that is dynamic, responsive, and complex.

It is to engage with justice and mercy not as competing systems to be reconciled, but as realities to be held together in ongoing interaction.

This way of living is demanding.

It requires attention, patience, humility, and the willingness to remain within uncertainty.

But it also opens the possibility for responses that are more aligned with the fullness of what is present.

Responses that do not reduce.

Responses that do not collapse.

Responses that emerge from within the tension itself.

And it is from within this practice that the next movement begins.

CHAPTER 23

The Role of the Church

PART 1: NOT THE MANAGER OF GRACE

IF GRACE CANNOT BE forced, cannot be rushed, cannot be reduced to a system, and cannot be contained within stable moral categories, then the question that follows is unavoidable: what, then, is the role of the Church? If grace resists control, what does it mean for an institution—structured, organized, and often oriented toward clarity and order—to participate in a reality that is inherently disruptive?

The temptation is immediate.

To manage.

To define.

To regulate.

Institutions exist, in part, to create coherence. They provide frameworks within which individuals can understand, participate, and act. They establish patterns, articulate expectations, and offer guidance. These functions are not inherently problematic. They allow for coordination, for shared life, for continuity over time.

But when applied to grace, they introduce risk.

Grace does not conform easily to structure.

It resists predictability.

It interrupts the very sequences that institutions often rely upon to maintain order. To attempt to manage grace is to place it within a framework that cannot contain it without altering it.

This alteration is subtle.

It does not necessarily appear as a rejection of grace.

It often appears as its organization.

The Church may develop language, practices, and processes that aim to facilitate grace—to make it accessible, to integrate it into communal life, to ensure that it is present within the rhythms of worship and relationship.

In doing so, it may begin to assume a role that extends beyond facilitation.

It becomes a mediator.

Not in the sense of pointing toward grace, but in the sense of administering it.

Determining when it is appropriate.

Defining how it should be expressed.

Establishing the conditions under which it is considered valid.

This movement shifts the position of the Church.

From participant to manager.

From witness to regulator.

Grace, in this context, is no longer encountered as something that disrupts expectation.

It becomes something that is anticipated, structured, and, to a degree, controlled.

This control provides stability.

It allows the Church to offer clear guidance, to define responses, to create systems that support communal life. It reduces uncertainty, providing members with a sense of how situations will be addressed, how conflicts will be resolved, how responses will be formed.

But it also constrains.

When grace is managed, its disruptive quality is diminished. The unexpected becomes expected. The unearned becomes conditioned. The interruption becomes a sequence.

The Church, in seeking to integrate grace, may inadvertently neutralize it.

This neutralization is not always recognized.

It can appear as faithfulness.

As the preservation of tradition.

As the maintenance of order.

The practices that emerge may be understood as necessary for communal life, as expressions of shared belief, as ways of embodying what is considered true.

And yet, within these practices, the edge of grace—the very quality that makes it what it is—can be softened.

The Church begins to speak of grace in ways that align with its structures, to interpret it through its systems, to apply it according to its frameworks.

In doing so, it risks losing the very thing it seeks to uphold.

This is the paradox.

The Church is called to bear witness to grace.

But it cannot control it.

It is tasked with proclaiming what it cannot manage.

With participating in what it cannot regulate.

With creating space for what it cannot produce.

To accept this limitation is difficult.

It challenges the institutional instinct.

It requires the Church to relinquish a form of control, to acknowledge that there are aspects of its central message that do not fit within its structures, that exceed its capacity to organize.

This relinquishment is not a failure.

It is a reorientation.

The Church is not the manager of grace.

It is the space in which grace may be encountered.

This distinction changes its role.

From administrator to host.

From regulator to witness.

From controller to participant.

As host, the Church creates environments in which people can engage with the realities that grace disrupts. It provides space for truth to be named, for offense to be expressed, for tension to be held. It does not determine the outcome of these engagements. It facilitates the conditions under which they can occur.

This facilitation is not passive.

It involves intentional practices, the cultivation of spaces that allow for complexity, the shaping of a culture that does not rush to resolution. It requires the Church to resist its own impulse to simplify, to allow for the presence of what cannot be easily integrated.

As witness, the Church points beyond itself.

It does not present grace as something it possesses.

It acknowledges that grace is encountered, not controlled.

It speaks of what it has seen, of what it has experienced, without claiming to determine how or when it will appear.

This witnessing is grounded in humility.

It recognizes the limits of the Church's role, the boundaries of its authority, the distinction between what it can do and what it can only receive.

As participant, the Church is not outside the disruption of grace.

It is within it.

It is subject to the same tensions, the same uncertainties, the same challenges that grace introduces. It does not stand above the reality it engages. It is shaped by it.

This participation requires openness.

The Church must be willing to be disrupted, to have its own categories challenged, its own structures questioned, its own assumptions exposed. It cannot remain unchanged while proclaiming a reality that changes everything it touches.

This openness is not easily sustained.

It requires ongoing reflection, continual adjustment, a willingness to examine how the Church's practices may be shaping or constraining the reality it seeks to hold.

It involves asking difficult questions.

Where are we managing what should not be managed?

Where are we imposing structure where openness is required?

Where are we substituting process for presence?

These questions do not have simple answers.

They must be revisited.

They must be engaged in different contexts, as situations arise, as patterns develop, as the Church continues to navigate the tension between its institutional nature and the disruptive reality of grace.

At this stage, the role of the Church is not to resolve this tension.

It is to remain within it.

To resist the impulse to control.

To create space without determining outcome.

To hold open what cannot be contained.

This is not a lesser role.

It is a different one.

It does not diminish the significance of the Church.

It redefines it.

The Church becomes the place where grace can disrupt without being suppressed, where tension can be held without being resolved prematurely, where individuals and communities can engage with realities that exceed their frameworks.

It is not the source of grace.

It is the environment in which grace can be encountered.

And it is from within this redefinition that the chapter continues.

PART 2: WHEN AUTHORITY TRIES TO CONTROL WHAT IT CANNOT HOLD

If the Church is not the manager of grace but the space in which it may be encountered, then the question that follows is how authority operates within that space. Institutions do not exist without authority. They require structures of leadership, mechanisms of decision-making, and forms of discipline that shape how communal life is ordered. Authority, in itself, is not the problem. It provides coherence, supports accountability, and enables the community to function in ways that are coordinated and sustained.

The difficulty arises when authority extends beyond its proper scope.

When it attempts to govern what it cannot contain.

Grace, as we have seen, resists control.

It does not conform to sequence.

It cannot be scheduled.

It cannot be enforced.

And yet, within the life of the Church, there is a persistent tendency to bring grace within the reach of authority—to define its expression, to regulate its timing, to determine its application.

This tendency often emerges in moments of tension.

When harm has occurred, when conflict arises, when relationships are strained, the community looks to its leaders for direction. There is a desire for clarity, for guidance, for a path forward that will restore order. Authority is called upon to interpret the situation and to prescribe a response.

In these moments, grace can become part of what is prescribed.

Leaders may call for forgiveness.

They may emphasize reconciliation.

They may frame certain responses as more aligned with the values of the community, encouraging members to move toward them. These actions are often motivated by a desire to heal, to restore, to prevent division.

But when grace is prescribed, it changes.

It becomes an expectation.

A requirement.

Something that can be measured and evaluated.

The individual is no longer free to engage with grace as it emerges within their experience.

They are expected to align with it as defined by the authority of the community.

This expectation introduces pressure.

The person who has been harmed may feel that their response is being guided, not by their own engagement with the situation, but by what is being communicated as appropriate. The space for their experience to unfold is narrowed, shaped by the expectations that authority has established.

This shaping can be subtle.

It may not take the form of direct command.

It may appear as strong encouragement, as the framing of certain responses as more mature, more faithful, more aligned with what the community values. The language used may be gentle, but the effect is directive.

Over time, this dynamic can create a pattern.

Members learn what is expected.

They understand how they are to respond in certain situations.

They internalize the framework that authority has established, shaping their own responses to align with it.

This alignment can create a form of compliance.

Individuals may adopt responses that fit within the expectations of the community, even when those responses do not fully reflect their internal experience. They may speak the language of grace without having engaged with it in a way that is real for them.

This compliance can be difficult to detect.

It does not appear as resistance.

It appears as agreement.

But beneath that agreement, there may be unresolved tension, unacknowledged harm, experiences that have not been fully engaged.

At the same time, authority can also manifest in the use of discipline.

When individuals do not align with the expected response, when they express anger, when they resist moving toward forgiveness, they may be seen as out of step with the community. Their response may be interpreted as problematic, as something that needs to be addressed.

Discipline, in this context, can be used to bring individuals back into alignment.

It may involve correction, admonition, or, in some cases, exclusion. The goal is to restore coherence, to ensure that members are operating within the framework that has been established.

This use of discipline can reinforce the control of grace.

It communicates that certain responses are not acceptable, that there are boundaries around how individuals are to engage with situations, that deviation from these expectations carries consequences.

This communication can create fear.

Members may become cautious in how they express themselves, aware that certain responses may lead to correction. They may limit their engagement, avoiding the articulation of experiences that do not align with what is expected.

This caution can reduce honesty.

The community may appear stable, unified, aligned.

But the depth of engagement is diminished.

The full range of experience is not present.

The data that anger and offense provide is not fully accessible.

Authority, in seeking to maintain order, may inadvertently suppress the very elements that would allow the community to engage more deeply with reality.

This suppression does not eliminate tension.

It relocates it.

The unresolved elements persist, shaping how individuals relate to one another, influencing the dynamics of the community, affecting the capacity for trust.

Over time, this can lead to disconnection.

Members may feel that they cannot bring their full experience into the community, that there are limits to what can be expressed, that certain realities must be managed privately rather than engaged collectively.

This disconnection is not always visible.

It may manifest as reduced participation, as guarded interactions, as a quiet distance that develops between individuals and the community.

At a deeper level, the use of authority to control grace alters how the Church understands itself.

It shifts from being a space of encounter to a system of regulation.

From a place where grace can disrupt to a place where it is managed.

This shift can be reinforced over time, as practices and patterns become established, as expectations are internalized, as the culture of the community is shaped by the use of authority.

To recognize this dynamic is not to reject authority.

It is to clarify its role.

Authority is necessary for the functioning of the community.

It provides structure, supports accountability, enables coordination.

But it is not the source of grace.

It cannot produce it.

It cannot determine its presence.

When authority attempts to do so, it moves beyond its scope.

The challenge, then, is to exercise authority in a way that does not attempt to control what cannot be held.

This involves restraint.

Knowing when not to prescribe.

When not to direct.

When not to enforce.

It requires the willingness to allow space for individuals to engage with grace in their own time, in their own way, without imposing a timeline or a specific outcome.

It also involves protection.

Creating an environment in which individuals can express their experience without fear of correction or exclusion, where the articulation of offense is not treated as deviation, but as part of the process of engagement.

This protective role is different from control.

It does not seek to shape the outcome.

It seeks to maintain the conditions under which engagement can occur.

At the same time, authority must remain attentive.

It cannot withdraw entirely.

It must engage with the dynamics of the community, with the relationships, with the situations that arise. It must hold the tension between providing structure and allowing openness, between guiding and not controlling.

This holding is not simple.

It requires discernment.

It involves ongoing reflection on how authority is being exercised, on the effects it is having, on the ways in which it may be shaping or constraining the reality it seeks to support.

The Church, in this sense, is continually learning.

Learning how to exercise authority without overreaching.

Learning how to create space without relinquishing responsibility.

Learning how to hold structure and openness together without collapsing one into the other.

This learning is not complete.

It continues.

As situations arise.

As patterns develop.

As the community engages with the realities that grace introduces.

And it is from within this ongoing learning that the chapter continues.

PART 3: A COMMUNITY THAT CAN WITHSTAND GRACE

If the Church is not the manager of grace and must resist the temptation to control or enforce it, then the question that remains is what kind of community it must become in order to hold grace without collapsing under its weight. Grace, as we have traced it throughout this work, is not a gentle addition to existing structures. It disrupts sequences, unsettles identities, fractures assumptions, and resists resolution. It does not simply pass through a community unchanged. It acts upon it.

To hold grace, then, is not to contain it.

It is to withstand it.

This distinction is essential.

Containment suggests control, the ability to manage what enters, to regulate its effects, to ensure that it aligns with existing structures. Withstanding suggests something different. It implies that the community will be acted upon, that it will be affected, that it will be required to absorb and engage with forces that it does not fully direct.

A community that can withstand grace must be shaped accordingly.

It must be able to remain present in the face of disruption, to sustain engagement when clarity is lost, to hold together when tensions arise. It must develop capacities that allow it to endure without retreating into control or collapsing into fragmentation.

The first of these capacities is resilience.

Not resilience in the sense of returning quickly to a previous state, but resilience as the ability to remain engaged when that previous state is no longer available. Grace disrupts the structures that provide stability. It alters the patterns that have been relied upon. A resilient community does not attempt to restore those patterns immediately. It remains present within the altered reality.

This presence requires strength.

The ability to tolerate uncertainty, to engage with situations that do not resolve, to hold together when members experience tension differently. Resilience allows the community to stay in the work, to continue engaging even when the path forward is not clear.

The second capacity is honesty.

A community that can withstand grace must be able to speak truthfully about its own experience. It must allow for the articulation of offense, the naming of harm, the expression of confusion and resistance. Without honesty, the effects of grace are obscured. The disruption is hidden, the tension unspoken, the reality unengaged.

Honesty creates visibility.

It brings into shared awareness the ways in which grace is affecting the community, the points at which it is resisted, the areas in which it is difficult to receive. This visibility is not comfortable, but it is necessary. It allows the community to engage with what is real rather than with what is assumed.

The third capacity is humility.

To withstand grace is to recognize that the community does not fully understand what it is engaging. Grace exceeds the frameworks through which it is interpreted. It operates in ways that are not predictable, that do not conform to established patterns.

Humility allows the community to acknowledge this limitation.

To admit that it does not have complete clarity, that its interpretations are partial, that its responses may need to be revised. It creates space for learning, for adjustment, for ongoing engagement.

Without humility, the community is more likely to move toward control, to assert its frameworks as definitive, to reduce the complexity of grace to manageable forms.

The fourth capacity is patience.

Grace does not operate on a schedule.

It does not align with the timelines that communities often prefer. The movement toward understanding, toward engagement, toward whatever form of response may emerge, takes time. It cannot be rushed without distortion.

A patient community allows this time.

It resists the urge to bring situations to quick resolution, to impose closure where it has not yet formed. It remains engaged over the long term, recognizing that the work of holding grace unfolds gradually.

This patience is not passive.

It involves sustained attention, continued presence, ongoing engagement. It is the willingness to stay with the work even when progress is slow or unclear.

The fifth capacity is relational depth.

Grace is encountered in relationship.

It affects how individuals engage with one another, how they interpret each other's responses, how they navigate tension. A community that can withstand grace must have relationships that are strong enough to hold this complexity.

These relationships are not defined by agreement.

They are defined by commitment.

A willingness to remain engaged even when there is difference, to continue in conversation when there is tension, to hold connection without requiring alignment. Relational depth allows the community to remain intact even as it is disrupted.

The sixth capacity is distributed responsibility.

The work of holding grace is not the task of a single leader or a small group. It is shared.

Each member of the community participates in creating and maintaining the space in which grace can be encountered. Each contributes to the posture of restraint, presence, curiosity, patience, and honesty that we have described.

This distribution prevents the concentration of control.

It ensures that the community does not rely on a single point of authority to manage what cannot be managed. It allows for a more organic engagement, shaped by the interaction of multiple perspectives.

Within a community formed by these capacities, grace can be held differently.

Not as something to be controlled, but as something to be engaged.

The disruptions it introduces are not immediately resolved.

They are sustained.

The tensions it creates are not suppressed.

They are explored.

The uncertainties it brings are not eliminated.

They are navigated.

This does not make the community stable in the traditional sense.

It does not provide the clarity that comes from fixed structures or predetermined responses. It introduces a different kind of stability, one that is grounded not in control, but in the capacity to remain present.

This presence is the defining characteristic.

The community does not withdraw from the effects of grace.

It does not attempt to neutralize them.

It stays.

It engages.

It holds.

This holding is not perfect.

The community will falter.

It will, at times, move toward control.

It will, at times, suppress expression.

It will, at times, seek resolution prematurely.

But if it is attentive, if it remains committed to the posture that allows grace to be encountered, it can return.

It can recalibrate.

It can continue.

This ongoing process is what defines the community.

Not the absence of failure, but the willingness to remain engaged, to learn, to adjust, to hold space even when it is difficult.

In this way, the Church becomes something different.

Not the place where grace is administered.

Not the system that regulates its presence.

But the community that can withstand it.

The place where its disruption is not feared.

Where its tension is not avoided.

Where its presence is allowed to reshape how life is lived together.

And it is from within this reshaping that the final movement of the book begins.

CHAPTER 24

What Grace Does Not Do

PART 1: THE LIMITS WE MUST NOT DENY

IF THE WORK OF this book has insisted that grace disrupts moral expectation, resists control, unsettles identity, and refuses premature resolution, then the final movement requires a different kind of clarity—not a clarification of what grace is, but of what it is not. This distinction is necessary because the language of grace, when left unexamined, is often extended beyond its limits, asked to do more than it can bear, and given functions that do not belong to it. And when this happens, harm follows.

Grace, in much of our discourse, is spoken of in expansive terms: it heals, restores, reconciles, makes things right. These statements are not entirely false, but they are often incomplete. They assume a sequence that is not guaranteed. They attribute to grace outcomes that are not always present. They create expectations that reality does not consistently fulfill. To speak truthfully about grace requires that we name its limits—not to diminish it, but to prevent its distortion.

The first limit is this: grace does not erase harm. This may seem obvious, and yet it is frequently obscured. When grace is invoked in response to harm, there can be an implicit assumption that forgiveness or mercy alters what has occurred—that it softens the reality of the event, reduces its impact, or meaningfully changes the past. But grace does not reach backward. It does not undo. The harm remains. The event has occurred. Its effects persist. The person who has been harmed continues to live with what has been done, with the ways it has shaped perception, trust, and experience.

To suggest that grace erases harm is to misrepresent both grace and reality. It places a burden on the harmed person to experience a change grace does not produce, implying that mercy should remove the weight of the past. When this does not happen, the person may feel at fault—as if they have failed to forgive correctly, are holding on, or are not receiving what has been offered. This is a misalignment. The failure is not in the person. It is in the expectation. Grace does not erase. It does not eliminate what has occurred or its effects. To acknowledge this is to allow the person to remain in reality, engaging what is true rather than what is expected.

The second limit follows closely: grace does not restore fairness. Fairness operates within proportion—it connects action and consequence, effort and outcome, harm and response. It assumes balance can be achieved. Grace does not operate within this framework; it interrupts it. It gives where there has not been earning. It releases where there has not been repayment. It does not calculate. And because it does not calculate, it does not restore balance.

When harm has occurred, fairness would require proportional response—that consequences reflect the weight of actions and that imbalance is addressed. Grace does not ensure this. It may accompany efforts toward fairness, but it does not guarantee them. This is difficult because fairness is tied to our sense of justice. We rely on it to believe the world holds together. When grace interrupts that structure, it does not replace it with a new equilibrium. It introduces a different reality—one that does not resolve imbalance.

This can feel like loss. The harmed person may experience grace as further disruption, removing the hope of fairness without providing a satisfying alternative. To claim grace restores fairness is to deny this experience, imposing meaning that does not align with reality. It suggests imbalance has been addressed when it has not.

The third limit extends further: grace does not guarantee reconciliation. Reconciliation requires relationship—mutual engagement, rebuilt trust, and conditions that support safe connection. Grace may make reconciliation possible, but it does not ensure it. The presence of grace does not restore trust automatically or change relational conditions. Reconciliation depends on more than grace—it requires sustained effort, mutual willingness, and the possibility that a relationship can be reformed in meaningful ways.

These conditions are not always present. To assume grace guarantees reconciliation places pressure on individuals to restore relationships prematurely or inappropriately. It can compel reengagement not because it is wise or safe, but because it is expected. This can be harmful, exposing individuals to further disruption and preventing necessary boundaries.

To speak truthfully about grace, then, is to refuse these assumptions: grace does not erase harm, does not restore fairness, does not guarantee reconciliation. This refusal is not rejection—it is protection. It prevents grace from being burdened with expectations it cannot fulfill and allows it to remain what it is. It also protects individuals from pressure to experience outcomes that are not guaranteed, creating space for truth, for harm to be acknowledged, imbalance to be named, and relationships to remain unresolved when necessary. This space does not resolve tension, but it is honest. And within that honesty, grace can be encountered without distortion—not as solution, but as presence within what is not fixed.

PART 2: WHAT REMAINS WHEN NOTHING IS FIXED

If grace does not erase harm, restore fairness, or guarantee reconciliation, then the question becomes unavoidable: what does grace do? The temptation is to compensate—to restore its appeal by reassigning functions, to ensure it still resolves. But this must be resisted. To move too quickly into affirmation risks reintroducing distortion. What can be said must be said carefully—not as correction, but as observation.

Grace does not fix. It remains.

To fix is to change conditions, to move from disruption to resolution. To remain is to be present within those conditions without removing them—to accompany rather than alter. Grace remains. It does not eliminate harm, remove imbalance, or restore what is lost. But it is present within those conditions.

This presence is subtle. It does not announce itself or produce visible change. It does not bring immediate relief, progress, or resolution. And yet, within those who encounter it, there is a shift—not external, but relational. The person remains within the same reality, but something in how they hold it changes.

The weight is not removed, but it is held differently. This is not relief or closure. It is the presence of something within the tension that allows continuation. Grace does not take the place of harm; it takes place alongside it. It accompanies rather than replaces.

This accompaniment is active. It is not mere absence of abandonment, but presence that engages without resolving, that holds without fixing. Within this presence, possibilities emerge—not guaranteed outcomes, but openings.

The person may find they can speak about what has occurred in new ways—not because harm has lessened, but because space has opened. Engagement with others may shift—not toward reconciliation necessarily, but toward less constrained interaction. Self-understanding may change—not erasing impact, but altering relation to it.

These are not produced by grace. They are made possible by it. Grace opens; it does not complete. It allows movement without determining direction.

These possibilities vary—some may experience forgiveness as possible, others release from the need to resolve, others continued engagement despite unresolved conditions. Grace does not stabilize these. It allows them.

At the same time, grace does not replace justice. Accountability, boundaries, and truth remain necessary. Grace does not resolve justice—it exists alongside it, complicating but not removing its demands.

To speak truthfully of grace is to remain within this complexity, resisting simplification. Grace is not solution but presence—not mechanism but reality. This does not diminish grace; it clarifies it. It allows grace to be encountered as it is, not as we wish it to be.

This encounter is not always comforting. It offers no guarantee that things will be made right. But it offers presence—not closure, but continuation.

PART 3: LIVING WITHOUT ILLUSION

If grace does not fix what is broken, then the question becomes how to live within a reality where resolution does not arrive. To live without illusion is to accept this reality without reshaping it through expectation. It is to refuse narratives that promise what grace does not deliver.

This refusal is not resignation. It is clarity. Resignation withdraws; clarity remains and engages without distortion.

To live without illusion is to hold truth as it is: harm remains harm, imbalance remains imbalance, relationships remain what they are. This requires continual return to reality, resisting the impulse to reinterpret or resolve prematurely.

Grace does not correct reality. It accompanies it.

This companionship allows a different form of endurance—not waiting for resolution, but continuing without it. This endurance is quiet, not triumphant. It is life lived within unresolved conditions.

Grace does not promise that endurance leads to resolution. It remains, allowing the person to remain.

Within this, subtle shifts occur. Harm no longer defines everything. Longing remains but does not determine participation. Relationships are engaged honestly—some continue, some do not.

Life itself is encountered differently—not as problem to solve, but as reality to inhabit.

Grace is not the answer. It is the presence.

It does not resolve tension. It allows it to be lived.

It does not complete the story. It allows it to continue.

This is not the ending we expect.

But it is honest.

And it is within this honesty that the work finds its conclusion.

CHAPTER 25

What Grace Makes Possible

PART 1: FUTURES THAT DO NOT REQUIRE REPAIR

IF GRACE DOES NOT erase harm, does not restore fairness, and does not guarantee reconciliation, and if what it offers is not resolution but presence, then the final question is not what has been solved, but what becomes possible when nothing has been solved. The instinct at the end of a work like this is to return to completion, to offer a final coherence that gathers the fragments and arranges them into something whole, but that instinct must be resisted. What emerges here is not completion. It is possibility.

This possibility does not arise from repair. It arises alongside what has not been repaired. Grace does not create futures by fixing the past. It does not reconstruct what has been broken or restore what has been lost in ways that erase their absence. The past remains. The harm remains. The imbalance remains. And yet, within this unchanged reality, something else begins to open—not because the conditions have shifted, but because the relationship to those conditions is no longer determined solely by their weight.

A future becomes possible where previously only repetition seemed available. This is the first movement—not a new beginning in the sense of starting over, but a continuation that is no longer confined to what has already occurred. The person is not released from the past. They are not separated from it. But they are no longer bound to repeat it in the same way, no longer required to move forward only along the lines that the past has established. This is not freedom in the sense of escape. It is freedom within constraint. The conditions remain, but the total determination of those conditions loosens. The person can act, can move, can engage in ways that are not entirely dictated by what has happened. This does not eliminate the influence of the past. It introduces the possibility that the past is not the only force at work.

Grace does not explain how this occurs. It does not provide a mechanism. It does not offer a sequence that can be followed to produce the same result. It is not transferable in that way. And yet, this opening appears—not as guarantee, but as possibility. This possibility is often quiet. It does not announce itself as transformation. It does not come with clarity or certainty. It may first appear as a slight shift—a willingness to take a step that would not have been taken before, an ability to remain in a space that would previously have been avoided, a change in how one engages with what is present. These shifts are not dramatic. They are not always visible to others. They may not even be fully recognized by the person experiencing them. And yet they mark a difference—a movement that was not previously available, a continuation that does not simply replicate what has already occurred.

This is the nature of a future that does not require repair. It does not wait for resolution in order to begin. It does not depend on the restoration of what has been lost. It unfolds within the conditions that remain. This does not mean that the desire for repair disappears. The longing for fairness, for reconciliation, for restoration continues. It remains part of the experience. But it is no longer the condition upon which the future depends. The person does not need the past to be fixed in order to move. They move within what has not been fixed. This movement is not linear. It does not follow a predictable path. There are moments of forward motion, moments of return, moments where the weight of the past feels as present as ever. The future does not replace the past. It coexists with it. This coexistence is part of the tension. The person lives within both—within what has been and what is becoming—without the ability to resolve one into the other. Grace does not remove this tension. It makes it livable.

This is the second movement: the possibility of presence without closure. Closure implies completion—an ending that resolves what has been open, a conclusion that brings the narrative to a point where it can be understood as finished. Grace does not provide this. The situations we have described throughout this work do not conclude in ways that bring full resolution. The harm is not undone. The imbalance is not corrected. The relationships are not always restored. And yet, life continues. Presence becomes possible without closure. The person is able to remain within what is unresolved, to engage with it, to inhabit it, without requiring that it be brought to completion. This presence is not passive. It is not resignation. It is active engagement with reality as it is, without the demand that it become something else.

To be present without closure is to live within open narratives—stories that do not end in the way we expect, that do not resolve into coherence, that remain unfinished. This unfinishedness can be difficult to bear. It challenges the desire for completion, for understanding, for the ability to look back and make sense of what has occurred. Grace does not provide that sense. It allows the person to continue without it. This continuation is not without meaning. It is not empty. Meaning is not derived from resolution. It emerges within the ongoing engagement with what is present—within the relationships that continue, the actions that are taken, the ways in which the person participates in life. Presence becomes its own form of coherence—not because it explains, but because it sustains.

The third movement extends further: transformation without explanation. In many narratives, transformation is tied to understanding. It is the result of insight, of realization, of a process that can be traced and articulated. We explain change. We locate its causes. We identify the steps that led from one state to another. Grace does not operate within this framework. The shifts it makes possible are not always explainable. The person may find that they are different in ways they cannot fully account for, that they are responding differently, engaging differently, inhabiting their experience in ways that do not align with what they would have expected. These changes do not always follow a clear sequence. They do not always correspond to identifiable moments. They may emerge gradually, without clear origin, without a point at which they can be said to have begun.

This lack of explanation can be unsettling. It resists the desire to understand, to control, to replicate. We often want to know how change occurs so that it can be reproduced. Grace does not provide this knowledge. It does not offer a method. It does not allow itself to be systematized. And yet, transformation happens—not as a process that can be mapped, but as a reality that can be observed. The person is not who they were, not because they have resolved what has occurred, but because they have continued within it, because something within that continuation has shifted. Grace does not explain this shift. It accompanies it. It remains within it. It makes it possible without making it predictable.

This is the final orientation—not toward resolution, not toward explanation, but toward possibility: futures that do not require repair, presence that does not depend on closure, transformation that does not rely on understanding. These are not guarantees. They are not outcomes that can be promised. They are possibilities that emerge within the reality that remains. Grace does not create them as solutions. It allows them as openings. And it is from within these openings that the final movement continues.

PART 2: A LIFE THAT CAN CONTINUE

If grace makes possible futures that do not require repair, presence that does not depend on closure, and transformation that does not rely on explanation, then the final question is not what grace accomplishes, but what kind of life becomes possible withinits presence. Not a life that has been resolved, clarified, or restored, but a life that continues—within the limits we have named, within the realities that remain unchanged, within the tensions that have not been reconciled.

To speak of a life that can continue is to resist a particular expectation: that meaningful life depends upon resolution. Much of what we have inherited assumes that in order to live fully, what has been broken must be repaired, what has been disrupted must be restored, what has been lost must somehow be recovered or replaced. Continuation, in this sense, is often imagined as the result of completion—the story brought to a point where it makes sense, where its elements can be integrated, where its tensions can be resolved.

But the work of this book has moved in a different direction. It has insisted that some things do not resolve, that harm remains, that imbalance persists, that relationships are not always restored, that questions do not always receive answers. And yet, within this unresolved reality, life does not end. It continues.

The possibility of continuation is not derived from the resolution of what has occurred, but from the presence that remains within it. Grace does not complete the story. It does not bring it to a point where it can be understood as finished. It allows the story to continue without that completion.

This continuation is not self-evident. It must be discovered—or perhaps more accurately, allowed. Because the instinct, when faced with unresolved reality, is often to stop: to withdraw, to disengage, to limit participation in order to avoid the weight of what has not been resolved. If the story cannot be completed, then perhaps it should not be continued.

Grace resists this movement—not by removing the weight, but by remaining within it. And in that remaining, it creates the possibility that continuation is not only necessary, but possible.

This possibility does not arrive as certainty. It does not guarantee that continuation will feel meaningful, that it will be free of struggle, or that it will lead to outcomes that justify the effort. It offers no such assurances. What it offers is presence. And within that presence, the person finds that they are able to take another step—not because the path is clear or the outcome known, but because the act of continuing is no longer dependent on those conditions.

A life that can continue is not defined by clarity. It is defined by participation. The person remains engaged—with their own experience, with others, with the world—without requiring that this engagement be resolved into coherence. They act, speak, respond, and relate even when the underlying conditions remain unsettled.

This participation is not the same as before. It is altered—not because tension has been removed, but because the person is no longer waiting for its removal in order to act. They no longer require the story to make sense in order to live within it. This shift is subtle, but decisive. It marks the difference between a life that is suspended—waiting for resolution—and a life that is active—continuing without it.

Within this continuation, certain qualities begin to take shape—not as goals to be achieved, but as characteristics that emerge from the practice of living within unresolved reality.

The first is steadiness. Not stability in the sense of unchanging conditions, but steadiness as the capacity to remain present despite them. The person is not easily displaced by the lack of resolution. They are not dependent on clarity in order to remain engaged. They can stay. This staying is not passive. It is an active endurance—a willingness to remain within what is difficult, to continue engaging even when conditions are not favorable, to resist the impulse to withdraw.

The second is openness—not vague receptivity, but a refusal to close the future based on the past. Even when the past has established patterns, the person does not assume those patterns must determine everything that follows. They remain open to the possibility that something else may emerge. This openness is not naive. It does not ignore what has occurred. It exists alongside it, acknowledging the past while refusing to let it define the limits of what is possible.

The third is honesty. A life that continues without illusion must be grounded in truth. The person does not pretend that harm has been erased, that fairness has been restored, or that reconciliation has been achieved when it has not. They live and speak within reality as it is. This honesty is not harsh. It is clear. It allows for engagement that is not distorted by expectation, that does not impose meaning where it does not exist, that does not require outcomes that are not present.

The fourth is relational integrity. The person engages others without forcing relationships into forms they cannot sustain. They do not require reconciliation where it is not possible, nor deny connection where it remains. They allow relationships to take the shape that reality supports. This integrity protects both the person and the other. It prevents the imposition of expectations that lead to further harm, allowing for connection where it can exist and distance where it must.

The fifth is humility—a recognition that the person does not fully understand what has occurred, what is occurring, or what may yet occur. They do not claim to have resolved the tension or arrived at final understanding. They remain open to what they do not know. This humility allows continued engagement, prevents premature closure, and sustains openness to the ongoing movement of life.

These qualities do not eliminate difficulty. They do not resolve the tensions that remain or transform the situation into something easier to inhabit. But they make it possible to live within it.

This is the work—not the resolution of what has been broken, but the continuation of life within what remains. Grace does not produce this life as an outcome. It makes it possible as a presence. It does not guarantee that the person will continue, but it creates the conditions in which continuation can occur.

This distinction matters because it preserves the reality of human participation. The person is not carried. They continue. They choose, in each moment, to remain engaged, to take another step, to participate in a life that has not been resolved.

Grace does not remove this responsibility. It accompanies it. It remains within it. And in that remaining, it makes possible a life that does not depend on resolution in order to be lived.

This is where the work ends. Not with answers, not with resolution, not with the restoration of what has been lost, but with the possibility of continuation—a life that can be lived within the limits we have named, within the tensions we have not resolved, within the presence that remains.

This is not the conclusion we often seek. But it is one that can be lived.

And that, finally, is enough.

Conclusion

Learning to Live in a World Where Grace Disrupts

IF THIS WORK HAS moved carefully through disruption, resistance, tension, and the limits of what grace does and does not do, then the conclusion does not introduce something new. It returns—not to repeat what has already been said, but to gather its movement into a final clarity: grace does not resolve the world we understand. It disrupts it. And the task is not to overcome that disruption, but to learn how to live within it.

From the beginning, the assumption has been that moral injury arises when the world violates what we believe should hold—when trust breaks, when harm is inflicted, when justice fails. That remains true. But this work has insisted on something more difficult to name: that disruption also occurs when grace enters where we do not believe it should—when mercy interrupts consequence, when forgiveness appears without repair, when the expected sequence does not complete itself.

This is the offense of grace—not that it is absent, but that it appears in ways that destabilize the moral structure we depend upon; not that it fails to act, but that it acts outside the framework we trust. It refuses proportion, resists predictability, and does not restore the balance we expect. Because of this, it does not always feel like good news.

We have traced what happens in that space. We have seen how people respond—not only with acceptance, but with anger, confusion, withdrawal, and resistance. We have seen how communities fracture when grace is interpreted differently, how institutions attempt to manage what cannot be controlled, and how individuals struggle to reconcile what they believe with what they are witnessing.

We have named the temptation to rush grace—to impose it prematurely, to use it to avoid the work of truth and justice—and we have seen how this distorts both grace and reality, silencing rather than healing and producing compliance instead of engagement. We have also named what grace does not do: it does not erase harm, does not restore fairness, and does not guarantee reconciliation. To say otherwise is to place upon grace a burden it cannot carry and upon people expectations that do not align with their lived experience.

And yet, grace remains—not as solution, but as presence; not as resolution, but as possibility; not as explanation, but as accompaniment within what has not been explained. This is where the work finally rests—not in what has been fixed, but in what remains possible when nothing has been fixed: a future that does not require repair, a presence that does not depend on closure, a transformation that does not rely on understanding, a life that can continue within unresolved reality.

This is not the conclusion we are trained to seek. We are formed to look for completion—for narratives that resolve, for tensions that are reconciled, for outcomes that justify what has been endured. We want the story to make sense. We want to look back and say that what has happened has led somewhere clear, somewhere coherent, somewhere that confirms the world still holds together.

Grace does not always offer that. It does not guarantee that the story will resolve in ways we can recognize. It does not ensure that what has been broken will be repaired or that what has been lost will be restored. What it offers is something more difficult and, perhaps, more necessary: the possibility of faithfulness—not faithfulness as certainty, nor as confidence that everything will be made right, but as the willingness to remain.

To remain present within what has not been resolved. To remain engaged within what does not make sense. To remain open within what resists closure.

This kind of faithfulness is not often celebrated. It is quiet. It does not announce itself as victory or provide the satisfaction of completion. It is the steady continuation of life within conditions that have not been altered—the ongoing participation in a world that has not been repaired.

And yet, it is here that grace is encountered most honestly—not in moments where everything aligns, but where it does not; where tension remains, where questions persist, where outcomes are uncertain. To live in a world where grace disrupts is to accept that this disruption will not be resolved. Grace will continue to appear where it unsettles, to interrupt where we expect sequence, to refuse the structures we rely upon.

The question, then, is not how to eliminate that disruption, but how to remain within it—without withdrawing, without closing, without forcing resolution where it has not come.

This is the invitation—not to understand grace completely, not to reconcile it with every expectation, not to make it fit, but to remain: to remain with the tension, with the questions, with the presence that does not resolve but does not leave.

This remaining is not passive. It is an active posture—a choice, repeated over time, to stay engaged with what is real, to resist the impulse to simplify, to allow complexity to remain. It is a way of living that does not depend on the world making sense in order to participate in it. It is, finally, a way of being faithful within a world that grace continues to disrupt.

And if that is where we end—not with resolution, but with presence; not with certainty, but with continuation—then perhaps we have not lost what we expected to find. Perhaps we have found something else.

Not an answer.

But a way to live.

And that is enough.

Epilogue

AFTER THE LAST WORD

There is a moment, after the last word, when nothing resolves. No final clarity arrives, no quiet sense that everything has been gathered and made whole—only a kind of stillness, and the life that remains.

You may find yourself returning to what has been named here—not to solve it, but to recognize it: a moment where grace unsettles rather than comforts, a response that does not fit what you expected, a tension that does not resolve when it should. When that happens, nothing in you needs to rush forward. Nothing needs to be fixed in order for you to continue. You are allowed to remain—not as someone who has figured it out, not as someone who has moved beyond disruption, but as someone still living within it.

There will be days when grace feels distant, when its presence is difficult to name, when what remains feels heavier than what is possible. There will be moments when the questions return unchanged and the desire for resolution presses again. Let it. You do not need to answer every question in order to stay. You do not need to reconcile every tension in order to move. You do not need to understand in order to continue.

There is a quiet kind of faithfulness that does not announce itself. It does not resolve or explain. It simply remains—in the conversation that did not end cleanly, in the relationship that did not return to what it was, in the memory that still carries weight, in the next small step that does not solve anything but is still taken.

This is not less than what you hoped for. It is simply different.

And if grace is present here—and it often is—it will not draw attention to itself. It will not explain what it is doing or make everything feel right. It will remain. And you will find, perhaps without noticing when it began, that you are still here—still living, still choosing, still able to take the next step.

Not because everything has been resolved.

But because it has not.

And that, too, is enough.

Acknowledgements

THIS BOOK DID NOT begin as a project. It began as a tension—one I could not resolve and, eventually, stopped trying to. Along the way, there were people who made it possible to remain within that tension long enough to write it.

I am grateful to those who trusted me with their stories. Some were shared in conversation, some in quiet moments, some in places where words came slowly or not at all. You may not see yourselves named here, but your experiences shaped this work in ways I could not have created on my own. I have tried to carry what you entrusted with care.

To those who have labored in the fields of moral injury, disaster response, pastoral care, and public life—you have given language to realities many people feel but cannot name. Your work made it possible for me to think more clearly and to write more honestly.

I am especially grateful for the communities I have been part of in disaster spiritual care and response. In those spaces, I have seen both the limits of our frameworks and the necessity of remaining present when those frameworks fail. The lessons learned there are woven throughout this book.

To colleagues, readers, and conversation partners who were willing to engage ideas that do not resolve easily—thank you for your patience and your honesty. Your questions sharpened this work. Your resistance clarified it.

To those who walk closely with me in life—family and friends who have allowed me to remain present even when I did not have answers—your presence has mattered more than anything I could name here. You have reminded me, again and again, that continuation is not abstract. It is lived.

To the communities of faith I have served and been formed by—you have shaped the questions that made this book necessary. You have also revealed, often without intending to, the tensions this book attempts to name. I remain grateful for both.

And finally, I offer thanks for the quiet, often unnoticed forms of grace that do not resolve, do not explain, and do not announce themselves, but remain. Without that presence, this work would not exist. With it, this work remains unfinished, as all such work must.

—Rev. Gregory C. Smith, PhD

About the Author

Rev. Gregory C. Smith, PhD, writes at the intersection of moral injury, faith, and lived human experience—particularly in places where clarity breaks down and easy answers fail. His work is shaped by years of engagement in disaster response, pastoral care, and public life, where he has accompanied individuals and communities navigating loss, disruption, and the limits of meaning-making.

Rather than offering resolution, his writing explores what remains when resolution does not arrive—how people continue, how faith is reformed, and how presence becomes possible in the absence of coherence. This book reflects that ongoing work: an attempt to speak honestly about grace not as solution, but as something encountered within the tensions it does not resolve.

He serves in leadership roles connected to disaster spiritual care and has been actively involved in supporting responders, survivors, and communities in the aftermath of crisis. These experiences continue to shape his understanding of moral complexity, institutional limits, and the quiet forms of endurance that often go unnamed.

Rev. Smith is the author of multiple works on moral injury, faith, and public life, as well as The Church Without Walls. Across his writing, he returns to a consistent question: what does it mean to remain human—and faithful—when the structures we depend on no longer hold?

He lives and works in the United States.

www.ingramcontent.com/pod-product-compliance
Lightning Source LLC
LaVergne TN
LVHW052251200926
848481LV00002B/334
9798385283927